BERLITZ®

Indonesian
PHRASE BOOK
& DICTIONARY

Easy to use features

- Handy thematic colour coding
- Quick Reference Guide—opposite page
- Tipping Guide—inside back cover
- Quick reply panels throughout

How best to use this phrase book

- We suggest that you start with the **Guide to pronunciation** (pp. 6-8), then go on to **Some basic expressions** (pp. 9-15). This gives you not only a minimum vocabulary, but also helps you get used to pronouncing the language. The phonetic transcription throughout the book enables you to pronounce every word correctly.
- Consult the **Contents** pages (3-5) for the section you need. In each chapter you'll find travel facts, hints and useful information. Simple phrases are followed by a list of words applicable to the situation.
- Separate, detailed contents lists are included at the beginning of the extensive **Eating out** and **Shopping guide** sections (Menus, p. 39, Shops and services, p. 97).
- If you want to find out how to say something in Indonesian, your fastest look-up is via the **Dictionary** section (pp. 164-189). This not only gives you the word, but is also cross-referenced to its use in a phrase on a specific page.
- If you wish to learn more about constructing sentences, check the **Basic grammar** (pp. 159-163).
- Note the **colour margins** are indexed in Indonesian and English to help both listener and speaker. And, in addition, there is also an index in Indonesian for the use of your listener.
- Throughout the book, this symbol ☛ suggests phrases your listener can use to answer you. If you still can't understand, hand this phrase book to the Indonesian-speaker to encourage pointing to an appropriate answer. The English translation for you is just alongside the Indonesian.

4th printing 1995 Printed in Switzerland

Contents

Acknowledgements
We are particularly grateful to Suwondo Budiardjo, Kate McLeod and Anton Alifandi for their help in the preparation of this book.

Guide to pronunciation

Indonesian language

Indonesian is a modern form of Malay, which was once written in the Arabic script. A couple of centuries ago English and Dutch missionaries devised spellings for it in the Latin alphabet. The spelling follows the pronunciation very closely, making it possible to read Indonesian with few difficulties. Moreover, the sound system of Indonesian is remarkably close to that of English, so that with care an English-speaking person can soon become a tolerable speaker of Indonesian. Unlike other languages of South-East Asia, there is no new script to be learned to read Indonesian and there are no tones to be learned to speak the language.

This and the following chapter are intended to make you familiar with the phonetic transcription we have devised and to help you get used to the sounds of Indonesian.

As a minimum vocabulary for your trip, we've selected a number of basic words and phrases under the title **Some basic expressions** (pages 10-15).

An outline of the spelling and sounds of Indonesian

Consonants

Letter	Approximate pronunciation	Symbol	Example	
b, d, f, l, m, n, v	are pronounced as in English			
c	like **ch** in **ch**ess	ch	**kecil**	k^e**cheel**
h	like **h** in **h**ot; pronounced rather more forcefully than in English as if sighing, particularly when it appears between similar vowels	h	**hari** **mahal**	**ha**ree **ma**hal
j	like **j** in **j**ug	j	**jalan**	**ja**lan

k	1) like **k** in **k**iss	k	**kopi**	**ko**pee
	2) at the end of a word it is cut short and is barely pronounced, as in a glottal stop	^{k}	**rokok**	**ro**ko^{k}
kh	as in the Scottish lo**ch**	kh	**khusus**	**khoo**soos
ng	like **ng** in si**ng**er	ng	**datang**	**da**tung
ngg	like **ng** in fi**ng**er	ngg	**minggu**	**ming**goo
ny	like ny in canyon, pronounced as one sound	ny	**nyonya**	**nyo**nya
p	like **p** in **p**ay	p	**apa**	apa
r	like **rr** in ba**rr**ow; always trilled like a Scottish **r**	r	**pasar**	**pa**sar
s	like **s** in **s**it	s	**bisaka**	**bee**saka
t	like **t** in **t**oe	t	**datang**	**da**tung
y	like **y** in **y**ou	y	**saya**	**sa**ya

Note

In Indonesian, the letters **k, p** and **t** are not aspirated as they are in English; when pronouncing them, try to prevent an expression of breath.

Vowels

a	like **a** in f**a**ther, or **u** in **u**p	a	**apa**	apa
ang	the same **a** sound as above; similar to the **ung** in l**ung** but longer	ung	**sedang**	s^{e}**dung**
e	1) like **a** in **a**lone	^{e}	**bekerja**	b^{e}k^{e}**rja**
	2) like **ay** in d**ay**	ay	**becak**	**bay**cha^{k}
	3) sometimes like **e** in b**e**t	e	**telepon**	**tel**epon
	4) sometimes omitted		**selamat**	**sla**mat
i	1) like **i** in macaron**i**	ee	**ini**	**ee**nee
	2) like **i** in h**i**t	i	**bichara**	**bicha**ra
o	like **o** in **o**pen	o	**orang**	**o**rung
u	like **oo** in t**oo** though slightly shorter	oo	**satu**	**sa**too

Diphthongs

ai	like **y** in m**y**	ai	**baik**	bai[k]
au	like **ow** in c**ow**	au	**mau**	mau

Note

To avoid possible confusion, hyphens are used in the transcriptions in this book where necessary to separate vowels that do not form diphthongs.

maaf — **ma**-af

Stress

The stress in Indonesian usually falls on the second last syllable of an Indonesian word.

makan — Jakar**ta**

However, if the vowel of the second last syllable is the neutral **e** (written as ^{e} in our transliteration), the stress usually falls on the last syllable;

b^{e}k^{e}**ja**

Pronunciation of the Indonesian Alphabet

A	ah	**N**	en
B	bay	**O**	o
C	chay	**P**	pay
D	day	**Q**	ki
E	ay	**R**	er
F	ef	**S**	es
G	gay	**T**	tay
H	ha	**U**	oo
I	ee	**V**	fay
J	jay	**W**	way
K	ka	**X**	eks
L	el	**Y**	yay
M	em	**Z**	zet

Indonesian and Malay

Malay and Indonesian are very similar languages. After years of negotiation, in 1972 Indonesia and Malaysia agreed on a standard spelling to be used in both countries. That is the spelling used in this phrase book. It is called E.Y.D. (*Ejaan yang disempurnakan*). You may still come across words written in the earlier spelling.

The pronunciation of Indonesian and Malay are rather different (it is comparable with the difference between English and American pronunciation) but speakers of either language have little difficulty in understanding the other. Most of the words used are common to both these languages, but there are differences. Some of the most common are listed below:

English	Indonesian	Malay
afternoon	**sore**	**petang**
can	**bisa**	**boleh**
car	**mobil**	**kereta**
cold	**dingin**	**sejuk**
cow	**sapi**	**lembu**
date	**tanggal**	**haribulan**
don't mention it/you're welcome	**kembali**	**sama-sama**
easy	**gampang**	**senang**
government	**pemerintah**	**kerajaan**
Mr.	**Bapak**	**Tuan**
Mrs.	**Ibu**	**Puan**
per cent	**persen**	**peratus**
plane	**pesawat**	**kapalterbang**
a quarter	**seperempat**	**sesuku**
room	**kamar**	**bilik**
shop	**toko**	**kedai**
staff	**pegawai**	**kakitangan**
time (of day)	**jam**	**pukul**
when	**kapan**	**bila**

Indonesian has many loan-words from Dutch, and Malay has as many from English. For example, for "office" Indonesian uses *kanto* and Malay uses *ofis*.

Some basic expressions

Yes.	**Ya.**	ya
No.	**Tidak.**	**tee**da^{k}
Please.	**Silahkan/tolong.**	see**lah**kan/**to**long
Thank you.	**Terima kasih.**	**tree**ma **ka**sih
Thank you very much.	**Terima kasih banyak.**	**tree**ma **ka**sih **ban**ya^{k}
That's all right/ You're welcome.	**Terima kasih kembali/Kembali.**	**tree**ma kasih k^{e}m**ba**lee/ k^{e}m**ba**lee

Greetings *Salam*

Good morning.	**Selamat pagi.**	**sla**mat **pa**gee
Good afternoon.	**Selamat siang.**	**sla**mat **see**ung
Good evening.	**Selamat malam.**	**sla**mat **ma**lam
Good night.	**Selamat tidur.**	**sla**mat **tee**door
Good-bye.	**Selamat tinggal.**	**sla**mat **ting**gal
See you later.	**Sampai jumpa nanti.**	**sam**pai **joom**pa **nan**tee
Hello/Hi!	**Halo!**	**ha**lo
This is Mr./Mrs./ Miss ...	**Tuan/Nyonya/ Nona ...**	**too**wan/**nyo**nya/**no**na
How do you do? (Pleased to meet you.)	**Senang berjumpa dengan anda.**	s^{e}**nung** b^{e}**rjoom** den**gan** **an**da
How are you?	**Apa kabar?**	**a**pa **ka**bar
Very well, thanks. And you?	**Baik, terima kasih. Dan anda sendiri?**	**ba**i^{k} **tree**ma **ka**sih. dan **an**da s^{e}n**dee**ree
How's life?	**Apa kabar?**	**a**pa **ka**bar
Fine.	**Baik.**	**ba**i^{k}

I beg your pardon?	**Maaf?**	**ma**-af
Excuse me. (May I get past?)	**Maaf. (Bolehkah saya lewat?)**	**ma**-af (**bo**layhkah **sa**ya **lay**wat)
Sorry!	**Maaf!**	**ma**-af

Questions *Pertanyaan-pertanyaan*

Where?	**Dimana?**	dee**ma**na
How?	**Bagaimana?**	**ba**gai**ma**na
When?	**Kapan?**	**ka**pan
What?	**Apa?**	**a**pa
Why?	**Mengapa?**	m^{e}ng**a**pa
Who?	**Siapa?**	see**a**pa
Which?	**Yang mana?**	yung **ma**na
Where is/are...?	**Dimana ... ?**	dee**ma**na
Where can I find/get...?	**Dimana saya bisa dapat ... ?**	dee**ma**na **sa**ya **bee**sa **da**pat
How far?	**Berapa jauh?**	**bra**pa **ja**ooh
How long? (time/distance)	**Berapa lama?/ Berapa panjang?**	**bra**pa **la**ma/**bra**pa **pan**jung
How much/How many?	**Berapa banyak?**	**bra**pa **ba**nya^{k}
How much does this cost?	**Berapa harganya ini?**	**bra**pa **har**ganya **ee**nee
When does... open/close?	**Kapan ... buka/ tutup?**	**ka**pan ... **boo**ka/**too**toop
What do you call this/that in...?	**Apakah ini namanya?**	apakah **ee**nee **na**manya
What does this/that mean?	**Apakah ini artinya?**	apakah **ee**nee arteenya

Do you speak...? *Apakah anda bisa bicara... ?*

Do you speak English?	**Apakah anda bisa bicara bahasa Inggeris?**	apakah **an**da **bee**sa bi**cha**ra ba**ha**sa **ing**grees
Does anyone here speak English?	**Apa ada yang bisa bicara bahasa Inggeris disini?**	apa **a**da yung **bee**sa bi**cha**ra ba**ha**sa **ing**grees dee**see**nee

I don't speak (much) Indonesian.	**Saya tidak bisa bicara (banyak) bahasa Indonesia.**	saya teeda^{k} beesa bichara (banya^{k}) bahasa indoneeseeya
Could you speak more slowly?	**Dapatkah anda berbicara lebih pelan-pelan?**	dapatkah anda berbichara l^{e}bih plan-plan
Could you repeat that?	**Bisakah anda mengulangi itu?**	beesakah anda m^{e}ngoolungee eetoo
Could you spell it?	**Bisakah anda mengeja itu?**	beesakah anda m^{e}ngayja eetoo
How do you pronounce this?	**Dapatkah anda mengucapkan ini?**	dapatkah anda m^{e}ngoochapkan eenee
Could you write it down, please?	**Dapatkah anda menulisnya?**	dapatkah anda m^{e}noolisnya
Can you translate this for me?	**Bisakah anda menterjemahkan ini untuk saya?**	beesakah anda m^{e}nt^{e}rj^{e}mahkan eenee oontoo^{k} saya
Can you translate this for us?	**Bisakah anda menterjemahkan ini untuk kami?**	beesakah anda m^{e}nt^{e}rj^{e}mahkan eenee oontoo^{k} kami
Could you point to the… in the book, please?	**Bisakah anda menunjuk kepada… didalam buku?**	beesakah anda m^{e}noonjoo^{k} k^{e}pada … deedalum bookoo
word	**kata**	kata
phrase	**ucapan**	oochapan
sentence	**kalimat**	kalimat
Just a moment.	**Tunggu sebentar.**	toonggoo s^{e}b^{e}ntar
I'll see if I can find it in this book.	**Saya lihat kalau ada di buku ini.**	saya leehat kalaoo ada dee bookoo eenee
I understand.	**Saya mengerti.**	saya m^{e}ng^{e}rtee
I don't understand.	**Saya tidak mengerti.**	saya teeda^{k} m^{e}ng^{e}rtee
Do you understand?	**Apakah anda mengerti?**	apakah anda m^{e}ng^{e}rtee

Can/May…? *Bisakah…?*

Can I have…?	**Bolehkah saya minta…?**	bolayhkan saya minta
Can we have…?	**Bolehkah kami minta…?**	bolayhkah kami minta

Can you show me...?	**Bisakah anda menunjukkan...?**	beesakah anda m^{e}noonjoo^{k}kan
I can't.	**Saya tidak bisa.**	saya teeda^{k} beesa
Can you tell me...?	**Dapatkah anda memberitahu saya... ?**	dapatkah anda m^{e}mb^{e}reetahoo saya
Can you help me?	**Dapatkah anda menolong saya?**	dapatkah anda m^{e}nolong saya
Can I help you?	**Apa yang bisa saya bantu?**	apa yung beesa saya bantoo
Can you direct me to...?	**Bisakah anda menunjukkan jalan ke... ?**	beesakah anda m^{e}noonjoo^{k}kan jalan k^{e}

Do you want...? *Apakah anda ingin... ?*

I'd like...	**Saya ingin...**	saya ingin
We'd like...	**Kami ingin...**	kami ingin
What do you want?	**Apa yang anda inginkan?**	apa yung anda inginkan
Could you give me...?	**Dapatkah anda memberikan...?**	dapatkah anda m^{e}mbreekan
Could you bring me...?	**Dapatkah anda mengambilkan...?**	dapatkan anda m^{e}ngambeelkan
Could you show me...?	**Bisakah anda menunjukkan kepada saya...?**	beesakah anda m^{e}noonjoo^{k}kan kepada saya
I'm looking/searching for...	**Saya sedang mencari...**	saya s^{e}dung m^{e}ncharee
I'm hungry.	**Saya lapar.**	saya lapar
I'm thirsty.	**Saya haus.**	saya haus
I'm tired.	**Saya lelah.**	saya l^{e}lah
I'm lost.	**Saya tersesat.**	saya t^{e}rs^{e}sat
It's important.	**Ini penting.**	eenee p^{e}nting
It's urgent.	**Ini mendesak.**	eenee m^{e}nd^{e}sa^{k}

It is/There is... *Ada...*

It is...	**Adalah...**	adalah
Is it...?	**Apakah...?**	apakah
It isn't...	**Ini tidak ...**	eenee teeda^{k}
Here it is.	**Inilah dia.**	eeneelah deeya

Here they are.	**Inilah mereka.**	**ee**neelah m^{e}**rayka**
There it is.	**Itulah dia.**	**ee**toolah deeya
There they are.	**Itulah mereka.**	**ee**toolah m^{e}**rayka**
There is/There are...	**Ada...**	ada
Is there/Are there...?	**Apakah ada... ?**	apakah ada
There isn't/aren't...	**Tidak ada...**	**tee**da^{k} ada
There isn't/aren't any.	**Tidak ada sama sekali.**	**tee**da^{k} ada **sama skal**ee

It's... *Adalah...*

beautiful/ugly	**cantik/jelek**	**chan**ti^{k}/j^{e}lay^{k}
better/worse	**lebih baik/lebih jelek**	l^{e}bih bai^{k}/l^{e}bih j^{e}lay^{k}
big/small	**besar/kecil**	b^{e}sar/k^{e}chil
cheap/expensive	**murah/mahal**	**moo**rah/**ma**hal
early/late	**pagi/terlambat**	**pa**gee/t^{e}**rlum**bat
easy/difficult	**mudah/sulit**	**moo**dah/**soo**lit
free (vacant)/ occupied	**kosong/isi**	**ko**song/**ee**see
full/empty	**penuh/kosong**	p^{e}**nooh**/**ko**song
good/bad	**baik/buruk**	bai^{k}/**boo**roo^{k}
heavy/light	**berat/ringan**	brat/**rin**gan
here/there	**disini/disana**	dee**see**nee/dee**sa**na
hot/cold	**panas/dingin**	**pa**nas/**din**gin
near/far	**dekat/jauh**	d^{e}kat/**ja**ooh
next/last	**berikut/terakhir**	b^{e}**ree**koot/t^{e}**rakh**eer
old/new	**lama/baru**	**la**ma/**ba**roo
old/young	**tua/muda**	**too**wa/**moo**da
open/shut	**terbuka/tertutup**	t^{e}r**boo**ka/t^{e}r**too**toop
quick/slow	**cepat/lambat**	ch^{e}pat/**lum**bat
right/wrong	**benar/salah**	b^{e}nar/**sa**lah

Quantities *Jumlah*

a little/a lot	**sedikit/banyak**	s^{e}dikit/**ba**nya^{k}
few/a few	**sedikit**	s^{e}dikit
much/many	**banyak**	**ba**nya^{k}
more/less (than)	**lebih banyak/lebih kurang (dari)**	l^{e}bih **ba**nya^{k}/l^{e}bih **koo**rung (**da**ree)
enough/too	**cukup/terlalu (banyak)**	**choo**koop/t^{e}**rla**loo (**ba**nya^{k})
some/any	**beberapa/ berapa saja**	b^{e}**bra**pa/**bra**pa **sa**ja

A few more useful words *Sedikit lebih banyak kata-kata berguna*

above	**di atas**	dee-**a**tas
after	**sesudah**	s^{e}**soo**dah
and	**dan**	dan
at	**di**	dee
before (time)	**sebelum**	s^{e}bloom
behind	**di belakang**	dee**bla**kung
below	**di bawah**	dee**ba**wah
between	**antara**	an**ta**ra
but	**tetapi**	t^{e}**ta**pee
down	**ke bawah**	k^{e} **ba**wah
downstairs	**ruang bawah**	roowung **ba**wah
during	**selama**	s^{e}**la**ma
for	**untuk**	**oon**too^{k}
from	**dari**	**da**ree
in	**di**	dee
inside	**di dalam**	dee**da**lum
near	**di dekat**	dee d^{e}kat
never	**tidak pernah**	**tee**da^{k} **p^{e}r**nah
next to	**berikut**	b^{e}**ree**koot
none	**tidak ada**	**tee**da^{k} ada
not	**tidak**	**tee**da^{k}
nothing	**tidak ada sama sekali**	**tee**da^{k} ada **sa**ma **ska**lee
now	**sekarang**	**ska**rung
on	**pada**	**pa**da
only	**hanya**	**han**ya
or	**untuk**	**oon**too^{k}
outside	**diluar**	dee**loo**war
perhaps	**barangkali**	**ba**rung**ka**lee
since	**sejak**	s^{e}ja^{k}
soon	**segera**	s^{e}gra
then	**lalu**	**la**loo
through	**melalui**	m^{e}**la**loo-ee
to	**ke**	ke
too (also)	**juga**	**joo**ga
towards	**terhadap**	t^{e}r**ha**dap
under	**dibawah**	dee**ba**wah
until	**sampai**	**sum**pai
up	**ke atas**	k^{e}-**a**tas
upstairs	**naik keatas**	nai^{k} k^{e}-**a**tas
very	**sekali**	**ska**lee
with	**dengan**	d^{e}ngan
without	**tanpa**	**tan**pa
yet	**masih**	**ma**sih

Arrival

Passport control *Pemeriksaan paspor*

To visit Indonesia you will need a passport valid at least 6 months after the date of entry and, if you are travelling for business reasons, you will also need a visa. You must have an onward ticket for leaving Indonesia. Your entry stamp on arrival gives you the right to spend two months in the country, though a special permit (*Surat Jalan*) is needed for visiting Irian Jaya.

Here's my passport.	**Ini paspor saya.**	**ee**nee **pas**por **sa**ya.
I'll be staying...	**Saya akan tinggal...**	saya akan **ting**gal
a few days	**beberapa hari**	b^e^**bra**pa **ha**ree
a week	**satu minggu**	sa**too** **ming**goo
2 weeks	**2 minggu**	doowa **ming**goo
a month	**satu bulan**	satoo **boo**lan
I don't know yet.	**Saya masih belum tahu.**	saya masih b^e^**loom ta**hoo
I'm here on holiday.	**Saya disini sedang libur.**	saya dee**see**nee s^e^dung **lee**boor
I'm here on business.	**Saya disini sedang ada urusan pekerjaan.**	saya dee**see**nee s^e^dung ada **oo**roosan p^e^rk^e^**rjaan**
I'm just passing through.	**Saya hanya lewat.**	saya **han**ya **lay**wat

If things become difficult:

I'm sorry, I don't understand.	**Maaf, saya tidak mengerti.**	**ma**-af saya **tee**da[k] m^e^ng^e^rtee
Does anyone here speak English?	**Apa ada yang bisa bicara bahasa Inggeris disini?**	apa ada yung **bee**sa **bi**chara ba**ha**sa **ing**grees dee**see**nee

PABEAN
CUSTOMS

After collecting your baggage at the airport (*lapangan terbang*) you have a choice: use the green exit if you have nothing to declare, or leave via the red exit if you have items to declare (in excess of those allowed).

barang untuk di laporkan goods to declare	**tiada sesuatu untuk dilaporkan** nothing to declare

You may bring in and take out as much foreign money as you wish but you may not enter or leave with more than 50 000 rp.

The chart below shows what you can bring in duty-free.

Cigarettes	Cigars	Tobacco	Spirits (Liquor)
200	50	100g	2 l

I have nothing to declare.	**Saya tiada sesuatu untuk dilaporkan.**	**sa**ya tee-**a**da s^{e}**swa**too **oon**too^{k} dee**la**porkan
I have...	**Saya punya...**	**sa**ya **poo**nya
a carton of cigarettes	**satu slof rokok**	**sa**too slof roko^{k}
a bottle of whisky	**satu botol wiski**	**sa**too botol **wis**kee
It's for my personal use.	**Itu hanya untuk keperluan saya pribadi.**	**ee**too **ha**nya **oon**too^{k} k^{e}**p^{e}r**loo-an **sa**ya pree**ba**dee
It's a gift.	**Itu hadiah.**	**ee**too **ha**dee-ah

Paspor anda.	Your passport, please.
Apa ada sesuatu yang perlu dilaporkan?	Do you have anything to declare?
Silahkan buka koper ini.	Please open this bag.
Anda harus bayar cukai untuk ini.	You'll have to pay duty on this.
Apakah anda punya barang-barang lain?	Do you have any more luggage?

Baggage—Porter *Koper—Porter*

Porters are clearly recognizable by their uniforms and have a fixed rate per item of baggage. Luggage trolleys are also available at airports.

Porter!	**Porter!**	port^{e}r
Please take (this/ my)…	**Tolong bawakan … (ini/saya).**	tolong bawakan … (eenee/ saya)
luggage	**barang**	barung
suitcase	**koper**	kop^{e}rr
(travelling) bag	**tas (perjalan)**	tas (p^{e}rjalan)
That one is mine.	**Barang ini saya punya.**	barung eenee saya poonya
Take this luggage…	**Bawa barang ini…**	bawa barung eenee
to the bus	**ke bis**	k^{e} bis
to the taxi	**ke taksi**	k^{e} taksee
How much is that?	**Berapa ongkosnya semua itu?**	brapa ongkosnya s^{e}moowa eetoo
There's one piece missing.	**Ada satu barang yang hilang.**	ada satoo barung yung heelung
Where are the luggage trolleys (carts)?	**Dimana kereta bagasi?**	deemana krayta bagasee

Changing money *Menukar uang*

Where's the nearest currency exchange office?	**Dimana kantor penukaran uang yang terdekat disini?**	deemana kantor p^{e}nookaran wung yung terd^{e}kat deeseenee
Can you change these traveller's cheques (checks)?	**Dapatkan anda menukar cek-cek wisata ini?**	dapatkan anda m^{e}nookar chek-chek weesata eenee
I want to change some dollars/pounds.	**Saya ingin menukar beberapa dollar/pon sterling.**	saya ingin m^{e}nookar b^{e}brapa dollar/pon sterling
Can you change this into rupiah/ Malaysian ringgit?	**Bisakah anda menukar ini ke rupiah/ringgit Malaysia?**	beesakah anda m^{e}nookarr eenee k^{e} roopeeyah/ringgit malaysia
What's the exchange rate?	**Berapakah nilai tukarnya?**	brapakah neelai tookarnya

BANK-CURRENCY, see page 129

Where is...? *Dimana... ?*

Where is the...?	**Dimana... ?**	dee**ma**na
booking office	**kantor pemesanan tempat**	**kan**tor p^e^**m^e^**sanan t^e^mpat
duty (tax)-free shop	**toko bebas cukai**	**to**ko **bay**bas **choo**kai
newsstand	**kios**	keeyos
restaurant	**restoran/rumah makan**	restoran/**roo**mah **ma**kan
How do I get to...?	**Bagaimana saya bisa pergi ke... ?**	**ba**gai**ma**na **sa**ya **bee**sa **p^e^r**gee k^e^
Is there a bus into town?	**Apakah ada bis ke kota?**	**a**pakah **a**da bis k^e^ **ko**ta
Where can I get a taxi?	**Dimana saya bisa dapat taksi?**	dee**ma**na **sa**ya **bee**sa **da**pat **tak**see
Where can I hire (rent) a car?	**Dimana saya bisa menyewa mobil?**	dee**ma**na **sa**ya **bee**sa m^e^**nyay**wa **mo**beel

Hotel reservation *Pemesanan tempat di hotel*

Do you have a hotel guide (directory)?	**Apakah anda punya buku petunjuk hotel?**	**a**pakah **an**da **poo**nya **boo**koo pe**toon**joo^k^ **ho**tel
Could you reserve a room for me?	**Bisakah anda pesan tempat untuk saya?**	**bee**sakah **an**da p^e^san t^e^mpat **oon**too^k^ **sa**ya
in the centre	**di tengah-tengah**	dee t^e^ngah-t^e^ngah
near the railway station	**di dekat setasion kereta-api**	dee d^e^kat **sta**seeyon **kray**ta-apee
a single room	**kamar untuk seorang**	**ka**mar **oon**too^k^ s^e^-**o**rung
a double room	**kamar untuk dua orang**	**ka**mar **oon**too^k^ doowa **o**rung
not too expensive	**jangan yang terlalu mahal**	**jun**gan yung t^e^**rla**loo **ma**hal
Where is the hotel/ guesthouse?	**Dimana letaknya hotel/wismatamu?**	dee**ma**na **l^e^**ta^k^nya **ho**tel/ **wis**matamoo
Do you have a street map?	**Apakah anda punya peta jalan?**	**a**pakah **an**da **poo**nya p^e^ta **ja**lan

HOTEL/ACCOMMODATION, see page 22

Car hire (rental) *Sewa mobil*

Visitors usually hire a car with driver or a taxi. Enquire from your hotel or a local travel agency such as Pacto or Nitour, both of which offer services throughout Indonesia. Your driver is responsible for fuel and car maintenance and will find his own accommodation and evening meal. It's usual to pay for his lunch and refreshment during the day. With a group of four or five, consider chartering a *bemo* or *oplet* (minivan) by the day.

Note: Traffic in Indonesia drives on the left.

I'd like to hire (rent) a car.	**Saya ingin menyewa mobil.**	saya **ing**in m^{e}**nyay**wa **mo**beel
small	**kecil**	k^{e}chil
medium-sized	**ukuran sedang**	**oo**kooran s^{e}dung
large	**besar**	b^{e}sar
automatic	**otomatis**	otomatees
I'd like it for a day/ a week.	**Saya ingin menyewa untuk satu hari/satu minggu.**	saya **ing**in m^{e}**nyay**wa **oon**too^{k} **sa**too **ha**ree/**sa**too **ming**goo
Do you have any special rates?	**Apakah anda punya tarip istimewa?**	apakah **an**da **poo**nya **ta**rip isti**may**wa
What's the charge per day/week?	**Berapa ongkos sewanya untuk satu hari/minggu?**	brapa ongkos **say**wanya **oon**too^{k} **sa**too **ha**ree/ **ming**goo
Is mileage included?	**Apakah ini tergantung jaraknya?**	apakah **ee**nee t^{e}**rgan**toong jara^{k}nya
What's the charge per kilometre?	**Berapa taripnya per kilometer?**	**bra**pa **ta**ripnya per **kee**lo**mayt**^{e}**r**
I'd like to leave the car in ...	**Saya ingin meninggalkan mobil di ...**	saya **ing**in m^{e}**ning**galkan **mo**beel dee
I'd like full insurance.	**Saya menginginkan asuransi penuh.**	**sa**ya m^{e}ng**ing**inkan asoo**ran**see p^{e}nooh
How much is the deposit?	**Berapa depositnya?**	brapa d^{e}**po**seetnya
I have a credit card.	**Saya punya kartu kredit.**	saya **poo**nya **kar**too kredit
Here's my driving licence.	**Ini surat izin mengemudi saya.**	**ee**nee **soo**rat **i**zin m^{e}ng^{e}**moo**dee **sa**ya

CAR, see page 75

Taxi

You'll find taxis clearly marked with *taksi* on the roof at airports, stations, hotels, where the staff will help you, or you can hail them in the street, using a downward waving motion of the hand. If hiring by the hour, the half-day or the day or using an unmetered or unofficial vehicle, negotiate the price before setting out. Alternatives to taxis for short distance travel are *helicaks* or *bajais*—two-passenger vehicles powered by a motor-cycle engine—and *becaks* or pedicabs.

Where can I get a taxi/helicak/bajaj?	**Dimana saya bisa dapat taxi/helicak/ bajaj?**	dee**ma**na **sa**ya **bee**sa **da**pat **tak**see/hel**ee**cha^{k}/**ba**jaj
Where is the taxi rank (stand)?	**Dimana pangkalan taksi?**	dee**ma**na **pung**kalan **tak**see
Could you get me a taxi?	**Bisakah anda mencarikan taksi untuk saya?**	**bee**sakah **an**da m^{e}n**cha**reekan **tak**see **oon**too^{k} **sa**ya
What's the fare to …?	**Berapa harga karcis ke … ?**	**bra**pa **har**ga **kar**chis k^{e}
That's too expensive.	**Itu terlalu mahal.**	**ee**too t^{e}**rla**loo **ma**hal.
How about … rupiah?	**Bagaimana kalau … rupiah?**	**ba**gai**ma**na **ka**laoo… roo**pee**yah
How far is it to …?	**Berapa jauh jaraknya ke … ?**	**bra**pa **ja**ooh **ja**ra^{k}nya k^{e}
Take me to …	**Bawalah saya ke …**	**ba**walah **sa**ya k^{e}
this address	**alamat ini**	alamat **ee**nee
the airport	**lapangan terbang**	**la**pungan **t^{e}r**bung
the town centre	**pusat kota**	**poo**sat **ko**ta
the … Hotel	**Hotel …**	**ho**tel
the railway station	**setasion kereta-api**	**sta**seeyon **kray**ta-**a**pee
Turn … at the next corner.	**Belok ke … di sudut jalan berikut.**	**bay**loo^{k} k^{e} dee **soo**doot **ja**lan b^{e}**ree**koot
left/right	**kiri/kanan**	**kee**ree/**ka**nan
Go straight ahead.	**Jalanlah lurus kedepan.**	**ja**lanlah **loo**roos k^{e}d^{e}pan
Please stop here.	**Silahkan berhenti disini.**	**see**lahkan b^{e}**rh^{e}n**tee dee**see**nee
I'm in a hurry.	**Saya tergesa-gesa.**	**sa**ya terg^{e}sa-g^{e}sa
Could you wait for me?	**Dapatkah anda menunggu saya?**	**da**patkah **an**da m^{e}**noong**goo **sa**ya
I'll be back in 10 minutes.	**Saya akan kembali dalam 10 menit.**	**sa**ya **a**kan k^{e}m**ba**lee **da**lum 10 menit

TIPPING, see inside back-cover

Hotel—Other accommodation

Advance reservation is essential for areas of strong touristic interest and major cities that are often the venue for exhibitions and conferences.

hotel (**ho**tel) — Major international hotels, located only in main cities and tourist centres, provide all the usual amenities of air-conditioning, western cuisine, swimming pools, room service and boutiques. Evening entertainment is likely to include local cultural performances (dance, *gamelan*).
Smaller business hotels in cities offer many of the same facilities on a less grand scale. Nostalgic old Dutch hotels are found in some of the high-country resorts.

wisma/pondok (**wis**ma/**pon**do[k]) — Usually family-run, these are modest hotels or guesthouses, friendly and clean, often with restaurant attached. Rooms are normally air-conditioned with an en suite shower and flush toilet. Note, however, that not everything marked *wisma* is a hotel: the word basically means "building".

losmen (**los**men) — Less expensive still, especially if you choose to share a room (normally up to four people). Toilet facilities are communal. You can request meals to be sent in.

penginapan (p[e]n**gee**napan) — A really inexpensive *losmen* and a *penginapan* are much the same. They can be good or bad, depending on luck. The worst is: uncomfortable or damp bedding; poor toilet and shower conditions; noise; heat; lack of privacy. Security may be bad and mosquitoes can make life a misery. Ask to have your room sprayed for insects if necessary.

graha wisata remaja (**gra**ha wee**sa**ta r[e]**ma**ja) — Youth hotel; basic and clean.

In villages without official accommodation, make your presence known to the headman. He can arrange for you to stay with a local family. Pay your hostess the price of the food and go prepared with small gifts.

Can you recommend a hotel/guesthouse?	**Dapatkah anda memberi nasehat tentang hotel/ wismatamu?**	**da**patkah **an**da m^{e}mbree **na**say-hat t^{e}ntung hotel/ **wis**matamoo

Checking in—Reception *Resepsi*

Especially in less expensive places you'll want to see the room. Indonesians place emphasis on different ideas of comfort from westerners and it may be that the room you consider superior is less expensive.

My name is...	**Nama saya adalah...**	**na**ma **sa**ya **a**dalah
I have a reservation.	**Saya telah memesan tempat disini.**	**sa**ya t^{e}lah m^{e}**m^{e}**san t^{e}mpat dee**see**nee
We've reserved 2 rooms/ an appartment.	**Kami telah pesan 2 kamar/apartemen.**	**ka**mi t^{e}lah p^{e}san 2 **ka**mar/ **apart**^{e}men
Here's the confirmation.	**Ini berita penegasannya.**	**ee**nee breeta p^{e}**n**^{e}gasannya
Do you have any vacancies?	**Apakah ada kamar kosong?**	apakah **a**da **ka**mar **ko**song
I'd like a...	**Saya ingin...**	**sa**ya **ing**in
single room	**satu kamar untuk seorang**	**sa**too **ka**mar **oon**too^{k} s^{e}-**o**rung
double room	**satu kamar untuk dua orang**	**sa**too **ka**mar **oon**too^{k} doowa **o**rung
We'd like a room...	**Kami ingin mendapat kamar...**	**ka**mi **ing**in m^{e}n**da**pat **ka**mar
with twin beds	**dengan dua tempat tidur**	d^{e}ngan doowa t^{e}mpat **tee**door
with a double bed	**dengan satu tempat tidur untuk dua orang**	d^{e}ngan **sa**too t^{e}mpat **tee**door **oon**too^{k} doowa **o**rung
with a bath	**dengan kamar mandi**	d^{e}ngan **ka**mar mundee
with a shower	**dengan kamar mandi air dus**	d^{e}ngan **ka**mar **mun**dee ay^{e}r doos
with a balcony	**dengan balkon**	d^{e}ngan balkon
with a view	**dengan pemandangan**	d^{e}ngan p^{e}**man**dungan
at the front	**di sebelah depan**	dee s^{e}blah d^{e}pan
at the back	**di sebelah belakang**	dee s^{e}blah **bla**kung

CHECKING OUT, see page 31

It must be quiet.	**Keadaannya pasti sepi.**	k^{e}-ada-annya pastee s^{e}pee
Is there...?	**Apakah ada... ?**	apakah ada
air conditioning	**alat pendingin**	alat p^{e}ndingin
a conference room	**kamar konperensi**	kamar konprensee
a laundry service	**pelayanan binatu**	p^{e}layanan binatoo
a private toilet	**kamar kecil pribadi**	kamar k^{e}chil preebadee
a radio/television in the room	**radio/televisi di kamar**	radeeyo/te-le-veesee dee kamar
a swimming pool	**kolam renang**	kolum r^{e}nung
hot water	**air panas**	ay^{e}r panas
room service	**pelayanan kamar**	p^{e}layanan kamar
running water	**air leding**	ay^{e}r layding
Could you put an extra bed/a cot in the room?	**Bisakah ditaruh tambahan tempat tidur/tempat tidur untuk bayi di kamar?**	beesakah deetarooh tumbahan t^{e}mpat teedoor/ t^{e}mpat teedoor ontoo^{k} bayee dee kamar

How much? *Berapa ongkosnya?*

What's the price...?	**Berapa harga-nya... ?**	brapa harganya
per day	**setiap hari**	s^{e}teeyap haree
per week	**setiap minggu**	s^{e}teeyap minggoo
for bed and breakfast	**untuk penginapan dan makan pagi**	oontoo^{k} p^{e}ngeenapan dan makan pagee
excluding meals	**diluar makan**	deeloo-ar makan
for full board (A.P.)	**untuk penginapan lengkan dengan makanan**	oontoo^{k} p^{e}ngeenapan l^{e}ngkan d^{e}ngan makanan
Does that include...?	**Apakah itu terma-suk... ?**	apakah eetoo t^{e}rmasoo^{k}
breakfast	**makan pagi**	makan pagee
service	**pelayanan**	p^{e}layanan
value-added tax (VAT)*	**pajak pertambahan nilai (ppn)**	paja^{k} p^{e}rtambahan neelai
Is there any reduction for children?	**Apakah ada reduksi untuk anak-anak?**	apakah ada raydooksee oontoo^{k} ana^{k}-ana^{k}
That's too expensive.	**Itu terlalu mahal.**	eetoo t^{e}rlaloo mahal
Do you have anything cheaper?	**Apakah ada yang lebih murah?**	apakah ada yung l^{e}bih moorah

NUMBERS, see page 147

How long? *Berapa lama?*

We'll be staying...	**Kami akan tinggal...**	**ka**mi **a**kan **ting**gal
overnight only	**hanya untuk satu malam**	**ha**nya **oon**too[k] **sa**too **ma**lum
a few days	**beberapa hari**	b[e]**bra**pa **ha**ree
a week (at least)	**satu minggu (paling sedikit)**	**sa**too **ming**goo (**pa**ling s[e]dikit)
I don't know yet.	**Saya masih belum tahu.**	**sa**ya **ma**sih b[e]loom **ta**hoo

Decision *Keputusan*

May I see the room?	**Bolehkah saya melihat kamarnya?**	**bo**layhkah **sa**ya m[e] **lee**hat **ka**marnya
That's fine. I'll take it.	**Baiklah itu. Saya akan mengambilnya.**	bai[k]lah **ee**too. **sa**ya **a**kan m[e]ng**um**bilnya
No. I don't like it.	**Saya tidak suka kamar itu.**	**sa**ya **tee**da[k] **soo**ka **ka**mar **ee**too
It's too...	**Terlalu...**	t[e]**rla**loo
cold/hot	**dingin/panas**	**ding**in/**pa**nas
dark/small	**gelap/kecil**	glap/k[e]chil
noisy	**berisik**	**bree**si[k]
I asked for a room with a bath.	**Saya minta kamar dengan kamar mandi.**	**sa**ya minta **ka**mar d[e]ngan **ka**mar **mun**dee
Do you have anything...?	**Apakah anda punya kamar...**	apakah **an**da **poo**nya **ka**mar
better	**yang lebih baik**	yung l[e]bih bai[k]
bigger	**yang lebih besar**	yung l[e]bih b[e]sar
cheaper	**yang lebih murah**	yung l[e]bih **moo**rah
quieter	**yang lebih sepi**	yung l[e]bih s[e]pee
Do you have a room with a better view?	**Apakah anda punya kamar dengan pemandangan yang lebih baik?**	apakah **an**da **poo**nya **ka**mar d[e]ngan p[e]**man**dungan yung l[e]bih bai[k]

NUMBERS, see page 147

Registration *Pendaftaran*

Upon arrival at a hotel or guesthouse you'll be asked to fill in a registration form (*formulir pendaftaran*).

Nama/Nama pertama	Name/First name
Tempat tinggal/Jalan/Nomor	Home town/Street/Number
Kebangsaan/Pekerjaan	Nationality/Occupation
Tanggal/ Tempat lahir	Date/Place of birth
Datang dari . . . / Pergi ke . . .	Coming from . . ./Going to . . .
Nomor Paspor	Passport number
Tempat/ Tanggal	Place/Date
Tanda tangan	Signature

What does this mean?	**Apakah ini artinya?**	apakah **ee**nee arteenya

Bolehkah saya lihat paspor anda?	May I see your passport, please?
Bisakah anda mengisi formulir pendaftaran ini?	Would you mind filling in this registration form?
Silahkan, beri tanda tangan disini.	Please sign here.
Berapa lama anda akan tinggal disini?	How long will you be staying?

What's my room number?	**Kamar saya nomor berapa?**	**ka**mar **sa**ya **no**mor **bra**pa
Will you have my luggage sent up?	**Bisakah anda suruh barang-barang saya diangkut ke-atas?**	**bee**sakah **an**da **soo**rooh ba**rung**-**ba**rung **sa**ya dee**ung**koot k^{e}-atas
Does the hotel have a garage?	**Apakah hotel punya garasi?**	apakah hotel **poo**nya gar**a**see
I'd like to leave this in the hotel safe.	**Saya ingin barang ini disimpan di lemari besi hotel.**	**sa**ya **in**gin **ba**rung **ee**nee dee**sim**pan dee l^{e}**ma**ree b^{e}see hotel

Hotel staff *Staf hotel*

hall porter	**portir ruang(an)**	**por**teer **roo**wung(an)
maid	**pembantu wanita**	p^{e}m**ban**too wa**nee**ta
manager	**manajer**	mana**jer**
porter	**portir**	**por**teer
receptionist	**resepsionis**	ray**sep**seeonis
switchboard operator	**operator**	op^{e}**ra**tor
waiter	**pelayan**	p^{e}**la**yan
waitress	**pelayan wanita**	p^{e}**la**yan wa**nee**ta

General requirements *Keperluan umum*

In small establishments you may be confronted with a waist-high tub of cold water in the bathroom *(mandi)*. Stand on the floor alongside, sluice yourself with water using the ladle, soap yourself, and rinse off. Don't get in the tub.

The key to room…, please.	**Tolong, kunci kamar nomor…**	**to**long **koon**chee **ka**mar **no**mor
Could you wake me at… please?	**Dapatkah anda membangunkan saya pada jam…?**	**da**patkah **an**da m^{e}m**bung**oonkan **sa**ya **pa**da jum
When is breakfast/ lunch/dinner served?	**Kapan disajikan makan pagi/ makan siang/ makan malam?**	**ka**pan deesa**jee**kan **ma**kan **pa**gee/**ma**kan **see**yung/ **ma**kan **ma**lum
May we have breakfast in our room, please?	**Bisakah kami diantar makan pagi di kamar?**	**bee**sakah **ka**mi dee-antar **ma**kan **pa**gee dee **ka**mar
Is there a bath on this floor?	**Apakah ada kamar mandi di lantai ini?**	apakah **a**da **ka**mar **mun**dee dee lantai **ee**nee
Where's the shaver socket (outlet)?	**Dimana stopkontak untuk alat cukur?**	dee**ma**na stopkonta^{k} **oon**too^{k} **a**lat **choo**koor
Can you find me a…?	**Dapatkah anda mencarikan… untuk saya?**	**da**patkah **an**da m^{e}n**cha**reekan … **oon**too^{k} **sa**ya
babysitter	**penjaga anak-anak**	p^{e}n**ja**ga **a**na^{k}-**a**na^{k}
secretary	**seorang sekretaris**	s^{e}-**o**rung sekre**ta**ris
typewriter	**sebuah mesin tik**	s^{e}**boo**wah m^{e}sin tik
May I have a/an/ some…?	**Bolehkah saya mendapat …?**	**bo**layhkah **sa**ya m^{e}n**da**pat
ashtray	**asbak**	asbak
bath towel	**handuk mandi**	**han**dook mundee

TELLING THE TIME, see page 153 er3

(extra) blanket	**(tambahan) selimut**	(**tumba**han) s^{e}**lee**moot
envelopes	**amplop-amplop**	amplop-amplop
hangers	**gantungan**	**gun**tongan
hot-water bottle	**botol air panas**	botol **ay**^{e}r **pa**nas
ice cubes	**es batu**	es **ba**too
needle and thread	**jarum dan benang**	**ja**room dan **b**^{e}nung
(extra) pillow	**(tambahan) bantal**	(tum**ba**han) bantal
reading lamp	**lampu baca**	**lum**poo **ba**cha
soap	**sabun**	**sa**boon
writing paper	**kertas tulis**	k^{e}rtas **too**lis
Where's the ...?	**Dimana ...?**	dee**ma**na
bathroom	**kamar mandi**	**ka**mar **mun**dee
dining-room	**kamar makan**	**ka**mar **ma**kan
emergency exit	**jalan keluar darurat**	**ja**lan k^{e}**loo**war da**roo**rat
lift (elevator)	**lift**	lift
Where are the toilets?	**Dimana kamar kecil?**	dee**ma**na **ka**mar k^{e}chil

Telephone—Post (mail) *Telepon—Pos*

Can you get me Jakarta 123-45-67?	**Bisakah anda mendapat hubungan telepon dengan Jakarta 123-45-67?**	**bee**sakah **an**da m^{e}n**da**pat **hoo**boongan te-le-pon d^{e}ngan ja**karr**ta 123-45-67
Do you have any stamps?	**Apakah anda punya perangko?**	apakah **an**da **poo**nya **prung**ko
Would you post this for me, please?	**Bisakah anda masukkan ini dalam pos untuk saya?**	**bee**sakah **an**da **ma**soo^{k}kan **ee**nee **da**lum pos **oon**too^{k} saya
Are there any letters for me?	**Apakah ada surat-surat untuk saya?**	apakah **a**da **soo**rat-**soo**rat **oon**too^{k} **sa**ya
Are there any messages for me?	**Apakah ada pesan-pesan untuk saya?**	apakah **a**da p^{e}san-p^{e}san **oon**too^{k} **sa**ya
How much is my telephone bill?	**Berapa rekening telepon saya?**	**bra**pa **rayk**^{e}ning te-le-pon **sa**ya

Difficulties *Kesulitan-kesulitan*

The ... doesn't work.	**... rusak.**	... **roo**sa^{k}
air conditioning	**alat pendingin/AC**	alat p^{e}ndingin/a**chay**
fan	**kipas angin**	**kee**pas **ung**een
heating	**pemanas**	p^{e}**ma**nas
light	**cahaya/sinar/ lampu**	cha**ha**ya/**see**narr/**lum**poo
radio	**radio**	**ra**deeyo
television	**televisi**	te-le-**vee**see

BREAKFAST, see page 38

The tap (faucet) is dripping.	**Keran menetes.**	kran m^e**nay**tays
There's no hot water.	**Tidak ada air panas.**	**tee**da^k **a**da **ay**^er **pa**nas
The washbasin is blocked.	**Wastafelnya tersumbat.**	was**ta**felnya t^er**soom**bat
The window is jammed.	**Jendelanya macet.**	j^en**day**lanya **ma**chet
The curtains are stuck.	**Gordennya macet.**	**gor**daynnya **ma**chet
The mesh screen is broken.	**Kasanya rusak.**	ka**sa**nya **roo**sa^k
The bulb is burned out.	**Bola lampu itu mati.**	**bo**la **lum**poo **ee**too **ma**tee
My bed hasn't been made up.	**Tempat tidur saya belum dibereskan.**	t^empat **tee**door **sa**ya b^eloom dee**be**reskan
The ... is broken.	**... patah.**	... **pa**tah
blind	**gorden**	**gor**dayn
lamp	**lampu**	**lum**poo
plug	**steker**	**stay**k^er
shutter	**daun penutup jendela**	daun p^e**noo**toop j^en**day**la
switch	**sakelar**	**sa**klar
Can you get it repaired?	**Bisakah itu diperbaiki?**	**bee**sakah **ee**too deeper**bai**kee
Can you spray the room, please?	**Bisakah anda menyemprot kamar ini?**	**bee**sakah **an**da meny^em**prot** kamar **ee**nee

Laundry—Dry cleaner's *Binatu—Binatu kemis*

I'd like these clothes...	**Saya ingin baju-baju ini...**	**sa**ya **ing**in **ba**joo-**ba**joo **ee**nee
cleaned/washed	**dicuci**	dee**choo**chee
ironed/pressed	**diseterika**	dee**stree**ka
When will they be ready?	**Kapan selesainya?**	**ka**pan s^el^e**sayn**nya
I need them...	**Saya memerlukannya...**	**sa**ya m^e**m^er**lookannya
today	**hari ini**	**ha**ree **ee**nee
tonight	**malam ini**	**ma**lum **ee**nee
tomorrow	**besok**	**bay**so^k
before Friday	**sebelum hari Juma'at**	s^ebloom **ha**ree **joo**ma-at

POST OFFICE AND TELEPHONE, see page 132

Can you ... this?	**Bisakah anda ... ini?**	**bee**sakah **an**da ... **ee**nee
mend	**memperbaiki**	m^{e}mp^{e}rbai^{k}ee
patch	**menambal**	m^{e}**nam**bal
stitch	**setik**	s^{e}ti^{k}
Can you get this stain out?	**Bisakah anda menghilangkan noda ini?**	**bee**sakah **an**da m^{e}ng**hee**lungkan **no**da **ee**nee
Is my laundry ready?	**Apakah cucian saya sudah siap?**	apakah **choo**chee-yan **sa**ya **soo**dah seeyap
This isn't mine.	**Ini bukan kepunyaan saya.**	**ee**nee **boo**kan k^{e}**poo**nya-an **sa**ya
There's something missing.	**Ada sesuatu yang hilang.**	ada s^{e}**swa**too yung **hee**lung
There's a hole in this.	**Ada lobang disini.**	ada **lo**bung dee**see**nee

Hairdresser—Barber *Penata rambut—Pemangkas rambut*

Is there a hairdresser/ beauty salon in the hotel?	**Apakah ada penata rambut/salon kecantikan di hotel ini?**	apakah **a**da p^{e}**na**ta **rum**boot/salon k^{e}**chan**tikan dee hotel **ee**nee
Can I make an appointment for Thursday?	**Bisakah saya buat janji untuk hari Kamis?**	**bee**sakah **sa**ya **boo**wat **jun**jee **oon**too^{k} **ha**ree **ka**mees
I'd like a cut and blow dry.	**Saya ingin rambut saya dipangkas dan diblow.**	**sa**ya **in**gin **rum**boot **sa**ya dee**pung**kas dan dee**blow**
I'd like a haircut, please.	**Saya ingin pangkas rambut.**	**sa**ya **in**gin **pung**kas **rum**boot
blow-dry	**blow**	blow
colour rinse	**bilasan warna**	**bee**lasan **warr**na
dye	**celup**	ch^{e}loop
face pack	**perawatan muka**	p^{e}**ra**watan muka
hair gel	**hair gel**	hair jel
manicure	**perawatan tangan dan kuku**	p^{e}**ra**watan **tun**gan dan **koo**koo
perm(anent)	**keriting permanen**	**kree**ting permanen
setting lotion	**pembersih penataan rambut**	p^{e}mb^{e}rsih p^{e}**na**ta-an **rum**boot
shampoo and set	**shampoo dan set**	sham**poo** dan set
with a fringe (bangs)	**dengan poni**	d^{e}ngan pony
Don't cut it too short.	**Jangan potong terlalu pendek.**	**jun**gan **po**tong t^{e}**rla**loo **pen**day^{k}

A little more off the...	**Potong sedikit lebih banyak di...**	**po**tong s^{e}dikit l^{e}bih **ba**nya^{k} dee
back	**bagian belakang**	**ba**geeyan **bla**kung
neck	**di sisi leher**	di seesee **lay**hair
sides	**kedua sisi**	k^{e}**doo**wa seesee
top	**atas**	**a**tas
I'd like a shave.	**Saya ingin cukur.**	**sa**ya **ing**in **choo**koor
Would you trim my..., please?	**Bisakah anda potong sedikit saja... saya?**	**bee**sakah **an**da **po**tong s^{e}dikit **sa**ja ... **sa**ya
beard	**jenggot**	**jeng**got
moustache	**kumis**	kumis
sideboards (sideburns)	**cambang**	**cham**bung

Checking out *Meninggalkan sesudah membayar*

May I have my bill, please?	**Bolehkah saya dapat rekening saya?**	**bo**layhkah **sa**ya **da**pat **rayk**^{e}ning **sa**ya
I'm leaving early in the morning.	**Saya akan pergi pagi-pagi besok.**	**sa**ya akan **p**^{e}**r**gee **pa**gee-**pa**gee **bay**so^{k}
Please have my bill ready.	**Harap rekening saya disiapkan.**	**ha**rap **rayk**^{e}ning **sa**ya deeseeyapkan
We'll be checking out around noon.	**Saya akan pergi kira-kira siang hari.**	**sa**ya akan **p**^{e}rgee **kee**ra-**kee**ra **see**yung **ha**ree
Can I pay by credit card?	**Bisakah saya membayar dengan kartu kredit?**	**bee**sakah **sa**ya m^{e}m**ba**yar d^{e}ngan **kar**too kredit
I think there's a mistake in the bill.	**Saya kira ada kesalahan dalam rekening.**	**sa**ya **kee**ra **a**da k^{e}**sa**lahan **da**lum **rayk**^{e}ning
Can you get us a taxi?	**Bisakah anda carikan taksi untuk kami?**	**bee**sakah **an**da **cha**reekan **tak**see **oon**too^{k} **ka**mi
Could you have our luggage brought down?	**Bisakah anda suruh barang-barang kami dibawa kebawah sini?**	**bee**sakah **an**da **soo**rooh **ba**rung-**ba**rung **ka**mi dee**ba**wa k^{e}**ba**wah seenee
Here's the forwarding address.	**Ini alamat untuk mengirimkan barang kami.**	**ee**nee **a**lamat **oon**too^{k} m^{e}ng**ee**rimkan **ba**rung **ka**mi
It's been a very enjoyable stay.	**Menyenangkan sekali selama kami tinggal disini.**	m^{e}**ny**^{e}nungkan **ska**lee s^{e}**la**ma **ka**mi **ting**gal dee**see**nee

TIPPING, see inside back-cover

Camping *Berkemah*

There are few western style camp grounds in Indonesia but ample opportunity for roughing it in nature reserves. Check with local forestry authorities to obtain permission before setting out. It's practical always to travel with a number of passport-sized photos to facilitate administrative matters. Indonesian guides ask a daily fee plus food.

Some nature reserves have *pasanggrahan* or *rumah-rumah kehutanan*, which are simple, very inexpensive forestry huts. There may also be *losmen* in the vicinity.

Is there a camp site near here?	**Apakah ada tempat untuk berkemah didekat sini?**	apakah **a**da t^{e}mpat **oon**too^{k} b^{e}**rkay**mah deed^{e}kat seenee
Can we camp here?	**Apakah kami boleh berkemah disini?**	apakah **ka**mi **bo**layh b^{e}**rkay**mah dee**see**nee
Do you have room for a tent/caravan (trailer)?	**Apakah ada ruang untuk tenda/kereta gandengan?**	apakah **a**da roowung **oon**too^{k} tenda/**kray**ta gan**den**gan
What's the charge...?	**Berapa ongkos-nya ...?**	**bra**pa ongkosnya
per day	**setiap hari**	s^{e}**tee**yap **ha**ree
per person	**untuk setiap orang**	**oon**too^{k} s^{e}**tee**yap **o**rung
for a car	**untuk satu mobil**	**oon**too^{k} **sa**too **mo**beel
for a tent	**untuk satu tenda**	**oon**too^{k} **sa**too tenda
for a caravan (trailer)	**untuk satu kereta gandengan**	**oon**too^{k} **sa**too **kray**ta gan**den**gan
Is there/Are there (a)...?	**Apakah ada ... ?**	apakah **a**da
drinking water	**air minum**	ay^{e}r **mi**noom
electricity	**listrik**	listrik
playground	**tempat bermain**	t^{e}mpat b^{e}rmain
restaurant	**restoran**	restoran
shopping facilities	**fasilitas berbelanja**	fas**i**litas b^{e}**rblan**ja
swimming pool	**kolam renang**	**ko**lum r^{e}nung
Where are the showers/toilets?	**Dimana tempat mandi air dus/ kamar kecil?**	deemana t^{e}mpat **mun**dee ay^{e}r doos/**ka**mar k^{e}chil
Where can I get butane gas?	**Dimana saya bisa dapat gas butan?**	dee**ma**na **sa**ya **bee**sa **da**pat gas **boo**tan

CAMPING EQUIPMENT, see page 106

Eating out

Indonesia boasts a fine and varied cuisine with a multitude of regional specialities. There's fish and tropical fruit in abundance; from cooler regions come magnificent fresh vegetables while subtle blends of spices add piquancy and chilies can set your palate on fire. Coconut and ginger are favourites for flavouring. There are some delicious surprises ahead. *Selamat makan*—Enjoy your meal!

warung
(**wa**roong)

Open-air food stalls are common throughout the islands and stay working till late at night when they're lit by kerosene or gas lamps. You sit at a wooden bench and eat at a long communal table. If you've found a place at one *warung* you can still buy food at others nearby to take back to your spot. The food is totally Indonesian, mostly soup, *sate*, rice and noodle dishes. Coffee shop *warung* are "men only" preserves.

rumah makan
(**roo**mah **ma**kan)

Literally an "eating house", this is in the midway category between the *warung* and the *restoran*. Although the food isn't necessarily better than at the open stalls, you're out of the dust and bustle of the street. A *rumah makan Padang* specializes in West Sumatran cooking. It's spicier than normal Indonesian fare. Order as many dishes as you like: you pay only for those you eat; accompanying sauces are free.

restoran
(restoran)

If the menu carries an English translation you're probably entering a higher price range with more westernized food. It may be good, though less authentic. Most Chinese restaurants carry the title *restoran*.

international
(eent^{e}rnash^{e}nal)

The big hotels offer international cuisine and, possibly, a specialized restaurant as well. Indonesia also has its share of fast-food chains with hamburgers, package ketchup, fried chicken, french fries and the usual assortment of soft drinks.

Indonesia is thronged with thousands of street vendors selling beverages or setting up temporary *sate* stands. Tiny chunks of meat on a bamboo skewer are grilled over charcoal braziers in the street and served with a variety of sauces, usually containing ground peanuts. Beverages, often brightly coloured and very sweet, are sold from carts. Another familiar sight is the *krupuk* vendor, balancing two enormous cans on a pole. These giant-sized savoury crackers replace bread and provide a good crunchy snack at any time. Innumerable fruit stalls provide the opportunity of sampling delectable tropical produce.

Note: During the Islamic fast month of Ramadan, restaurants in many parts of the country close until sunset. Chinese restaurants remain open. Food and hygiene are likely to be good; prices are usually higher than in similar Indonesian outlets.

Meal times *Jam makan*

It may sometimes seem as though Indonesians eat all day long! Main meals are named by the time of day:

Breakfast—*makan pagi*—is available from very early and, even in simpler establishments, you'll almost certainly have a choice of fresh fruit, European-style bread and spreads and tea or coffee.
Lunch—*makan siang*—is best kept to a light snack because of the heat; yet more rice, served with two or three meat and vegetable dishes, washed down with water or tea, then fresh fruit to cleanse the palate before the siesta.
Dinner—*makan malam*—is the main meal of the day, eaten in the cool of the evening as soon as darkness falls around 6.30pm. Rice will be served with a variety of meat and vegetable dishes—a family meal will number four or five dishes, even more if guests are invited, as the tradition of hospitality is to serve more than could possibly be eaten. The first course will usually be *sate* (satay), grilled meat served with a spicy peanut-based sauce. Remember to drink plenty of fluids in the course of the day. Dehydration is a danger in this climate.

How to eat *Cara makan*

In strongly Islamic areas (West Sumatra, for example), it's the custom to eat with the tips of the fingers of your right hand. Use the right hand to pass dishes (the left is kept for the toilet and is considered unclean). If you're a guest, wait for your host or hostess to indicate when to begin eating or drinking. It's considered good manners not to drain your glass but to leave a little at the bottom. Sometimes food arrives tastefully served on a banana leaf. In traditional restaurants, help yourself plenteously to the rice first, then add to it from side dishes.

Indonesian cuisine *Masakan Indonesia*

Many influences have gone into Indonesian cuisine. Arabian countries, India, China, Japan and European nations, Holland in particular, have all brought their influence to bear. Ingredients vary from place to place over this enormous expanse of islands. Rice is the staple with *nasi goreng* (fried rice) the most common of all dishes. Indonesians are very discerning about the quality of rice, which is considered superior when it comes from certain areas. However, it doesn't grow everywhere and, depending on where you travel, you may find it replaced by corn (maize), potatoes, sweet potatoes or sago. Soya beans are also used in a variety of ways. Any dish with *mie* in it means that noodles are served instead of rice. An abundance of fresh vegetables from high country market gardens enhances the meal; mango, papaya, and bamboo shoots are also used.

Fish, seafood, eggs, poultry and meat are added to the basic rice in small quantities, merely to give savour. Delicious sauces are provided in abundance. The most common meat snack is *sate*, tiny kebabs reflecting the Arabian influence. If you're not a chilli lover, hold back on *sambal*, a chilli, prawn and lime paste. Bread is replaced by large crackers called *krupuk*.

Muslims don't eat pork or shellfish and don't drink alcohol. Hindus don't eat beef. Depending on the region, you may be offered either of these as well as goat and buffalo. You may even encounter grilled dragonflies (in Bali) or puppy dog (North Sulawesi). Duck is a common Balinese speciality. West Sumatra boasts the spiciest cuisine. Anything with *padang* in its name is likely to be hot.

Anda ingin makan apa?	What would you like?
Saya menyarankan ini.	I recommend this.
Anda ingin minum apa?	What would you like to drink?
Kami tidak punya . . .	We don't have . . .
Apakah anda ingin . . . ?	Would you like . . .?

Hungry? *Laparkah?*

I'm hungry/I'm thirsty.	**Saya lapar/Saya haus.**	saya **la**par/**sa**ya haus
Can you recommend a good restaurant?	**Dapatkah anda menyarankan suatu restoran yang baik?**	**da**patkah **an**da me**ya**rankan **swa**too restoran yung bai^{k}
Are there any inexpensive restaurants around here?	**Apakah ada restoran yang tidak mahal di sekitar sini?**	apakah **a**da restoran yung **tee**da^{k} **ma**hal dee s^{e}**kee**tar seenee

If you want to be sure of getting a table in a well-known restaurant, it may be better to book in advance.

I'd like to reserve a table for 4.	**Saya ingin pesan meja untuk 4 orang.**	sa**y**a **in**gin p^{e}san **may**ja **oon**too^{k} 4 **o**rung
We'll come at 8.	**Kami akan datang jam 8.**	**ka**mi akan **da**tung jum 8
Could we have a table . . .?	**Bisakah kami dapat meja untuk . . . ?**	**bee**sakah **ka**mi **da**pat **may**ja **oon**too^{k}
in the corner	**di pojok**	dee **po**jo^{k}
by the window	**di dekat jendela**	dee d^{e}kat j^{e}n**day**la
outside	**di luar**	dee **loo**war
on the terrace	**di teras**	di **te**ras
in a non-smoking area	**di ruang tidak merokok**	di roowung **tee**da^{k} m^{e}**ro**ko^{k}

Asking and ordering *Minta dan memesan*

Waiter/Waitress!	**Pelayan pria/ Pelayan wanita!**	p^{e}**la**yan preeya/p^{e}**la**yan wa**nee**ta
I'd like something to eat/drink.	**Saya ingin makan/ minum.**	**sa**ya **ing**in **ma**kan/**min**oom
May I have the menu, please?	**Bolehkan saya dapat menu?**	**bo**layhkan **sa**ya **da**pat m^{e}noo
Do you have a set menu?	**Apakah ada menu khusus?**	**a**pakah **a**da m^{e}noo **khoo**soos
What do you recommend?	**Apa yang anda sarankan?**	**a**pa yung **an**da **sa**rankan
Do you have anything ready quickly?	**Apakah anda ada sesuatu yang cepat siap?**	**a**pakah **an**da **a**da s^{e}**swa**too yung ch^{e}pat seeyap
I'm in a hurry.	**Saya terburu-buru.**	**sa**ya t^{e}r**boo**roo-**boo**roo
I'd like...	**Saya ingin...**	**sa**ya **ing**in
Could we have a/ an..., please?	**Bolehkah kami dapat... ?**	**bo**layhkah **ka**mee **da**pat
ashtray	**asbak**	**as**bak
cup	**cangkir**	**chung**keer
fork	**garpu**	**gar**poo
glass	**gelas**	glass
knife	**pisau**	**pee**sau
napkin (serviette)	**serbet**	serbet
plate	**piring**	**pee**ring
spoon	**sendok**	sen-do^{k}
May I have some...?	**Bolehkah saya minta... ?**	**bo**layhkah **sa**ya **min**ta
bread	**roti**	**ro**tee
butter	**mentega**	m^{e}n**tay**ga
lemon	**jeruk sitrun**	j^{e}roo^{k} sitroon
oil	**minyak**	minya^{k}
pepper	**merica**	m^{e}**ree**cha
salt	**garam**	**ga**rum
seasoning	**bumbu**	**boom**boo
sugar	**gula**	**goo**la
vinegar	**cuka**	**choo**ka

Special diet *Diet khusus*

Some useful expressions for those with special requirements:

I'm on a diet.	**Saya sedang menjalankan diet.**	**sa**ya s^{e}dung men**ja**lankan dee-yet
I'm vegetarian.	**Saya seorang vegetaris.**	saya s^{e}-**or**ung vege**ta**ris
I don't drink alcohol.	**Saya tidak minum alkohol.**	saya **tee**da^{k} **mi**noom alkohol
I don't eat meat.	**Saya tidak makan daging.**	saya **tee**da^{k} **ma**kan **da**ging
I mustn't eat food containing…	**Saya tidak boleh makan makanan yang mengandung…**	saya **tee**da^{k} **bo**layh **ma**kan **ma**kanan yung m^{e}ng**an**doong
flour/fat	**tepung/lemak**	t^{e}poong/l^{e}ma^{k}
salt/sugar	**garam/gula**	**ga**rum/**goo**la
Do you have… for diabetics?	**Apakah anda punya… untuk penyakit gula?**	apakah **an**da **poo**nya… **oon**too^{k} p^{e}**nya**kit **goo**la
cakes	**kue**	kway
fruit juice	**air/sari buah**	ay^{e}r/**sa**ree **boo**wah
a special menu	**menu khusus**	menoo **hoo**soos
Do you have any vegetarian dishes?	**Apakah anda punya daftar makanan vegetaris?**	apakah **an**da **poo**nya **daf**tar **ma**kanan vege**ta**ris
Could I have cheese/ fruit instead of dessert?	**Bolehkah saya dapat keju/buah-buahan sebagai pengganti kue-kue?**	**bo**layhkah **sa**ya **da**pat **kay**joo/**boo**wah-**boo**wah s^{e}**ba**gai p^{e}ng**gan**tee kway-kway
Can I have an artificial sweetener?	**Bolehkah saya minta pemanis buatan?**	**bo**layhkah **sa**ya **min**ta p^{e}**ma**nis **boo**watan

And…

I'd like some more.	**Saya ingin sedikit tambah.**	**sa**ya **in**gin s^{e}**di**kit tambah
Can I have more…, please?	**Bolehkah saya tambah…?**	**bo**layhkah **sa**ya tambah
Just a small portion.	**Sedikit saja.**	s^{e}dikit **sa**ja
Nothing more, thanks.	**Cukup, terima kasih.**	**choo**koop **tree**ma **ka**sih
Where are the toilets?	**Kamar kecilnya ada dimana?**	**ka**mar k^{e}chilnya **a**da dee**ma**na

What's on the menu? *Ada apa di daftar makanan?*

Under the headings below, you'll find alphabetical lists of dishes that might be offered on an Indonesian menu with their English equivalent. You can simply show the book to the waiter. If you want some fruit, for instance, let *him* point to what's available on the appropriate list. Use pages 37 and 38 for ordering in general.

Reading the menu *Membaca menu*

anggur	**ung**goor	wine
ayam	**a**yum	chicken
binatang berburu	bi**na**tung b^{e}r**boo**roo	game
bir	beerr	beer
buah	**boo**wah	fruit
burger	b^{e}rg^{e}r	burgers
eskrim	eskrim	ice cream
hidangan pembuka	**hee**dungan p^{e}m**boo**ka	entrees
hidangan telur	**hee**dungan t^{e}loorr	egg dishes
ikan	**ee**kan	fish
kue-kue	kway-kway	deserts
makanan hasil laut	**maka**nan **ha**sil laut	seafood
makanan kecil	**maka**nan k^{e}chil	snacks
masakan telur	**ma**sakan t^{e}loorr	egg dishes
minuman	**min**ooman	beverages
pasta	pasta	pasta
pengantar (makanan pembuka)	p^{e}**ngan**tar (**ma**kanan p^{e}m**boo**ka)	appetizers
sayur-mayur	**sa**yoor-**ma**yoor	vegetables
selada	s^{e}**la**da	salads
sup	soop	soups
unggas	**oong**gas	poultry

Breakfast *Makan pagi*

A typical Indonesian breakfast will consist of a rice dish - usually *nasi goreng* (fried rice), made from the night before's leftovers. This may be served with *telur mata sapi*, a fried or "ox eye" egg on top, or strips of omelette. Alternatively, papaya flesh can be served mixed with rice and *santen* (coconut milk).

I'd like breakfast, please.	**Bolehkah saya makan pagi?**	**bo**layhkah **sa**ya **ma**kan **pa**gee
I'll have a/an/ some...	**Saya ingin...**	**sa**ya **ing**in
bacon and eggs	**bacon dan telur**	**ba**kon dan t^{e}**loorr**
boiled egg	**telur rebus**	t^{e}**loorr** r^{e}boos
soft/hard	**setengah matang/direbus sampai matang**	s^{e}t^{e}ngah **ma**tung/ deer^{e}boos **sum**pai **ma**tung
cereal	**hasil biji-bijian**	**ha**sil **bee**jee-**bee**jee-an

eggs	**telur/telor**	t^{e}loorr
fried eggs	**telor matasapi**	t^{e}loorr matasapee
scrambled eggs	**telor aduk goreng**	t^{e}loorr adoo^{k} goreng
fruit juice	**sari buah**	saree boowah
grapefruit	**jeruk besar**	j^{e}roo^{k} b^{e}sar
orange	**jeruk manis**	j^{e}roo^{k} manis
ham and eggs	**daging babi dan telur goreng**	daging babee dan t^{e}loorr goreng
jam	**sele**	s^{e}lay
marmalade	**sele jeruk**	s^{e}lay j^{e}roo^{k}
toast	**roti panggang**	rotee punggung
yoghurt	**yogurt**	yogoort
May I have some...?	**Bolehkah saya minta...?**	bolayhkah saya minta b^{e}brapa
bread	**roti**	rotee
butter	**mentega**	m^{e}ntayga
(hot) chocolate	**cokelat (panas)**	chok^{e}lat (panas)
coffee	**kopi**	kopee
decaffeinated	**tanpa kafein**	tanpa kafayn
black/with milk	**hitam/dengan susu**	heetam/d^{e}ngan soosoo
honey	**madu**	madoo
milk	**susu**	soosoo
cold/hot	**dingin/panas**	dingin/panas
pepper	**merica**	m^{e}reecha
rolls	**roti kadet**	rotee kadet
salt	**garam**	garum
tea	**teh**	teh
with milk	**dengan susu**	d^{e}ngan soosoo
with lemon	**dengan jeruk sitrun**	d^{e}ngan j^{e}roo^{k} sitroon
(hot) water	**air (panas)**	ay^{e}r (panas)

Starters (Appetizers) *Pengantar*

I'd like an appetizer.	**Saya ingin makanan pembuka.**	saya ingin makanan p^{e}mbooka
What would you recommend?	**Apa yang anda nasehatkan?**	apa yung anda nasayhatkan
kacang bawung	kachung bawung	fried peanuts with garlic and onion
kacang goreng	kachung goreng	fried peanuts
krupuk udang	kroopoo^{k} oodung	prawn crackers
lemper	l^{e}mper	sticky rice stuffed with meat

lumpia	**loom**ya	spring roll
martabak	mar**taba**^{k}	savoury meat pancakes
perkedel kentang	p^{e}rk^{e}**del** k^{e}**ntung**	potato cakes
rempeyek bayem	r^{e}mpeye^{k} **ba**yum	fried spinach in batter
serundeng	**srun**deng	pan-fried coconut with peanuts
serundeng daging sapi	**srun**deng **da**ging **sa**pee	spiced beef and coconut balls

perkedel jagung (p^{e}rk^{e}**del ja**goong) corn fritters. Rice-flour batter fritters, flavoured with chilli and cumin.

pangsit (**pung**sit) fried wun-tun. These are small, deep-fried dumplings, made from a thin pastry resembling the Chinese wonton, filled with a pork or prawn based stuffing.

perkedel kentang daging sapi (p^{e}rk^{e}**del** k^{e}**ntung** daging **sa**pee) meat and potato balls. Flavoured with nutmeg and garlic, these meatballs, usually made with beef, can be served hot or cold.

rempeyek kacang (r^{e}m**pe**ye^{k} **ka**chung) savoury peanut fritters. This spicy, crispy snack can also be made with sweetcorn or shrimps.

Soups *Sup*

In Indonesia, soup is rarely served at the start of a meal. More usually it forms part of the main meal, accompanying or containing rice or noodles. The two kinds you will encounter will be *soto*, a thick, spicy and filling soup, and *sop*, a thin and lighter soup.

mi bakso	mee **bak**so	meatball soup with noodles
sop bakso	sop **bak**so	meatballs with vegetable soup
sop sawi dengan babi	sop **sa**wee d^{e}ngan **ba**bee	chinese cabbage and pork soup
sop udang	sop **oo**dung	prawn and courgette soup
soto ayam bumbu kari	**so**to ayam **boom**boo **ka**ree	curried chicken soup
soto daging	**so**to **da**ging	spicy beef soup
soto ikan	**so**to **ee**kan	fish soup
soto udang	**so**to **oo**dang	prawn soup

sayur lodeh
(**sa**yoor **lo**deh)
Javanese vegetable soup. Coconut milk is added to this delicious spicy soup, making it thick and creamy.

sop buntut
(sop **boon**toot)
spicy oxtail soup. A very popular dish, probably of Dutch origin. Oxtails can be seen in the market places, hanging in a line with a candle burning under each to keep the flies away.

sop kol rebung
(sop kol **re**boong)
bamboo shoots and cabbage soup. A thick, filling soup, flavoured with ginger and served with boiled rice. The rice is moistened with stock and the vegetables spooned over it, with the rest of the stock served in a separate bowl.

soto ayam
(**so**to **a**yam)
spiced chicken soup. In one variation of this popular soup, each diner can make up his or her own soup, selecting a combination of cooked ingredients from those on offer, usually including beansprouts, cabbage, noodles, chicken and eggs, then adding the basic stock.

Egg dishes *Masakan telur*

Dishes using eggs are common both in Indonesian and Chinese restaurants. The best omelettes are Chinese. Duck's eggs are a speciality in some areas.

acar telur	**a**char t^{e}**loorr**	eggs in a piquant sauce

omelet
(omlet)
Indonesian omelette. The basic omelette is flavoured with onion and chilli peppers, and may be served with a variety of ingredients.

omelet kecap	omlet **k^{e}**chap	soya sauce omelette
omelet udang	omlet **oo**dang	prawn omelette
orak arik	**o**ra^{k} **a**ree^{k}	fried cabbage with eggs
tahu telur	**ta**hoo t^{e}**loorr**	bean curd omelette
telur bumbu bali	t^{e}**loorr boom**boo **ba**lee	eggs in tomato and chilli sauce
telur dadar padang	t^{e}**loorr da**darr **pa**dung	duck egg and coconut omelette
telur isi	t^{e}**loorr ee**see	stuffed eggs

Fish and seafood *Ikan dan makanan hasil laut*

Indonesia offers an astounding choice of seafood and fish, even inland, where freshwater species are farmed in pools and rice fields. The Mahakam River (Kalimantan) is renowned for enormous, freshwater shrimps, while eels and frogs are cultivated in some parts (especially Bali).

I'd like some fish.	**Saya ingin makan ikan.**	saya ingin makan eekan
What kind of seafood do you have?	**Makanan hasil laut yang mana yang anda punya?**	makanan hasil laut yung mana yung anda poonya
bandeng	band^e^ng	freshwater milk fish
bawal	bawal	silver pomfret
belut	b^e^loot	eel
cakalang	chakalung	skipjack
cumi-cumi	choomee choomee	squid
glodok	glodo^k^	mud skipper
ikan gurita	eekan gooreeta	octopus
ikan laut	eekan la-oot	sea fish
ikan mas	eekan mas	golden freshwater carp
ikan pari	eekan paree	ray
ikan tambak	eekan tamba^k^	freshwater fish
ikan tongkol	eekan tongkol	tuna
ikan todak	eekan toda^e^	swordfish
kakap	kakap	giant perch
kakap merah	kakap mayrah	red snapper
karper	karp^e^rr	carp
kepah	k^e^pah	mussels
kepiting	k^e^peeting	crab
remis	r^e^mees	mussels
sarden	sarden	sardines
tenggiri	t^e^nggeeree	Spanish mackerel
tiram	teeram	oysters
udang karang	oodang karang	lobster

baked	**dikukus**	deekoosoos
fried	**digoreng**	deegoreng
grilled	**dipanggang**	deepunggung
marinated	**diasinkan**	deeasinkan
poached	**direbus**	deer^e^boos
sautéed	**digoreng sebentar**	deegoreng s^e^b^e^ntar
smoked	**diasap**	dee-asap
steamed	**dikukus**	deekoosoos

Fish dishes *Beberapa masakan ikan*

ikan bumbu kuning	**ee**kan **boom**boo **koo**ning	fish fried with turmeric
ikan cuka	**ee**kan **choo**ka	fried fish with vinegar
ikan kari	kan **ka**ree	fish curry
ikan panggang	**ee**kan **pung**gung	grilled fish
ikan panggang kecap	**ee**kan **pung**gung k^{e}chap	marinated fish with chili sauce
ikan santan	**ee**kan **san**tun	fish in coconut milk
kepiting pedas	k^{e}**pee**ting p^{e}**das**	spicy crab
otak-otak ikan dan udang	**o**ta^{k} **o**ta^{k} **ee**kan dan **oo**dung	fish and prawn rolls
sambal goreng cumi-cumi	**sam**bal **go**reng **choo**mee **choo**mee	squid in chilli sauce
udang goreng	**oo**dung **go**reng	fried prawns
udang goreng bumbu	**oo**dung **go**reng **boom**boo	spicy fried prawns
udang masak bumbu	**oo**dung **ma**sa^{k} **boom**boo	curried prawns

ikan asam manis
(**ee**kan **a**sam **ma**nis)
fish in sweet and sour sauce. The fish used for this delicious dish is *gurami*, a freshwater fish with tasty, thick white meat. The sour tastes of mustard, vinegar and lemon blend with the sweet candlenuts and sugar.

goreng teri
(**go**reng **t^{e}**ree)
fried dried anchovies. *Teri* are very small fish, young anchovies of only a thumb's width, which are dried and salted, then fried in garlic and chillies.

ikan panggang santan
(**ee**kan **pung**gung **san**tun)
fish with coconut milk. This dish, layers of river fish and kale and onions, originates in West Sumatra and is richly flavoured with spiced coconut milk.

ikan goreng
(**ee**kan **go**reng)
fried fish with five sauces. A basic fried fish is enhanced with a variety of flavours, dipped in a choice of spicy-sweet, tomato, black bean, onion, and coconut-peanut sauces.

pais udang
(**pa**-ees **oo**dang)
prawn parcels. The parcels are made from banana leaves, which are wrapped around prawns and spices (ginger, turmeric, basil and chillies), then grilled on a charcoal stove.

Meat *Daging*

The pork is excellent in Bali where *babi guling* (roast suckling pig) is a highly-reputed dish. Javanese Muslims eat a lot of goat, delicious in stews and curries. High-grade beef and lamb are imported. Buffalo, the local alternative to beef, can be very tough.

Some traditional eating houses display samples of their wares in the window. If you can't translate the menu, simply point out what you fancy. Offal (liver, kidneys, brains) are frequently served. If they don't appeal, learn the phrase to turn them down.

I'd like some...	**Saya ingin...**	sa**ya** **ingin**
beef	**daging sapi**	**da**ging **sa**pee
lamb	**daging kambing**	**da**ging **kum**bing
pork	**daging babi**	**da**ging **ba**bee
veal	**daging anak sapi**	**da**ging **ana**[k] **sa**pee
I don't want that.	**Saya tidak mau.**	**saya tee**da[k] ma-oo

babi yang masih menyusu	**ba**bee yung **ma**sih m[e]**nyoo**soo	suckling pig
bakso	bakso	meatballs
bistik	**bee**stee[k]	steak
buntut sapi	**boon**toot **sa**pee	oxtail
daging babi (diasap)	**da**ging **ba**bee (dee-asap)	(smoked) ham
daging kambing	**da**ging **kum**bing	mutton
daging kelenjar perut	**da**ging k[e]**l**[e]**n**jar p[e]root	sweetbreads
daging kerbau	da**ging** k[e]**rba**-oo	water buffalo
daging pinggang	**da**ging **ping**gung	sirloin
ginjal	ginjal	kidneys
kaki babi	**ka**kee **ba**bee	pig's trotters
kaki (kambing)	**ka**kee (**kum**bing)	leg (of lamb)
kelinci	klinchee	rabbit
kepala babi	k[e]**pa**la **ba**bee	pig's head
lidah	**lee**dah	tongue
potongan	**po**tongan	chop
sayatan	**sa**yatan	cutlet
sepek	spek	bacon
sosis	sosis	sausage

baked	**dimasak**	dee**masa**[k]
barbecued	**dipanggang**	dee**pung**gung
boiled	**direbus**	deer[e]boos
fried	**digoreng**	dee**gor**eng
grilled	**dibakar**	dee**ba**kar
roast	**panggang**	**pung**gung
sautéed	**digoreng sebentar**	dee**gor**eng s[e]b[e]ntar
stewed	**direbus**	deer[e]boos
underdone (rare)	**kurang matang**	**koo**rung **ma**tung
medium	**setengah matang**	s[e]t[e]ngah **ma**tung
well-done	**dimasak matang-matang**	dee**masa**[k] **ma**tung-**ma**tung

Some meat specialities *Beberapa masakan daging*

babi asam pedas	**ba**bee **a**sam p[e]das	pork in hot and sour sauce
babi kecap	**ba**bee **k[e]**chap	fried pork in soya sauce
daging asam manis	**da**ging **a**sam **ma**nis	sweet and sour beef
daging bumbu bali	**da**ging **boom**boo **ba**lee	beef in chilli and tamarind sauce
daging pedas	**da**ging p[e]das	beef stew with hot pepper sauce
daging tomat	**da**ging **to**mat	stewed beef with tomatoes
dendeng ragi	**d[e]n**d[e]ng **ra**gee	crisp fried meat with coconut
gulai jawa	**goo**lai **ja**wa	chillied lamb curry
gulai kambing	**goo**lai **kam**bing	lamb curry
gulai otak	**goo**lai **o**ta[k]	brains in spicy coconut sauce
hati goreng Bali	**ha**tee **gor**[e]ng **ba**lee	liver with peanut and coconut Balinese style
jilabulo	jila**boo**lo	chicken livers in sago and coconut

kari kambing padang	**ka**ree **kam**bing **pa**dung	Sumatran lamb chop curry
panggang kambing	**pung**gung **kam**bing	spit-roasted lamb
perkedel babi goreng	p[e]rk[e]**del ba**bee **go**reng	spicy pork meatballs
sambal goreng babi	**sam**bal **go**reng **ba**bee	chillied pork in coconut milk
sate kambing	**sa**tay **kum**bing	lamb satay
sate pentul	**sa**tay p[e]ntool	minced pork satay
semur lidah	s[e]moor **lee**dah	boiled tongue in soya sauce

daging manis
(**da**ging **ma**nis)
dry fried sweet beef. Lean strips of beef are marinated in cumin, ginger, tamarind and brown sugar, then fried until crisp. This dish may then also be served roasted—*dendeng*—accompanied by rice and sambals.

goreng babat asam pedas
(**go**reng **ba**bat **a**sam p[e]das)
hot and sour fried tripe. Tripe is a popular delicacy in Indonesia, here fried with chillies and lemon grass to give a sharp, sour flavour.

gulai kambing
(**goo**lai **kam**bing)
lamb stew. More like a thick soup, served spooned over boiled rice, this dish is spiced with galangal, lemon grass, cinnamon and coconut.

lapis daging semarang
(**la**pees **da**ging s[e]**ma**reng)
beef Semarang style. A thick, sweet tomato stew, with thin strips of beef marinaded in nutmeg and garlic.

sate
(**sa**tay)
meat satay. Lean cubes of pork, beef, lamb or chicken, barbecued and served with peanut-based sauces, from sweet and sour to fiery chilli hot.

semur babi
(smoor **ba**bee)
pork with vermicelli. Thin slices of pork are cooked with garlic, green chillies and tomatoes, with transparent vermicelli made from green bean starch.

Game and poultry *Binatang buruan dan unggas*

Chicken is appreciated throughout Indonesia. The Balinese rear ducks in the rice fields and produce a memorable speciality: *bebek betutu*, duck broiled in banana leaves.

anak itik	ana^k **ee**ti^k	duckling
angsa	**ung**sa	goose
ayam	ayum	chicken
dada/kaki/sayap	**da**da/**ka**kee/**sa**yap	breast/leg/wing
ayam panggang	ayum **pung**gung	barbecued chicken
ayam kebiri	ayum k^e**bee**ree	capon
ayam mutiara	ayum mootee-**a**ra	guinea fowl
babi hutan	**ba**bee **hoo**tan	wild boar
bebek	**bay**bay^k	duck
bebek kecil	**bay**bay^k k^{e}chil	teal
burung dara	**boo**roong dara	pigeon
burung puyuh	**boo**roong **poo**yooh	quail
itik	**ee**ti^k	duck
kalkun	**kal**koon	turkey
kelinci	klinchee	hare
menjangan	**m^e**njungan	venison
terwelu	t^e**rway**loo	hare

These are some dishes you'll find hard to resist:

ayam goreng	ayum **go**reng	Indonesian spicy fried chicken
ayam goreng bulat	ayum **go**reng **boo**lat	stuffed braised chicken
ayam panggang	ayum **pung**gung	marinaded grilled chicken
ayam panggang bumbu besengek	ayum **pung**gung **boom**boo b^{e}s^{e}nge^k	roasted chicken with coconut sauce
ayam panike	ayum pa**nee**kay	chicken in aromatic sauce
ayam santan	ayum **san**tun	boiled chicken in coconut milk
bebek bumbu cabe	**bay**bay^k **boom**boo **chabay**	duck in chilli sauce
bebek tauco	**bay**bay^k **tau**cho	duck with salted yellow beans
opor bebek	**o**por **bay**bay^k	duck in coconut sauce
sate ayam	**sa**tay **a**yum	chicken satay
semur ayam	smoor **a**yum	chicken in soya sauce
tumis ayam dengan jamur	**too**mis **a**yum **den**gan **ja**moor	chicken with mushrooms

bebek hijau	(**bay**bay[k] **hee**jau)	duck in green chilli sauce. A West Sumatran dish, with lime leaves and lemon grass. Very hot and strongly flavoured.
gudeg	(**good**[e]g)	chicken with jackfruit. The most famous of all Javanese traditional dishes, a thick coconut sauce with tender spicy chicken.
gulai ayam	(**goo**lai ayum)	Javanese chicken curry. A distinctive taste is lent to this hot curry by the addition of a paste made from dry-fried grated coconut.
lapis ayam	(**la**pees **a**yum)	layered steamed chicken. Layers of chicken, spiced with galangal, coriander and chilli, wrapped in banana-leaf parcels and steamed over charcoal.

Rice and noodles *Nasi dan mi*

Anything on the menu with *nasi* in it means that it either contains rice or that rice is served with it. With *mie* dishes, the rice is replace by noodles.

The Dutch invented the *rijstaffel* (rice table) and, although it may not be quite authentic, it's an excellent way of trying yourself out on a wide range of delectable Indonesian foods. Many of the hotels and tourist restaurants service this positive banquet of rice with a mouth-watering array of side dishes. However hungry you are, remember, for health reasons, to wash the street dust off your hands before plunging in.

ketan	k[e]tan	sticky (glutinous) rice
mie ayam godog	mee ayum **go**dog	noodles in chicken soup
mie goreng kuah	mee **go**reng kuah	braised noodles
mie goreng sapi	mee **go**reng **sa**pee	fried noodles with beef and prawns
nasi goreng	**na**see **go**reng	fried rice
nasi kuning bumbu	**na**see **koon**ing **boom**boo	yellow rice with spices
nasi santan	**na**see **san**tun	rice in coconut milk

mie jawa
(mee **jawa**)

Javanese fried or boiled noodles. Originating in China, this dish can be served either as a noodle soup or fried with cabbage leaves, beansprouts, beef or pork and flat-leaved parsley.

nasi goreng istimewa
(**na**see **go**reng **ees**tim**ay**wa)

special fried rice. A basic *nasi goreng*, but served with a variety of cold meats, mushrooms and peanuts, and garnished with strips of omelette and prawn crackers.

nasi tumpeng
(**na**see **toom**peng)

festive rice cone. This dish is one always seen at celebrations or festivities in Indonesia: a beautiful mound of delicately flavoured yellow rice served with any number of accompaniments, from meatballs and prawn crackers to marbled eggs and a whole roast chicken.

Sauces *Saus*

Sauces and relishes form a very important part of Indonesian meals, adding flavours and heat to the main dishes. People unused to very hot food should take *sambal* sauce in moderation, as the most common ingredient is fiery hot chillies!

acar ketimun	**a**char k^{e}teemoon	cucumber pickle
sambal bajak	**sam**bal **ba**ja^{k}	spicy chilli sauce
sambal cuka	**sam**bal **choo**ka	vinegar and chilli sauce
sambal jelentah	**sam**bal j^{e}l^{e}ntah	garlic and chilli sauce
sambal terasi	**sam**bal **tra**see	shrimp paste relish
sambal terong	**sam**bal t^{e}rong	aubergine relish
sambal tomat	**sam**bal **to**mat	tomato and chilli sauce
sambal ulek	**sam**bal **oo**le^{k}	chilli paste
saos kacang	saus **ka**chung	peanut sauce

bumbu kacang pedas
(**boom**boo **ka**chung p^{e}**das**)

satay sauce. This sauce, usually hot and spicy with a base of ground peanuts, will always accompany barbecued skewers of marinaded meat. A milder variety is *bumbu kacang*.

sambal ikan
(**sam**bal **ee**kan)

fish relish. This can be made from tuna or eel, a sour, hot relish to accompany anchovy or fish dishes.

sambal kelapa
(**sam**bal **kla**pa)

coconut sauce. This can be served as a side dish or sprinkled directly over food, a delicious sweet and spicy sauce which complements many main dishes.

Vegetables and salads *Sayur-mayur dan selada*

When you're sweltering in the heat of the city, it's barely credible that, up in the hills, they're growing marvellous cauliflowers, cabbages, carrots, corn (maize), onions - all the familiar cool climate produce.

Vegetarians are well catered for in a country where the emphasis is on grains, vegetables and fruit.

adas	adas	fennel
apokat	apokat	avocado
asparagus/asperges	as**par**agus	asparagus
bawang	**ba**wung	onions
bawang perai	**ba**wung prai	leeks
bayam	**ba**yum	spinach
brambang	**brum**bung	leeks
buah gambas	**boo**wah **gum**bas	squash
buah tomat	**boo**wah tomat	tomatoes
cabe rawit	**cha**bay **ra**wit	chili
cendawan	ch^{e}**nda**wan	mushrooms
daun sla	daun sla	lettuce
ercis	^{e}rchis	peas
jagung	**ja**goong	corn
jagung manis	**ja**goong **ma**nis	sweetcorn
jalar	**ja**lar	sweet potatoes
jamur	**ja**moor	mushrooms
kacang-kacangan	**ka**chung-**ka**chungan	beans
kacang hijau	**ka**chung **hee**jau	mung beans
kacang merah	**ka**chung **may**rah	kidney beans
kacang pendek	**ka**chung **pen**day^{k}	French beans
kacang polong	**ka**chung **po**long	peas
kapri	**ka**pree	peas
kastanye	**kas**tanya	chestnuts
kentang	k^{e}ntung	potatoes
ketimun	k^{e}**tee**moon	cucumber
kobis	kobis	cabbage
kol	kol	cabbage
kol kembang	kol **k^{e}**mbung	cauliflower
labu	**la**boo	pumpkin
lobak cina	**lo**ba^{k} **chee**na	turnips
lobak	**lo**ba^{k}	radishes
lombok besar	**lom**bo^{k} b^{e}sar	(sweet) peppers
berbentuk bel hijau/merah	b^{e}**rb^{e}**ntoo^{k} bel **hee**jau/**may**rah	green/red
miju-miju	**mee**joo-**mee**joo	lentils
oyong	**o**yong	squash

rades	**ra**des	radishes
rambat	**rum**bat	sweet potatoes
sayur campuran	**sa**yoor **chum**pooran	mixed vegetables
selada	**sla**da	lettuce
seledri	s^{e}laydree	celery
terong	t^{e}rong	aubergine (eggplant)
ubi manis	**oo**bee **ma**nis	sweet potatoes
wortel	**wort**^{e}l	carrots

Raw salads should be eaten only in places where you are sure they have been hygienically prepared. The local variety, a favourite luncheon dish, is *gado-gado*, lightly steamed vegetables with peanut sauce. *Tahu* (bean curd) and *tempe* are made from soya beans, which form the basis of many tasty dishes replacing meat.

acar kuning	**a**char **koo**ning	mixed vegetables in vinegar
buncis tumis	**boon**chis **too**mis	spicy fried green beans
gado-gado	**ga**do **ga**do	mixed vegetables with peanut sauce
gadon tahu	**ga**don **ta**hoo	bean curd with coconut and chilli
kari sayur	**ka**ree **sa**yoor	vegetable curry
rujak	**roo**ja^{k}	fruit and vegetable salad
sayur bayem jagung	**sa**yoor **bay**^{e}m **ja**goong	spinach and sweetcorn salad
sayur tumis	**sa**yoor **too**mis	stir-fried vegetables
slada kangkung	**sla**da **kung**koong	watercress and cucumber salad
slada saos kelapa	**sla**da saus **kla**pa	green salad with coconut sauce
slada wortel	**sla**da **wort**^{e}l	carrot and apple salad
tahu campur	**ta**hoo **cham**poor	bean curd with vegetables
tempe goreng tepung	tempay **go**reng t^{e}poong	tempe deep-fried in batter
terik tempe	t^{e}ri^{k} tempay	tempe with thick candlenut sauce
terong goreng	t^{e}rong **go**reng	fried aubergines
urap	**oo**rap	mixed vegetables with coconut sauce
urap panggang	**oo**rap **pung**gung	vegetables and coconut baked with egg

Herbs and spices *Rempah-rempah*

After all, you're in the land of the Spice Islands! Although cloves, cinnamon and nutmeg were the lure which drew long-ago adventurers to Maluku (the Moluccas) where they grew, these are not normal flavours in Indonesian cooking. Cloves, it's true, are used to scent local *kretek* cigarettes but in the kitchen the favourite seasonings are ginger, coconut, peanuts, lime, turmeric, soy sauce and chillis.

Many Indonesian dishes aren't spicy hot but it's just as well to know how to say: "Not too spicy" (*Jangan terlalu pedas*).

adas manis	adas **ma**nis	aniseed
asam	asam	tamarind
bawang benggala	**ba**wung b^{e}ng**ga**la	chives
bawang putih	**ba**wung **poo**tih	garlic
brambang	**brum**bung	shallot
buah ketimun muda	**boo**wah k^{e}**tee**moon **moo**da	gherkins
bumbu cengkeh	**boom**boo **ch^{e}ng**kayh	pimiento
cengkeh	**ch^{e}ng**kayh	clove
dasun	**da**soon	garlic
daun salam	daun **sa**lam	bay leaf
garam	**ga**rum	salt
jahe	**ja**hay	ginger
jemuju	j^{e}**moo**joo	caraway
jintan	**jin**tan	caraway
kayu manis	**ka**yoo **ma**nis	cinnamon
kemangi	k^{e}**mun**gee	basil
ketumbar	k^{e}**toom**bar	coriander
kunyit	**koo**nyit	saffron
lada	**la**da	pepper
lokio	**lo**keeyo	chives
merica	m^{e}**ree**cha	pepper
pala	**pa**la	nutmeg
panili	**pa**nilee	vanilla
paprika	pa**pree**ka	paprika
permen	p^{e}rmen	mint
peterseli	**payt^{e}rsay**lee	parsley
selasih	s^{e}**la**sih	basil
seledri air	s^{e}laydree **ay**^{e}r	watercress
tanaman lobak	**ta**naman **lo**ba^{k}	horseradish

Fruit and nuts *Buah-buahan dan kacang-kacangan*

There's an amazing treat in store! The fruit is so delectable, so varied and so little known to many westerners that we've included a list to help you identify the colourful produce you see all around, some of it found only in Indonesia. Note that all fruit should be washed and peeled.

Do you have any fresh fruit?	**Apakah anda punya buah-buahan segar?**	a**pa**kah **an**da **poo**nya **boo**wah-**boo**wahan s^{e}gar
I'd like a (fresh) fruit cocktail.	**Saya ingin koktail buah-buahan segar.**	**sa**ya **ing**in koktail **boo**wah-**boo**wahan s^{e}gar

anggur	**ung**goor	grapes
apel	**a**pel	apple
aprikot	a**pree**kot	apricots
arbei	**ar**bei	strawberries
badam	**ba**dum	almonds
buah ara	**boo**wah **a**ra	figs
buah-buahan kering	**boo**wah-**boo**wahan kring	dried fruit
buah ceri	**boo**wah cherree	cherries
buah frambus	**boo**wah **fram**boos	raspberries
buah kemiri	**boo**wah k^{e}**mee**ree	hazelnuts
buah per	**boo**wah per	pear
buah prem	**boo**wah prem	plums
frambus	**fram**boos	gooseberries
jeruk besar	j^{e}roo^{k} b^{e}sar	grapefruit
jeruk limau	j^{e}roo^{k} **lee**mau	lime
jeruk manis	j^{e}roo^{k} **ma**nis	orange
jeruk sitrun	j^{e}roo^{k} **si**troon	lemon
kacang tanah	**ka**chung **ta**nah	peanuts
kastanye	**kas**tanya	chestnuts
kelapa	**kla**pa	coconut
kenari	k^{e}**na**ree	walnuts
kismis	**kis**mis	raisins
kurma	**koorr**ma	dates
limau	**lee**mau	lemon
nanas	**na**nas	pineapple
persik	p^{e}rsi^{k}	peach
pisang	**pee**sung	banana
semangka	s^{e}**mung**ka	melon

apokat
(**apo**kat) — avocado: here it's whipped into unforgettable creamy beverages with tinned milk and flavouring or served in a combination with ice cream.

belimbing
(**blim**bing) — starfruit; crunchy and thirst-quenching. The name comes from the star shape it presents in cross section.

duku
(**doo**koo) — small, yellowish, anonymous-looking fruit which peel open to give a taste thrill midway between a lychee and a grape.

durian
(**doo**reeyan) — expensive, by Indonesian standards, and seasonal. Once you've bought it, you have to live with the odour until you eat it! Opinions are divided over whether to love or hate this spiky, large fruit which is supposed to have aphrodisiac qualities.

jeruk
(j^e^roo^k^) — citrus fruit; apart from lemons and limes, much used in flavouring, you'll find sweet oranges (*jeruk manis*), the giant pomelo (*jeruk muntis*)—a little like a grapefruit but less acid—and a type of tangerine (*jeruk baras*).

kelapa
(**kla**pa) — coconut; of course you'll recognize them! Here you'll appreciate the refreshing quality of the milk and the delicate taste of the jelly-like flesh around.

mangga
(**mang**ga) — mango; there are many varieties. The slightly turpentine flavour is an acquired taste.

manggis
(**mang**gis) — mangosteen; purple skin with a white interior. A most delightfully perfumed taste. Queen Victoria, having heard of it, offered to reward any traveller who could come back with a mangosteen in good condition.

marquisa
(markweesa) — it looks and tastes like a giant passion fruit. Purple seeds are embedded in moist, yellow, semi-liquid flesh.

nangka
(**nung**ka) — jackfruit; It's enormous. Inside, the texture is chewy and pleasantly astringent in small doses.

papaya (pa**pa**ya)	fairly well known and readily available in the West. This large, yellow-skinned fruit was introduced into Indonesia. It tastes a little like a mango but is more solid.
pisang (**pee**sung)	banana; there are over 40 varieties ranging from the sweet finger banana (*pisang mas*) to the giant *pisang raja* with fruit almost two feet long. Larger kinds are used for cooking. *Pisang mas* (gold banana) and *pisang susu* (milk banana) make excellent eating.
rambutan (ram**boo**tan)	this rosy, spiny fruit, once slipped from its shell, is juicy and sweet like a lychee.
sawo (**sa**wo)	the exterior is a dour, brown camouflage for the honey flavour it contains.
salak (**sa**la^{k})	snakefruit; named for its mottled brown skin. It has a flavour all its own.
tuih (**too**-ih)	smooth and flavoured like a coconut.
sirsak (**seer**sak)	custard apple; it's sometimes known as soursop and contains a tangy, soft interior under that warty hide. They're ripe when they give slightly under the pressure of your thumb, the case with many tropical fruit.

Desserts *Kue kering*

I'd like a dessert, please.	**Bolehkah saya dapat kue-kue?**	**bo**layhkah **sa**ya **da**pat kway-kway
What do you recommend?	**Apa yang anda sarankan?**	**a**pa yung **an**da **sa**rankan
Something light, please.	**Sesuatu yang ringan.**	s^{e}**swa**too yung ringan
Just a small portion.	**Sedikit saja.**	s^{e}dikit **sa**ja

buah avokat	**boo**ah a**vo**kat	avocado dessert
eskrim	^{e}skreem	ice-cream
getuk lindri	g^{e}took **lin**dree	sweet potato cake
kolak ubi	**ko**la^{k} **oo**bee	sweet potatoes in coconut syrup
kue talam pisang	kway **ta**lum **pee**sung	banana batter pudding
nagasari	naga**sa**ree	rice cake with banana
panekuk pisang	pa**ne**kook **pee**sung	banana pancakes
pisang goreng	**pee**sung **go**reng	banana fritters
semar mendem	s^{e}mar m^{e}nd^{e}m	coconut filled pancakes

onde-onde (**on**day **on**day)	rice cakes in coconut. Attractive fresh-green rice cakes, coloured and scented with the fragrant duan pandan leaf, rolled in fresh grated coconut.
rujak (**roo**ja[k])	hot spicy fruit salad. A refreshing dessert: a variety of fruits soaked in salted water, served with a syrupy sweet-sour sauce.
serikaya (se**ree**kaya)	kenari-nut cake. A delicious steamed cake, originating in Alor, which can be served with a thick coconut sauce.

Drinks *Minuman*

Tap water is dangerous throughout Indonesia (even for cleaning your teeth). To be safe, it must be boiled for at least 20 minutes, then stored in a sterilized container. This has been done for the carafe water in your hotel room and that available in reliable restaurants. Use your discretion in other places. It's probably best to drink the irresistible tropical street juices without ice until you adjust to the country.

Alcohol is not permitted by the Muslim religion although, occasionally, your Indonesian friends may enjoy a beer. There's good beer available (*Bintang* and *Ankar*), as well as a mild beer-lemonade shandy, *Green Sands*. They all go well with Indonesian food.

Beer *Bir*

What would you like to drink?	**Anda ingin minum apa?**	anda **ing**in **min**oom **a**pa
I'd like a beer, please.	**Saya ingin bir.**	**sa**ya **ing**in beerr
Have a beer!	**Minumlah bir!**	min**oom**lah beerr
A bottle of lager, please.	**Satu botol bir yang tidak keras.**	**sa**too botol beerr yung **tee**da[k] kras
A bottle of mild beer, please.	**Satu botol bir ringan.**	**sa**too botol beerr ringan

Wine *Minuman anggur*

A little wine is now produced in Java, but it will be rare for you to come across it. You are more likely to be offered foreign wines, which you'll find in international places. They can be very expensive.

May I have the wine list?	**Bolehkah saya lihat daftar minuman anggur?**	**bo**layhkah **sa**ya **lee**hat **daf**tar **min**ooman **ung**goor
I'd like a ... of red wine/white wine.	**Saya ingin satu ... minuman anggur merah/putih.**	**sa**ya **ing**in **sa**too ... **min**ooman **ung**goor **may**rah/**poo**tih
a bottle	**satu botol**	**sa**too botol
half a bottle	**setengah botol**	s^e^t^e^ngah botol
a carafe	**satu karaf**	**sa**too karaf
a small carafe	**karaf kecil**	karaf k^e^chil
a glass	**gelas**	glass
How much is a bottle of champagne?	**Berapa harganya satu botol sampanye?**	**bra**pa **har**ganya **sa**too botol sam**pa**nya
Bring me another bottle/glass of ..., please.	**Tolong ambilkan satu botol/gelas ... lagi.**	**to**long ambilkan **sa**too botol/glass ... lagi
Where does this wine come from?	**Minuman anggur ini datang dari negeri mana?**	**min**ooman **ung**goor **ee**nee **da**tung **da**ree n^e^gree **ma**na

red	**merah**	**may**rah
white	**putih**	**poo**tih
rosé	**merah jambu**	**may**rah **jum**boo
sweet	**manis**	**ma**nis
dry	**kering**	kring

Other alcoholic drinks *Minuman lain yang mengandung alkohol*

What you will find in some districts is foaming, pleasant-tasting *tuak*. It's brewed from palms and gets stronger as it matures. In the markets it's sold in hollow bamboo canes. *Brem* and *badik* are both rice-based alcoholic beverages. Chinese restaurants may serve strong *arak*, also made from rice.

I'd like a/an...	**Saya ingin suatu...**	saya ingin swatoo
aperitif	**perangsang makan**	p^{e}rungsung makan
cognac	**konyak**	konyak
gin	**gin**	jin
liqueur	**liqueur**	likyoor
rum	**rum**	room
vermouth	**vermouth**	v^{e}rmooth
vodka	**vodka**	vodka
whisky	**wiski**	wiskee
neat (straight)	**murni**	moornee
on the rocks	**sama es**	sama es
with a little water	**dengan sedikit air**	d^{e}ngan s^{e}dikit ay^{e}r
Give me a large gin and tonic, please.	**Tolong beri saya satu gelas besar gin dan tonic.**	tolong bree saya satoo glass b^{e}sar jin dan tonik
Just a dash of soda, please.	**Bolehkah saya dapat sedikit soda.**	bolayhkah saya dapat s^{e}dikit soda

Nonalcoholic Drinks *Minuman tanpa alkohol*

Non-alcoholic beverages include a myriad fresh fruit drinks, normal bottled soft drinks and mineral water. Cold, sweetened bottled tea is an excellent dehydrant.

apple juice	**sari buah apel**	saree boowah apel
fruit juice	**sari buah**	saree boowah
grapefruit juice	**sari buah jeruk besar**	saree boowah j^{e}roo^{k} b^{e}sar
herb tea	**teh jamu**	teh jamoo
lemon juice	**sari buah jeruk sitrun**	saree boowah j^{e}roo^{k} sitroon
lemonade	**limun/limonade**	leemoon/leemonada
milk	**susu**	soosoo
milkshake	**milkshake**	milkshaik
mineral water	**air mineral**	ay^{e}r min^{e}ral
fizzy (carbonated)	**membuih**	m^{e}mboo-ih
still	**biasa**	beeyasa
orange juice	**sari jeruk manis**	saree j^{e}roo^{k} manis
orangeade	**air jeruk**	ay^{e}r j^{e}roo^{k}
tomato juice	**sari tomat**	saree tomat
tonic water	**tonikum**	toneekoom

Hot beverages *Minuman panas*

Tea and coffee are both grown in Indonesia. China tea is practically the national beverage.

I'd like a/an...	**Saya ingin...**	**sa**ya **ing**in
(hot) chocolate	**cokelat panas**	**chok**^{e}lat **pa**nas
coffee	**kopi**	**ko**pee
black	**hitam**	**hee**tam
with cream	**dengan kepala susu**	d^{e}ngan k^{e}**pa**la **soo**soo
with milk	**dengan susu**	d^{e}ngan **soo**soo
caffein-free	**tanpa kafein**	tanpa **ka**fein
espresso coffee	**yang sangat keras**	yung **sun**gat kras
tea	**teh**	teh
cup of tea	**secangkir teh**	s^{e}**chung**keer teh
iced tea	**teh es**	teh es
with milk/lemon	**dengan susu/ jeruk sitrun**	d^{e}ngan **soo**soo/j^{e}roo^{k} sitroon

Complaints *Pengaduan*

There's a plate/glass missing.	**Ada piring/gelas yang hilang.**	**a**da **pee**ring/glass yung **hee**lung
I don't have a knife/ fork/spoon.	**Saya tidak punya pisau/garpu/sen-dok.**	**sa**ya **tee**da^{k} **poo**nya **pee**sau/**gar**poo/**sen**-do^{k}
That's not what I ordered.	**Ini bukan yang saya pesan.**	**ee**nee **boo**kan yung **sa**ya p^{e}san
I asked for...	**Saya minta...**	**sa**ya **min**ta
There must be some mistake.	**Tentu ada kesala-han.**	**t^{e}n**too **a**da k^{e}**sa**lahan
May I change this?	**Bolehkah saya menukar ini?**	**bo**layhkah **sa**ya m^{e}**noo**kar **ee**nee
The meat is...	**Dagingnya...**	**da**gingnya
overdone	**terlalu lama dimasak**	t^{e}**rla**loo **la**ma dee**ma**sa^{k}
underdone	**kurang masak**	**koo**rung **ma**sa^{k}
too rare	**terlalu mentah**	t^{e}**rla**loo **m^{e}n**tah
too tough	**terlalu liat**	t^{e}**rla**loo leeyat
This is too...	**Ini terlalu...**	**ee**nee t^{e}**rla**loo
bitter/salty/sweet	**pahit/asin/manis**	**pa**hit/**a**sin/**ma**nis
I don't like this.	**Saya tidak suka ini.**	**sa**ya **tee**da^{k} **soo**ka **ee**nee

The food is cold.	**Makanannya dingin.**	**maka**nannya **ding**in
This isn't fresh.	**Ini tidak segar.**	**ee**nee **tee**da^k s^{e}gar
What's taking you so long?	**Apa yang bikin anda begitu lama?**	apa yung **bee**kin **an**da b^e**gee**too **la**ma
Have you forgotten our drinks?	**Apakah anda lupa akan minuman kita?**	apakah **an**da **loo**pa akan **min**ooman **kee**ta
This isn't clean.	**Ini tidak bersih.**	**ee**nee **tee**da^k b^{e}rsih
Would you ask the head waiter to come over?	**Bisakah anda tolong panggilkan kepala pelayan?**	**bee**sakah **an**da **to**long **pung**geelkan k^e**pa**la p^e**la**yan

The bill (check) *Rekeningnya*

In small eating houses where individuals have made an effort to please you, it would be polite to leave something in response. It is not expected. Tipping is basically discouraged but it is, after all, a personal recognition of service.

I'd like to pay.	**Saya ingin bayar.**	**sa**ya **ing**in **ba**yar
We'd like to pay separately.	**Kami ingin bayar sendiri-sendiri.**	**ka**mi **ing**in **ba**yar s^e**ndee**ree-s^e**ndee**ree
I think there's a mistake in this bill.	**Saya kira ada kesalahan dalam rekening ini.**	**sa**ya **kee**ra **a**da k^e**sa**lahan **da**lum **rayk**^{e}ning **ee**nee
What's this amount for?	**Jumlah ini untuk apa?**	**joom**lah **ee**nee **oon**too^k **a**pa
Is service included?	**Apakah ongkos pelayanan termasuk didalamnya?**	apakah ongkos p^e**la**yanan t^e**rma**soo^k dee**da**lumnya
Is the cover charge included?	**Apakah ongkos tambahan termasuk didalamnya?**	apakah ongkos **tum**ba**han** t^e**rma**soo^k dee**da**lumnya
Do you accept traveller's cheques?	**Apakah anda menerima cek wisata?**	apakah **an**da m^{e}n^e**ree**ma chek wi**sa**ta
Can I pay with this credit card?	**Bolehkah saya membayar ini dengan kartu kredit?**	**bo**layhkah **sa**ya m^{e}m**ba**yar **ee**nee d^{e}ngan **kar**too kredit
Please round it up to…	**Tolong bulatkan menjadi…**	**to**long **boo**latkan m^e**nja**dee

Keep the change.	**Biarkanlah uang kembalinya.**	**bee**yarkanlah wung k^e^m**ba**leenya
That was delicious.	**Itu sungguh lezat betul.**	**ee**too **soong**goh l^e^zat b^e^**tool**
We enjoyed it, thank you.	**Kami senang sekali, terima kasih.**	**ka**mi s^e^nung **ska**lee **tree**ma **ka**sih

PELAYANAN TERMASUK
SERVICE INCLUDED

Snacks—Picnic *Makanan kecil—Piknik*

Unless you're going to a nature reserve, you won't have to think in advance about outdoor eating supplies. Roadside fruit stalls and inexpensive eating places will keep you going through your travels. However, whether on foot or in a vehicle, you may wish to make sure you have some form of bottled beverage with you to ensure your liquid intake. Some visitors choose to travel with water purification tablets.

Give me two of these and one of those.	**Tolong beri saya dua biji dari yang ini dan satu dari yang itu.**	**to**long bree **sa**ya **doo**wa **bee**jee **da**ree yung **ee**nee dan **sa**too **da**ree yung **ee**too
to the left/right	**ke kiri/kanan**	k^e^ **kee**ree/**ka**nan
above/below	**atas/bawah**	atas/**ba**wah
It's to take away.	**Untuk dibawa pulang.**	**oon**too^k^ dee**ba**wa **poo**lung
I'd like a piece of cake.	**Saya ingin sepotong kue kering.**	**sa**ya **ing**in s^e^**po**tong kway kring
fried sausage	**sosis goreng**	sosis **go**reng
omelet	**telur dadar**	t^e^**loorr da**dar
open sandwich	**satu sandwich**	**sa**too **sand**wich
with ham	**dengan ham**	d^e^ngan ham
with cheese	**dengan keju**	d^e^ngan **kay**joo
potato salad	**kentang dan selada**	k^e^ntung dan s^e^**la**da

You can snack away happily on a multitude of sweet or savoury titbits. There are ever-popular peanuts, sugary or tasty pancakes (*martabak*); sticky rice flavoured with meat attractively enveloped in banana leaf, seemingly everybody's favourite at local airports (*lemper*); a similarly wrapped soy-bean cake, sweet and chili-spiced (*tempe*). In North Sulawesi they snack on a kind of crystallized mace; in West Sumatra some of the *krupuk* (crackers) are violently coloured shocking pink. The Balinese go for crunchy, fried baby eels. Sweets are available almost everywhere. Keep a few packs on you always for the children in remoter areas who cluster around, clowning and giggling and, like youngsters back home, are happy to have an unexpected treat.

Here's a basic list of food and drink that might come in useful when shopping for a picnic.

I'd like a/an/ some…	**Saya ingin satu…**	saya **in**gin
apples	**apel**	apel
bananas	**pisang**	**pee**sung
biscuits (Br.)	**biskuit**	**bis**koot
beer	**bir**	beerr
bread	**roti**	**ro**tee
butter	**mentega**	m^{e}**ntay**ga
cheese	**keju**	**kay**joo
chips (Am.)	**keripik**	**kreepi**^{k}
chocolate bar	**sebatang cokelat**	s^{e}**ba**tung **chok**^{e}lat
coffee	**kopi**	**ko**pee
cookies	**kue**	kway
crisps	**garing/kering**	**ga**ring/kring
eggs	**telor/telur**	t^{e}**loorr**
gherkins (pickles)	**ketimun kecil**	k^{e}**tee**moon k^{e}chil
grapes	**buah anggur**	**boo**wah **ung**goor
ice-cream	**eskrim**	eskrim
milk	**susu**	**soo**soo
oranges	**jeruk manis**	j^{e}roo^{k} **ma**nis
pepper	**merica**	m^{e}**ree**cha
roll	**roti kadet**	**ro**tee kadet
salt	**garam**	**ga**rum
sausage	**sosis**	sosis
soft drink	**minuman tanpa alkohol**	**min**ooman tanpa alkohol
sugar	**gula**	**goo**la
tea bags	**teh celup**	teh ch^{e}loop
yoghurt	**yogurt**	**yo**goort

TIPPING, see inside back-cover

Travelling around

It would take a lifetime exploring and understanding this intricate archipelago republic. A first encounter with Java or Bali will only whet your appetite for more. Trains are fine for Java and Sumatra – slower than buses but more comfortable and less tiring. There's a range of ferries and boats. You can also try adventurer's luck with the rakish *pinisi* (sailing ships) which ply to some islands. Mostly, though, you'll be island-hopping by plane.

Plane *Pesawat terbang*

Garuda is the national airline, complemented by Merpati Nusantara, Bouraq and Mandala Airlines.
Note: Flights are often delayed by weather conditions.

Is there a flight to Balikpapan?	**Apakah ada penerbangan ke Balikpapan?**	apakah **a**da p^{e}n^{e}r**bung**an k^{e} **bal**ik**pa**pan
Is it a direct flight?	**Apakah itu penerbangan langsung?**	apakah **ee**too p^{e}n^{e}r**bung**an **lung**soong
When's the next flight to Medan?	**Kapankah penerbangan yang berikutnya ke Medan?**	**ka**pankah p^{e}n^{e}r**bung**an yung b^{e}**ree**kootnya k^{e} **may**dan
Is there a connection to Padang?	**Apakah ada sambungan ke Padang?**	apakah **a**da **sam**boongan k^{e} **pa**dung
I'd like to book a ticket to Sabang.	**Saya ingin beli karcis ke Sabang.**	saya **ing**in blee **kar**chis k^{e} **sa**bung
single (one-way)	**karcis satu jalan**	**kar**chis **sa**too **ja**lan
return (round trip)	**karcis pulang-pergi**	**kar**chis **poo**lung-**p^{e}r**gee
business class	**kelas bisnis**	klas **bis**nis
aisle seat	**tempat duduk dekat gang**	**t^{e}m**pat **doo**do^{k} d^{e}kat gung
window seat	**tempat duduk dekat jendela**	**t^{e}m**pat **doo**do^{k} d^{e}kat j^{e}n**day**la
What time do we take off?	**Jam berapa kita berangkat?**	jum b^{e}**ra**pa **kee**ta **b^{e}rung**kat
What time should I check in?	**Jam berapa saya harus mendaftarkan diri untuk naik kapal?**	jum b^{e}**ra**pa **sa**ya **ha**roos m^{e}n**daf**tarkan **dee**ree **oon**too^{k} nai^{k} **ka**pal

Is there a bus to the airport?	**Apakah ada bis ke lapangan terbang?**	apakah **a**da bis k^{e} **la**pungan **t^{e}r**bung
What's the flight number?	**Ini penerbangan nomor berapa?**	**ee**nee p^{e}n^{e}r**bung**an **no**mor b^{e}**ra**pa
What time do we arrive?	**Jam berapa kita tiba?**	jum b^{e}**ra**pa **kee**ta **tee**ba
I'd like to ... my reservation.	**Saya ingin ... pesanan tempat saya.**	**sa**ya **in**gin ... **p^{e}**sanan **t^{e}**mpat **sa**ya
cancel	**membatalkan**	m^{e}mba**ta**lkan
change	**merobah**	m^{e}**ro**bah
confirm	**menegaskan**	m^{e}**n^{e}**gaskan

KEDATANGAN
ARRIVAL

KEBERANGKATAN
DEPARTURE

Train *Kereta-api*

Indonesia's state railway system PJKA runs trains on Java, Madura and Sumatra. It's simplest to get a travel agent to book you. Make sure you understand departure details: Jakarta and Surabaya have several stations. Javanese main routes are Jakarta - Yogya - Solo - Surabaya, and Jakarta - Semarang - Surabaya. The two link up.

Travel by train in Indonesia is very cheap by Western standards. Fares vary by train and by class; similarly the presence of air conditioning or electric fans depends on the train. These are some of the train services you may encounter:

Bima (**bee**ma) — night express (via Yogya); air conditioned luxury train; the only service offering sleeping accommodation.

Mutiara Utara (moo**ti**ara oo**ta**ra) — fast express train via Semarang; has air conditioning and reclining seats.

Parahiyangah (parahee**yung**ah) — fast trains travelling the relatively short distance from Jakarta to the high country resort, Bandung; departs several times daily.

Expres Siang (ek**spres** siang) — day express trains connecting Bandung and Surabaya via Yogya.

GBM Cepat (gbm **che**pat) — slow and generally very crowded; best avoided.

Note: Trains may not run strictly to time. Your ticket may work out to an extremely minimal amount more than quoted because of a station fee (*bea stasiun*). Day travel gives you a better view of the country but Indonesians themselves often prefer cooler night travel.

To the railway station *Ke setasion kereta-api*

Where's the railway station?	**Dimana setasion kereta-api?**	dee**ma**na **sta**seeyon **kray**ta-**a**pee
Taxi!	**Taksi!**	**tak**see
Take me to the...	**Bawa saya ke...**	**ba**wa **sa**ya k^{e}
main railway station	**setasion kereta-api**	**sta**seeyon **kray**ta-**a**pee
What's the fare?	**Berapa ongkosnya?**	b^{e}**ra**pa **ong**kosnya

JALAN MASUK	ENTRANCE
JALAN KELUAR	EXIT
KE PERON	TO THE PLATFORMS
INFORMASI/KETERANGAN	INFORMATION

Where's the...? *Dimana... ?*

Where is/are (the)...?	**Dimana... ?**	dee**ma**na
bar	**bar**	bar
booking office	**kantor pemesanan tempat**	**kan**tor p^{e}**m**^{e}**s**anan **t**^{e}**m**pat
currency exchange office	**kantor penukaran uang**	**kan**tor p^{e}**noo**karan wung
left-luggage office (baggage check)	**kantor penitipan koper**	**kan**tor p^{e}**nee**tipan **ko**per
lost property (lost and found) office	**kantor barang-barang hilang**	**kan**tor **ba**rung-**ba**rung **hee**lung
newsstand	**kios**	keeyos
platform 7	**peron**	**pe**ron
reservations office	**kantor pemesanan tempat**	**kan**tor p^{e}**m**^{e}**s**anan **t**^{e}**m**pat
restaurant	**restoran**	**res**toran
snack bar	**warung makanan kecil**	**wa**roong **ma**kanan k^{e}chil

ticket office	**tempat penjualan karcis**	t^{e}mpat p^{e}njoowalan karchis
waiting room	**ruang tunggu**	roowung toonggoo
Where are the toilets?	**Dimana kamar kecil?**	deemana kamar k^{e}chil

Inquiries *Keterangan*

When is the ... train to Pekalongan?	**Kapan kereta-api ... ke Pekalongan?**	kapan krayta-apee ... k^{e} p^{e}kalongan
first/last/next	**yang pertama/yang terakhir/yang berikutnya**	yung p^{e}rtama/yung t^{e}raheer/yung b^{e}reekootnya
What time does the train to Semarang leave?	**Jam berapa kereta-api ke Semarang berangkat?**	jum b^{e}rapa krayta-apee k^{e} s^{e}marung b^{e}rungkat
What's the fare to Surabaya?	**Berapa harga karcisnya ke Surabaya?**	b^{e}rapa harga karchisnya k^{e} soorabaya
Is there a connection to ...?	**Apakah ada sambungan ke ... ?**	apakah ada samboongan k^{e}
Do I have to change trains?	**Apakah saya harus ganti sepur?**	apakah saya haroos gantee spoor
Is the train running on time?	**Apakah kereta-api jalan tepat pada waktunya?**	apakah krayta-apee jalan t^{e}pat pada waktoonya
What time does the train arrive in Bogor?	**Jam berapa kereta-api sampai di Bogor?**	jum b^{e}rapa krayta-apee sumpai dee bogor
Does the train stop in Cirebon?	**Apakah kereta-api berhenti di Cirebon?**	apakah krayta-apee b^{e}rh^{e}ntee dee cheerebon
Which platform does the train to Yogyakarta leave from?	**Kereta-api ke Yogyakarta berangkat dari peron mana?**	krayta-apee k^{e} jogjakarta b^{e}rungkat daree peron mana
Which platform does the train from Solo arrive at?	**Kereta-api dari Solo datang di peron mana?**	krayta-apee daree solo datung dee peron mana
I'd like a timetable.	**Saya ingin daftar perjalanan.**	saya ingin daftar p^{e}rjalanan

TAXI, see page 21

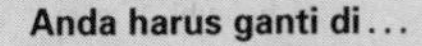

Anda harus ganti di...	You have to change at...
Ada kereta-api ke... pada jam...	There's a train to... at...
Kereta-api anda akan berangkat dari peron 2.	Your train will leave from platform 2.
Akan ada kelambatan... menit.	There will be a delay of... minutes.
Kelas satu di depan/di tengah/di belakang.	First class at the front/in the middle/at the rear.

Tickets *Karcis*

I'd like a ticket to Purwokerto.	**Saya mau beli karcis ke Purwokerto.**	**sa**ya mau blee **kar**chis k^e poorwo**k^{e}r**to
single (one-way)	**untuk satu jalan**	**oon**too^k **sa**too **ja**lan
return (round trip)	**untuk perjalanan pulang-pergi**	**oon**too^k p^e**rja**lanan **poo**lung-**p^{e}r**gee
first/second class	**kelas satu/dua**	klas **sa**too/dua
half price	**setengah harga**	s^{e}t^{e}ngah **har**ga

Reservation *Pesanan tempat*

I'd like to reserve a...	**Saya ingin memesan...**	**sa**ya **ing**in m^e**m^e**san
seat (by the window)	**tempat duduk (didekat jendela)**	**t^{e}m**pat **doo**do^k (deed^{e}kat j^{e}n**day**la)
berth	**tempat tidur**	**t^{e}m**pat **tee**door
upper	**di sebelah atas**	dee s^{e}blah **a**tas
middle	**di sebelah tengah**	dee s^{e}blah t^{e}ngah
lower	**di sebelah bawah**	dee s^{e}blah **ba**wah
berth in the sleeping car	**tempat tidur di kereta tidur**	**t^{e}m**pat **tee**door dee **kray**ta **tee**door

All aboard *Di atas*

Is this the right platform for the train to Jakarta?	**Apakah ini benar peron untuk kereta-api yang pergi ke Jakarta?**	apakah **ee**nee b^{e}nar **pe**ron **oon**too^k **kray**ta-apee yung **p^{e}r**gee k^e ja**kar**ta
Is this the right train to Malang?	**Apakah ini betul kereta-api yang pergi ke Malang?**	apakah **ee**nee b^e**tool** **kray**ta-apee yung **p^{e}r**gee k^e **ma**lung

Does this train go to...?	**Apakah kereta-api ini pergi ke... ?**	apakah **kray**ta-apee **ee**nee p^{e}**r**gee k^{e}
Excuse me. Could I get past?	**Maaf. Bolehkah saya lewat?**	ma-af. **bo**layhkah **saya** **lay**wat
Is this seat taken?	**Apakah tempat duduk ini sudah ada yang mengambil?**	apakah **t^{e}mpat doodo^{k}** eenee **soo**dah ada yung m^{e}ngumbil

PEROKOK
SMOKER

BUKAN PEROKOK
NONSMOKER

I think that's my seat.	**Saya kira inilah tempat duduk saya.**	saya **kee**ra **ee**neelah **t^{e}mpat doodo^{k} saya**
Would you let me know before we get to Kroya?	**Dapatkah anda kasih tahu saya sebelum kita sampai di Kroya?**	**dapatkah anda kasih tahoo** saya sebelum **keeta** sumpai dee **kro**ya
What station is this?	**Setasion manakah ini?**	**sta**seeyon **ma**nakah **ee**nee
Is the next station...?	**Apakah setasion yang berikutnya ini... ?**	apakah **sta**seeyon yung b^{e}**ree**kootnya **ee**nee
How long does the train stop here?	**Berapa lama kereta-api berhenti disini?**	b^{e}**ra**pa **lama kray**ta-apee b^{e}rh^{e}ntee dee**see**nee
When do we arrive in Madiun?	**Bila kita sampai di Madiun?**	**bee**la **kee**ta **sum**pai **dee** **mad**yoon

Sleeping *Tidur*

Are there any free compartments in the sleeping car?	**Apakah ada kompartemen kosong di gerbong tidur?**	apakah ada kom**part^{e}**men **ko**song dee **g^{e}r**bong **tee**door
Where's the sleeping car?	**Dimanakah kereta tidur?**	dee**ma**nakah **kray**ta **tee**door
Where's my berth?	**Dimana tempat tidur saya?**	dee**ma**na **t^{e}**mpat **tee**door **saya**
I'd like a lower berth.	**Saya ingin tempat tidur sebelah bawah.**	saya **in**gin **t^{e}**mpat **tee**door s^{e}blah **ba**wah

Would you make up our berths?	**Dapatkah anda membereskan tempat tidur kami?**	dapatkah anda m^{e}mbereskan t^{e}mpat teedoor kamee
Would you wake me at 7 o'clock?	**Dapatkah anda membangunkan saya pada jam 7?**	dapatkah anda m^{e}mbungoonkan saya pada jum 7

Baggage—Porters *Bagasi—Kuli-kuli*

Porter!	**Kuli!**	koolee!
Can you help me with my luggage?	**Dapatkah anda tolong bawakan begasi saya?**	dapatkah anda tolong bawakan b^{e}gasee saya
Where are the luggage trolleys (carts)?	**Dimana ada kereta begasi?**	deemana ada krayta b^{e}gasee
Where are the luggage lockers?	**Dimanakah lemari-lemari untuk menyimpan bagasi?**	deemanakah l^{e}maree-l^{e}maree oontoo^{k} m^{e}nyimpan b^{e}gasee
Where's the left-luggage office (baggage check)?	**Dimana kantor untuk menitipkan barang-barang?**	deemana kantor oontoo^{k} m^{e}nitipkan barung-barung
I'd like to leave my luggage, please.	**Saya ingin menitipkan bagasi saya.**	saya ingin m^{e}nitipkan b^{e}gasee saya
I'd like to register (check) my luggage.	**Saya ingin mendaftarkan barang-barang saya.**	saya ingin m^{e}ndaftarkan barung-barung saya

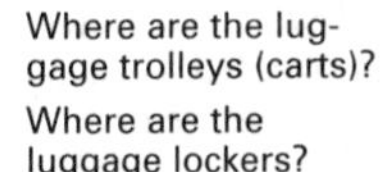

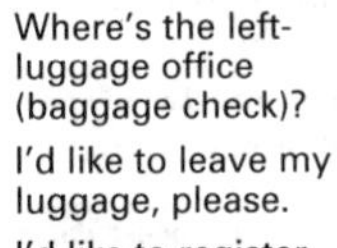

MENDAFTARKAN BARANG-BARANG
REGISTERING (CHECKING) BAGGAGE

Coach (long-distance bus) *Bis jarak-jauh*

An overnight express bus (*bis malam*) is the best way to travel long distances. These can only be boarded at city terminals. *Oplets*, *bemos* (short for *becak motors*) and *colts* run short to middle distances between cities and towns. They're hot, crowded, uncomfortable, and the driving can be dangerous. They're also inexpensive and friendly. The number of passengers on these "mini-buses" varies from about 6 to 20.

PORTERS, see also page 18

When's the next coach to...?	**Kapankah berang-kat bis jarak-jauh yang berikutnya ke... ?**	**ka**pankah b^{e}**rung**kat bis jara^{k}-jaooh yung b^{e}**ree**kootnya k^{e}
Does this coach stop at...?	**Apakah bis ini ber-henti di... ?**	apakah bis **ee**nee b^{e}rh^{e}ntee dee
How long does the journey (trip) take?	**Perjalanan ini makan waktu berapa lama?**	p^{e}**r**jalanan **ee**nee **ma**kan **wak**too b^{e}**ra**pa **la**ma

Bus *Bis*

Within town, you can take a local bus (*bis kota*) or whirl around in a *helicak* or *bajaj*. These "cabins" with driver and motor-cycle engine seat two people. The traditional *becak* or pedicab has been phased out in Jakarta, although you'll see scores of them in some other places.
In some areas you can take a *dokar*, a form of horse-drawn cart, around town or from village to village.

Which bus goes to the town centre?	**Bis yang manakah pergi ke pusat kota?**	bis yung **ma**nakah **p**^{e}**r**gee k^{e} **poo**sat **ko**ta
Where can I get a bus to Freedom Square?	**Dimana saya bisa dapat bis untuk pergi ke Medan Merdeka?**	dee**ma**na **sa**ya **bee**sa **da**pat bis **oon**too^{k} **p**^{e}**r**gee k^{e} m^{e}dan m^{e}rd^{e}ka
Which bus do I take to Taman Mini Indonesia?	**Bis yang mana yang mesti saya ambil untuk pergi ke Taman Mini?**	bis yung **ma**na yung m^{e}stee **sa**ya **um**bil **oon**too^{k} **p**^{e}**r**gee k^{e} **ta**man **mee**nee
Where's the bus stop?	**Dimanakah seta-sion bis?**	dee**ma**nakah **sta**seeyon bis
When is the... bus to Salatiga?	**Kapankah bis yang... ke Sala-tiga?**	**ka**pankah bis yung ... k^{e} **sa**la**tee**ga
first/last/next	**yang pertama/yang terakhir/yang beri-kutnya**	yung p^{e}**rta**ma/yung t^{e}**ra**heer/yung b^{e}**ree**kootnya
How much is the fare to...?	**Berapakah harga karcis ke... ?**	b^{e}**ra**pakah **har**ga **kar**chis k^{e}
Do I have to change buses?	**Apakah saya harus ganti bis?**	apakah **sa**ya **ha**roos **gan**tee bis

How many bus stops are there to...?	**Ada berapa setasion bis dalam perjalanan ke... ?**	ada b^{e}**ra**pa **sta**seeyon bis **da**lum p^{e}**rja**lanan k^{e}
Will you tell me when to get off?	**Bisakah anda beritahu saya bila saya harus turun?**	**bee**sakah **an**da bree**ta**hoo **sa**ya **bee**la **sa**ya **ha**roos **too**roon
I want to get off at the National Museum.	**Saya ingin turun di Gedung Gajah.**	**sa**ya **ing**in **too**roon dee g^{e}**doong ga**ja

PEMBERHENTIAN BIS	BUS STOP
BERHENTI ATAS PERMINTAAN	REQUEST STOP

Boat service *Dinas perjalanan kapal*

Water transport matches land transport in picturesque variety. Regular passenger and vehicular ferries run between the most popular islands (Java - Madura, for example).

Pelni, the national shipping line, offer a two-week round-trip taking in Java, Sulawesi, Kalimantan and Sumatra. Other shipping lines have cheaper fares and rougher conditions. Ask a travel agent about them.

In East Kalimantan the Mahakam River trip is an unforgettable experience on a grand old houseboat. Sailboats, outriggers (*prahu*) or motorized craft (*kapal motor*) can be hired at most beach fronts. To travel on the larger sailing ships (*kapal layar*), inquire in person at the ports where they berth.

When does the next boat for... leave?	**Kapankah kapal yang berikutnya ke... berangkat?**	**ka**pankah **ka**pal yung b^{e}**ree**kootnya k^{e}... b^{e}**rung**kat
Where's the embarkation point?	**Dimanakah tempat embarkasi?**	dee**ma**nakah **t**^{e}**m**pat embar**ka**see
How long does the crossing take?	**Penyeberangan makan waktu berapa lama?**	p^{e}ny^{e}**brung**an **ma**kan **wak**too b^{e}**ra**pa **la**ma
Which ports do we stop at?	**Di pelabuhan-pelabuhan mana kita singgah?**	dee p^{e}**la**boohan-p^{e}**la**boohan **ma**na **kee**ta **sing**gah

I'd like to take a tour of the harbour.	**Saya ingin mengadakan pelayaran keliling di pelabuhan.**	saya **ing**in m^{e}ngadakan p^{e}**la**yaran k^{e}**lee**ling dee p^{e}**la**boohan
boat	**kapal/perahu**	kapal/**pra**hoo
cabin	**kamar (di kapal)**	**ka**mar (dee **ka**pal)
single/double	**untuk seorang/ untuk dua orang**	**oon**too^{k} s^{e}-**o**rung/ **oon**too^{k} **doo**wa **o**rung
deck	**geladak**	g^{e}**la**da^{k}
ferry	**ferry**	**f^{e}**rree
hydrofoil	**hidrofoil**	hid**ro**foil
life belt/boat	**rompi pelampung/ sekoci penolong**	**rom**pee p^{e}**lam**poong/ s^{e}**ko**chee p^{e}**no**long
port	**pelabuhan**	p^{e}**la**boohan
river cruise	**pelayaran sungai**	p^{e}**la**yaran **soong**ai
ship	**kapal**	**ka**pal
steamer	**kapal api/uap**	**ka**pal **a**pee/**wap**
reclining seat	**tempat duduk berbaring**	**t^{e}**mpat **doo**do^{k} b^{e}r**ba**ring

Other means of transport *Lain-lain alat pengangkutan*

Considering the heat and the cheap forms of transport available, hitching becomes unappealing. Women should dress discreetly and not travel alone.

to hitchhike	**membonceng**	m^{e}m**bon**cheng
to walk	**jalan kaki**	**ja**lan **ka**kee

Bicycle hire *Sewa sepeda*

Bicycles are available for hire in Bali and Yogyakarta. In other places where you can't hire, you can always buy a secondhand model. Check it over well, especially brakes and tread. Most roads in Java and Bali are sealed and some have cycle tracks. There are plenty of repair shops.

Buses and boats will transport bikes.

I'd like to hire a...	**Saya ingin menyewa...**	saya **ing**in m^{e}**nyay**wa
bicycle	**sepeda**	**spay**da
moped	**sepeda kumbang**	**spay**da **koom**bang
motorbike/scooter	**sepeda motor/sekuter**	**spay**da **mo**torr/**skoo**t^{e}r

Car *Mobil*

Short-stay visitors usually hire a taxi or chauffeur-driven car. Although roads and bridges are being built at great pace in Indonesia, local road conditions can be unpredictable and, in places, appalling. In addition, driving around the busy steets of Indonesia's towns and cities can be extremely stressful and fought with hazards - so leave all the problems connected with motoring to your driver (*sopir*). Your hotel reception or a local tourist office can generally recommend you a good driver.

Where's the nearest (self-service) filling station?	**Dimana pompa bensin (pelayanan sendiri) yang terdekat?**	dee**ma**na **pom**pa **ben**seen (p^e**la**yanan s^e**ndee**ree) yung terd^ekat
Fill it up, please.	**Silahkan diisi penuh.**	**see**lahkan dee**ee**see p^enooh
Give me ... litres of petrol (gasoline).	**Tolong berikan saya ... liter bensin.**	**to**long breekan **sa**ya ... liter **ben**seen
super (premium)/ regular/unleaded/ diesel	**bensin premium/ biasa/tidak mengandung timah/ solar**	**ben**seen pre**mee**oom/ **bee**yasa/**tee**da^k m^eng**an**doong **tee**mah/ **so**lar
Please check the ...	**Tolong periksa ...**	**to**long priksa
battery	**aki**	**a**kee
brake fluid	**oli rem**	**o**lee rem
oil/water	**minyak/air**	minya^k/**a**yer
Would you check the tyre pressure?	**Bisakah tolong periksa tekanan ban?**	**bee**sakah **to**long priksa t^e**ka**nan ban
1.6 front, 1.8 rear.	**1.6 ban depan, 1.8 ban belakang.**	1.6 ban d^epan 1.8 ban **bla**kung
Please check the spare tyre, too.	**Bisakah juga tolong periksa tekanan ban serep?**	**bee**sakah **joo**ga **to**long priksa t^e**ka**nan ban **say**rap
Can you mend this puncture (fix this flat)?	**Dapatkah anda menambal ban ini?**	**da**patkah **an**da m^e**nam**bal ban **ee**nee
Would you clean the windscreen (windshield)?	**Dapatkah anda membersihkan kipas kaca mobil?**	**da**patkah **an**da m^em**ber**sihkan **kee**pas **ka**cha **mo**beel

Would you change the... please?	**Dapatkah anda mengganti... ?**	dapatkah anda m^{e}nggantee
bulb	**bola lampu**	bola lampoo
fan belt	**tali kipas**	talee keepas
spark(ing) plugs	**busi**	boosee
tyre	**ban**	ban
wipers	**kipas kaca mobil**	keepas kacha mobeel

Asking the way—Street directions *Menanyakan jalan—Petunjuk-petunjuk jalan*

Can you tell me the way to...?	**Bisakah anda kasih tahu saya jalan ke... ?**	beesakah anda kasih tahoo saya jalan k^{e}
In which direction is...?	**Ke jurusan manakah jalan ke... ?**	k^{e} jooroosan manakah jalan k^{e}
How do I get to...?	**Bagaimana caranya saya bisa pergi ke... ?**	bagai mana charanya saya beesa p^{e}rgee k^{e}
Are we on the right road for...?	**Apakah kita ada di jalan yang benar menuju ke... ?**	apakah keeta ada dee jalan yung b^{e}nar m^{e}noojoo k^{e}
How far is the next village?	**Berapa jauhkah desa yang berikutnya?**	b^{e}rapa jaoohkah daysa yung b^{e}reekootnya
How far is it to... from here?	**Berapa jauh jaraknya dari sini ke... ?**	b^{e}rapa jaooh jara^{k}nya daree seenee k^{e}
Is there a motorway (expressway)?	**Apakah ada jalan tol?**	apakah ada jalan tol
How long does it take...?	**Perjalanan... memerlukan waktu berapa lama?**	p^{e}rjalanan... m^{e}m^{e}rlookan waktoo b^{e}rapa lama
by car/on foot	**dengan mobil/ dengan jalan kaki**	d^{e}ngan mobeel/d^{e}ngan jalan kakee
Can I drive to the centre of town?	**Bolehkah saya mengendarai mobil sampai ke pusat kota?**	bolayhkah saya m^{e}ng^{e}ndara-ee mobeel sumpai k^{e} poosat kota
Is traffic allowed in the town centre?	**Apakah lalu-lintas dibolehkan di pusat kota?**	apakah laloo-lintas deebolayhkan dee poosat kota

CAR HIRE, see page 20

Can you tell me where… is?	**Dapatkah anda beri tahu saya dimana… ?**	**da**patkah **an**da bree **ta**hoo **sa**ya dee**ma**na
How can I find this place/address?	**Bagaimana saya bisa menemukan tempat/alamat ini?**	**ba**gai **ma**na **sa**ya **bee**sa m^en^emookan **t^em**pat/ **a**lamat **ee**nee
Where's this?	**Dimanakah ini?**	dee**ma**nakah **ee**nee
Can you show me on the map where I am?	**Bisakah anda menunjukkan saya di peta dimana saya berada?**	**bee**sakah **an**da m^e**noon**jookkan **sa**ya dee **pay**ta dee**ma**na **sa**ya b^e**ra**da
Where are the nearest public toilets?	**Dimanakah kamar kecil untuk umum yang terdekat?**	dee**ma**nakah **ka**mar k^echil **oon**too^k **oo**moom yung terd^ekat

Anda berada di jalan yang salah.	You're on the wrong road.
Pergilah lurus terus.	Go straight ahead.
Ada disana di sebelah kiri/kanan.	It's down there on the left/right.
di seberang/di belakang… **di sebelahnya/sesudah…**	opposite/behind… next to/after…
utara/selatan **timur/barat**	north/south east/west
Pergilah ke persimpangan jalan yang pertama/kedua.	Go to the first/second crossroads (intersection).
Beloklah ke kiri pada lampu lalu-lintas.	Turn left at the traffic lights.
Beloklah ke kanan pada sudut jalan yang berikutnya.	Turn right at the next corner.
Ambillah jalan…	Take the… road.
Jalan itu adalah jalan satu jurusan.	It's a one-way street.
Anda harus kembali ke…	You have to go back to…
Ikuti tanda-tanda untuk Garut.	Follow signs for Garut.

Parking *Memarkir*

Have low-denomination notes on you for parking fees, which are very frequently demanded. Note that if you hire a taxi, these fees are also your responsibility, not the driver.

Where can I park?	**Dimana saya bisa memarkir?**	dee**mana** saya **bee**sa m^{e}**mar**keer
Is there a car park nearby?	**Apakah ada lapangan parkir dekat sini?**	apakah **a**da **la**pungan par**keer** d^{e}kat **see**nee
May I park here?	**Bolehkah saya memarkir disini?**	**bo**layhkah **sa**ya m^{e}**mar**keer dee**see**nee
What's the charge per hour?	**Berapa ongkosnya untuk satu jam?**	b^{e}**ra**pa **ong**kosnya **oon**too^{k} **sa**too jum

Breakdown—Road assistance *Kerusakan—Pertolongan jalan*

Where's the nearest garage?	**Diamanakah bengkel mobil yang terdekat?**	Dee **ma**nakah **beng**kel **mo**beel yung terd^{e}kat
My car has broken down.	**Mobil saya rusak.**	**mo**beel **sa**ya **roo**sa^{k}
Where can I make a phone call?	**Dimana saya bisa memakai telepon?**	dee**mana** **saya** **bee**sa m^{e}**ma**kai **te**lepon
I've had a breakdown at...	**Saya ada kerusakan mobil di...**	**sa**ya **a**da k^{e}**roo**sa^{k}an **mo**beel dee
Can you send a mechanic?	**Bisakah anda mengirim seorang montir?**	**bee**sakah **an**da m^{e}ng**ee**rim s^{e}-**o**rung monteer
My car won't start.	**Mobil saya tak mau hidup mesinnya.**	**mo**beel **sa**ya ta^{k} mau **hee**doop m^{e}sinnya
The battery is dead.	**Akinya mati.**	**a**keenya **ma**tee
I've run out of petrol (gasoline).	**Saya kehabisan bensin.**	**sa**ya k^{e}**ha**bisan **ben**seen
I have a flat tyre.	**Saya punya ban kempes.**	**sa**ya **poo**nya ban **kem**pes
The engine is overheating.	**Mesinnya terlalu panas.**	m^{e}sinnya t^{e}**r**laloo **pa**nas
There's something wrong with the...	**Ada sesuatu yang rusak dengan...**	**a**da s^{e}**swa**too yung **roo**sa^{k} d^{e}ngan
brakes	**rem**	rem
carburettor	**karburator**	**kar**boorator
exhaust pipe	**knalpot**	knalpot
radiator	**radiator**	radiator
wheel	**roda**	**ro**da

Can you send a break-down van (tow truck)?	**Bisakah anda kirim mobil derek?**	**bee**sakah **an**da **kee**reem **mo**beel d^{e}ray^{k}
How long will you be?	**Berapa lama anda bisa ditunggu?**	b^{e}**ra**pa **la**ma **an**da **bee**sa dee**toong**goo
Can you give me an estimate?	**Bisakah anda memberi saya perkiraan?**	**bee**sakah **an**da m^{e}m**bree** **sa**ya p^{e}r**kee**ra-an

Accident—Police *Kecelakaan—Polisi*

Please call the police.	**Tolong panggilkan polisi.**	**to**long **pung**geelkan **po**leesee
There's been an accident. It's about 2 km. from...	**Ada terjadi kecelakaan. Kira-kira 2 km. dari...**	ada t^{e}**rja**dee k^{e}ch^{e}**la**ka-an. **kee**ra-kira 2 km **da**ree
Where's there a telephone?	**Dimana ada telepon?**	dee**ma**na **a**da **te**lepon
Call a doctor/an ambulance quickly.	**Tolong cepat panggilkan dokter/ambulans.**	**to**long ch^{e}pat **pung**geelkan dokter/**am**boolans
Here's my driving licence.	**Ini sim saya.**	**ee**nee sim **sa**ya
What's your name and address?	**Siapa nama anda dan dimana alamat anda?**	see**a**pa **na**ma **an**da dan dee**ma**na **a**lamat **an**da
What's your insurance company?	**Manakah perusahaan asuransi anda?**	**ma**nakah p^{e}**roo**saha-an asoo**ran**see **an**da

Road signs *Tanda-tanda jalan*

BAHAYA	Danger
BELOKAN	Bend
DILARANG BELOK	No turning
DILARANG LEWAT	No passing
DILARANG MASUK	No entry
DILARANG PARKIR	No parking
HATI-HATI! PERBAIKAN JALAN!	Caution Roadworks
KELUAR	Exit
KENDARAAN DILARANG MASUK	No vehicles
PELAN-PELAN	Drive slowly
PENGALIHAN LALU-LINTAS	Diversion (Detour)
STOP	Stop

Sightseeing

Maps can be found at hotel desks, travel agencies, local tourist offices and bookshops. Giveaway tourist newspapers contain information about places of interest and forthcoming events, as do the English-language papers. Guides are provided on organized tours. You can hire a guide for a set fee at places of special interest.

Where's the tourist office?	**Dimanakah kantor turis?**	dee**ma**nakah **kan**tor **too**ris
What are the main points of interest?	**Mana tujuan wisata yang menarik?**	mana **too**juan wee**sa**ta yung m^{e}narik
We're here for…	**Kami disini selama…**	**ka**mee dee**see**nee **sla**ma
only a few hours	**hanya beberapa jam saja**	**ha**nya b^{e}b^{e}**ra**pa jum **sa**ja
a day	**satu hari**	**sa**too **ha**ree
a week	**satu minggu**	**sa**too minggoo
Can you recommend a sightseeing tour?	**Bisakah anda memberi saran tentang perjalanan tamasya?**	**bee**sakah **an**da m^{e}m**bree** **sa**ran t^{e}ntung p^{e}r**ja**lanan tamasha
Where do we leave from?	**Kita berangkat dari mana?**	**kee**ta b^{e}**rung**kat **da**ree **ma**na
Will the bus pick us up at the hotel?	**Apakah bisnya akan menjemput kami di hotel?**	apakah **bis**nya akan m^{e}nj^{e}mpoot **ka**mee dee hotel
How much does the tour cost?	**Berapa ongkosnya perjalanan wisata?**	b^{e}**ra**pa **ong**kosnya p^{e}r**ja**lanan wee**sa**ta
What time does the tour start?	**Jam berapa perjalanan dimulai?**	jum b^{e}**ra**pa p^{e}r**ja**lanan dee**moo**lai
What time do we get back?	**Jam berapa kita akan tiba kembali?**	jum b^{e}**ra**pa **kee**ta akan **tee**ba k^{e}**mba**lee
Do we have free time in…?	**Apakah kita punya waktu bebas di… ?**	apakah **kee**ta **poo**nya **wak**too **bay**bas dee
Is there an English-speaking guide?	**Apakah ada pengantar tamasya yang bisa bicara bahasa Inggeris?**	apakah **a**da p^{e}**ngan**tar tamasha yung **bee**sa **bi**chara **ba**hasa ing-grees

I'd like to hire a private guide for...	**Saya ingin memakai seorang pramuwisata pribadi untuk...**	saya ingin m^{e}makai s^{e}-orung pramooweesata preebadee oontoo^{k}
half a day	**setengah hari**	s^{e}t^{e}ngah haree
a day	**satu hari**	satoo haree
Where is/Where are the...?	**Dimana...?**	deemana
art gallery	**balai/gedung kesenian**	balai/g^{e}doong k^{e}s^{e}nee-an
botanical gardens	**kebun raya**	k^{e}boon raya
building	**gedung**	g^{e}doong
business district	**daerah bisnis**	da-irah bisnis
castle	**kastil**	kastil
catacombs	**kuburan dibawah tanah**	koobooran dee bawah tanah
cave	**gua**	go-a
cemetery	**kuburan**	koobooran
city centre	**pusat kota**	poosat kota
chapel	**kapel**	kapel
church	**gereja**	grayja
concert hall	**ruang konser**	roowung konser
court house	**gedung pengadilan**	g^{e}doong p^{e}ngadilan
downtown area	**daerah perdagangan**	da-irah p^{e}rdagungan
embankment	**tambak/tanggul**	tumba^{k}/tunggool
exhibition	**pameran**	pamayran
factory	**paberik**	pabreek
fair	**pasar malam**	pasar malam
flea market	**pasar loak**	pasar lowa^{k}
fortress	**benteng**	benteng
fountain	**air mancur**	ayer manchoor
gardens	**kebun**	k^{e}boon
harbour	**pelabuhan**	p^{e}laboohan
lake	**danau/telaga**	danow/t^{e}laga
library	**perpustakaan**	p^{e}rpoostaka-an
market	**pasar**	pasar
memorial	**tanda peringatan**	tanda p^{e}ringatan
monastery	**biara**	beeyara
monument	**monumen**	monoomen
museum	**museum**	mooseeoom
old town	**kota lama**	kota lama
National museum	**Museum nasional**	mooseeoom naseeyonal
palace	**istana**	istana
park	**taman**	taman

parliament building	**gedung parlemen**	g^{e}**doong par**laymen
planetarium	**planetarium**	planet**a**ree-oom
royal palace	**istana kerajaan**	istana k^{e}**raja**-an
ruins	**puing-puing**	pwing-pwing
shopping area	**daerah pertokoan**	**da**-irah p^{e}**rtoko**-an
square	**alun-alun/lapangan**	aloon-aloon/**la**pungan
stadium	**stadion**	**sta**deeyon
statue	**patung**	**pa**toong
stock exchange	**bursa saham**	**boor**sa **sa**-ham
temple	**candi**	**chan**dee
theatre	**sandiwara**	sandee**wa**ra
tomb	**makam**	**ma**kam
tower	**menara**	m^{e}**nara**
town hall	**balai kota**	**ba**lai **ko**ta
university	**universitas**	ooneeversee**tas**
zoo	**kebun binatang**	k^{e}boon bin**a**tung

Admission *Izin masuk*

Most museums shut early afternoon, before noon on Friday and all day Monday.

Is… open on Sundays?	**Apakah… buka pada hari Minggu?**	apakah… **booka pada** haree minggoo
What are the opening hours?	**Kapankah jam-jam buka tempat ini?**	**ka**pankah jum-jum **booka** t^{e}**mpat eenee**
When does it close?	**Kapan dia tutup?**	kapan **deea too**toop
How much is the entrance fee?	**Berapa harga karcis masuknya?**	b^{e}**rapa har**ga **kar**chis masoo^{k}nya
Is there any reduction for (the)…?	**Apakah ada reduksi untuk…?**	apakah ada ray**dook**see **oon**too^{k}
children	**anak-anak**	anak-ana^{k}
disabled	**orang cacat**	orung **cha**chat
groups	**rombongan**	**rom**bongan
pensioners	**orang pensiunan**	orung pen**syoo**nan
students	**pelajar**	p^{e}**la**jar
Do you have a guidebook (in English)?	**Apakah anda punya buku pedoman (dalam bahasa Inggeris)?**	apakah **an**da **poo**nya **boo**koo p^{e}**do**man (**da**lum **ba**hasa ing-grees)
Can I buy a catalogue?	**Bolehkah saya beli satu katalog?**	**bo**layhkah **sa**ya blee **sa**too katalog

Is it all right to take pictures?	**Apakah diperbolehkan untuk mengambil gambar?**	**a**pakah deep^e^r**bo**layhkan **oon**too^k^ m^e^ng**um**bil **gum**bar

BOLEH MASUK/BEBAS MASUK	ADMISSION FREE
TIDAK DIPERBOLEHKAN MEMBAWA KAMERA/ALAT POTRET	NO CAMERAS ALLOWED

Is there easy access for the disabled?	**Apakah mudah masuk bagi orang cacat?**	**a**pakah **moo**dah **ma**soo^k^ **ba**gee **o**rung **cha**chat
Are there facilities/activities for children?	**Apakah ada fasilitas-fasilitas/kegiatan-kegiatan bagi anak-anak?**	**a**pakah **a**da fa**sil**itas-fa**sil**itas/k^e^**gee-at**an-k^e^**gee-at**an **ba**gee **a**nak-**a**na^k^

Who-What-When? *Siapa-Apa-Kapan?*

What's that building?	**Gedung apakah itu?**	g^e^**doong a**pakah **ee**too
Who was the...?	**Siapakah... ?**	see**a**pakah
architect	**arsiteknya**	arsiteknya
artist	**senimannya**	s^e^neemannya
painter	**pelukisnya**	p^e^**loo**kisnya
sculptor	**pemahatnya**	p^e^**ma**hatnya
Who built it?	**Siapa yang membangunnya?**	see**a**pa yung m^e^m**bang**oonnya
Who painted that picture?	**Siapa yang melukis lukisan itu?**	see**a**pa yung m^e^**loo**kiss **loo**kissan **ee**too
When did he live?	**Dia hidup di tahun-tahun berapa?**	**dee**a **hee**doop dee **ta**hoon-**ta**hoon b^e^**ra**pa
When was it built?	**Kapan ia dibangun?**	**ka**pan **ee**a dee**bung**oon
Where's the house where... lived?	**Dimanakah rumahnya dimana... tinggal dikala masa hidupnya?**	dee**ma**nakah **roo**mahnya dee**ma**na... **ting**gal dee**ka**la **ma**sa **hee**doopnya
We're interested in...	**Kami mempunyai perhatian terhadap...**	**ka**mee m^e^m**poo**nya-ee p^e^r**ha**tee-an t^e^r**ha**dap
antiques	**barang-barang antik**	**ba**rung-**ba**rung anteek
archaeology	**arkeologi**	arkay**o**logee
art	**seni**	s^e^nee
botany	**botani**	**bo**tanee

ceramics	**keramik**	k^{e}**ra**mik
coins	**uang logam**	wung **lo**gum
fine arts	**kesenian murni**	k^{e}s^{e}nee-an **moor**nee
furniture	**mebel**	**mayb**^{e}**l**
geology	**geologi**	gay**o**logee
handicrafts	**kerajinan tangan**	k^{e}**ra**jinan **tung**an
history	**sejarah**	s^{e}**ja**rah
medicine	**ilmu kedokteran**	ilmoo k^{e}**dok**t^{e}ran
music	**musik**	**moo**seek
natural history	**ilmu pengetahuan alam**	ilmoo p^{e}ng^{e}**ta**hoo-an **a**lam
ornithology	**ilmu burung**	ilmoo **boo**roong
painting	**lukisan**	**loo**kissan
pottery	**barang tembikar**	**ba**rung t^{e}m**bee**kar
religion	**agama**	a**ga**ma
sculpture	**patung**	**pa**toong
zoology	**zoologi**	zoo-**o**logee
The ... is ...	**...nya**	...nya
amazing	**mengagumkan**	m^{e}nga**goom**kan
awful	**mengerikan**	m^{e}ng^{e}**ree**kan
beautiful	**cantik**	**chan**ti^{k}
gloomy	**muram**	**moo**rum
impressive	**mengesankan**	m^{e}ng^{e}**san**kan
interesting	**interesan**	inte**re**san
magnificent	**bagus sekali**	**ba**goos **ska**lee
pretty	**molek**	**mo**lay^{k}
strange	**aneh**	**a**nayh
superb	**hebat**	**hay**bat
terrifying	**mengerikan**	m^{e}ng^{e}**ree**kan
ugly	**jelek**	**j**^{e}**lay**^{k}

Religious services *Kebaktian keagamaan*

Indonesians respect every religion and are suspicious of acknowledged atheism. Ninety per cent of the population is Muslim with a complex background tradition of Hinduism and animism. Bali is almost entirely Hindu. There are also Buddhists, Taoists and Christians. There is no active synagogue.

Wear discreet clothing to visit holy places, which include the Sultans' palaces. Remove your shoes to enter a mosque; women should cover their heads and upper arms. Depending on the religious tradition of the monument, you may be asked to don a *sarung* or a temple sash, available for hire at a tiny fee.

Is there a . . . near here?	**Apakah ada . . . didekat sini?**	apakah ada . . . deed^{e}kat seenee
mosque	**masjid/mesjid**	masjid/m^{e}sjid
Catholic church	**gereja Katolik**	grayja katoleek
Protestant church	**gereja Protestan**	grayja protestan
temple	**candi**	chandee

In the countryside *Daerah pedesaan*

How far is it to . . .?	**Berapa jauhkah jalan ke . . . ?**	b^{e}rapa jaoohkah jalan k^{e}
Can we walk there?	**Apakah kita bisa jalan kaki kesana?**	apakah keeta beesa jalan kakee k^{e}sana
What kind of . . . is that?	**. . . macam apa itu?**	. . . machum apa eetoo
animal/bird	**binatang/burung**	binatung/booroong
flower/tree	**bunga/pohon**	boonga/pohon
buffalo/crocodile	**kerbau/buaya**	k^{e}rbau/boowaya
monkey/snake	**monyet/ular**	mony^{e}t/oolar

Landmarks *Tanda penunjuk*

bridge	**jembatan**	j^{e}mbatan
cliff	**jurang**	joorung
farm	**tanah pertanian**	tanah p^{e}rtaneeyan
field	**lapangan**	lapungan
forest	**hutan**	hootan
garden	**kebun**	k^{e}boon
hill	**bukit**	bookit
house	**rumah**	roomah
lake	**danau**	danow
meadow	**padang rumput**	padung roompoot
mountain	**gunung**	goonoong
path	**jalan kecil**	jalan k^{e}chil
peak	**puncak**	pooncha^{k}
pond	**kolam**	kolum
river	**sungai**	soongai
road	**jalan**	jalan
sea	**laut**	lout
spring	**mata air**	mata ayer
valley	**lembah**	l^{e}mbah
village	**desa**	daysa
wall	**tembok**	tembo^{k}
waterfall	**air terjun**	ayer t^{e}rjoon
wood	**kayu**	kayoo

ASKING THE WAY, see page 76

Relaxing

Most of the usual kinds of entertainment are available, but visitors are more intent on uncovering local cultural performances: *wayang*, dance and *gamelan*. Be sure to obtain a copy of the Directorate of Tourism's *Calendar of Events* with exact times for main attractions in all areas. Hotel reception desks and tourist offices are an excellent source of information.

Cinema (movies)—Theatre *Gedung bioskop—Teater*

What's on at the cinema tonight?	**Film apa dimainkan di gedung bioskop malam ini?**	film apa dee**main**kan dee g^e**doong bee**yoskop **ma**lam **ee**nee
What's playing at the... Theatre?	**Apa yang sedang dipertunjukkan di Teater...?**	apa yung s^edung deep^e**rtoon**jookan dee **ta**yat^er
What sort of play is it?	**Sandiwara macam apakah itu?**	sandee**wa**ra **ma**chum apakah **ee**too
Who's it by?	**Siapakah penulisnya?**	seeapakah p^e**noo**lisnya
Can you recommend a...?	**Bisakah anda menyarankan suatu...?**	**bee**sakah **an**da m^e**nya**rankan **swa**too
good film	**film yang baik**	film yung bai^k
comedy	**komedi**	**ko**maydee
musical	**komedi musik**	**ko**maydee **moo**seek
Where's that new film directed by... being shown?	**Film baru yang disutradarai oleh... itu sedang dimainkan dimana?**	film **ba**roo yung deesootra**da**ra-ee **o**layh... **ee**too s^edung dee**main**kan dee**ma**na
Who's in it?	**Siapa yang main didalamnya?**	see**a**pa yung main dee**da**lumnya
Who's playing the lead?	**Siapa yang main peran utamanya?**	see**a**pa yung main p^e**ran** oota**ma**nya
Who's the director?	**Siapa sutradaranya?**	see**a**pa sootra**da**ranya
Is there a shadow puppet show on somewhere?	**Apakah ada pertunjukan wayang kulit disini?**	apakah **a**da p^e**rtoon**jookan **wa**yung **koo**lit dee**see**nee
What time does it begin?	**Jam berapa dia mulai?**	jum b^e**ra**pa **dee**a moolai

Are there any seats for tonight?	**Apakah ada tempat duduk kosong untuk malam ini?**	apakah ada t^{e}mpat doodo^{k} kosong oontoo^{k} malam eenee
How much are the seats?	**Berapa harganya karcis untuk tempat duduk itu?**	b^{e}rapa harganya karchis oontoo^{k} t^{e}mpat doodo^{k} eetoo
I'd like to reserve 2 seats for the show on Friday evening.	**Saya ingin memesan 2 karcis untuk pertunjukan pada hari Jumat malam.**	saya ingin m^{e}m^{e}san 2 karchisoontoo^{k} p^{e}rtoonjoo^{k}an pada haree joomat malam
Can I have a ticket for the matinée on Tuesday?	**Bisakah saya dapat karcis untuk pertunjukan siang pada hari Selasa?**	beesakah saya dapat karchis oontoo^{k} p^{e}rtoonjoo^{k}an see-ung pada haree slasa
I'd like a seat ...	**Saya ingin dapat tempat duduk ...**	saya ingin dapat t^{e}mpat doodo^{k}
not too far back	**jangan terlalu jauh ke belakang**	jungan t^{e}rlaloo jaooh k^{e} blakung
somewhere in the middle.	**kira-kira di tengah**	keera-keera dee t^{e}ngah
How much are the seats in the circle (mezzanine)?	**Berapa harganya karcis untuk tempat duduk di loteng tengah?**	b^{e}rapa harganya karchis oontoo^{k} t^{e}mpat doodo^{k} dee loteng t^{e}ngah
May I have a programme, please?	**Bisakah saya dapat buku acara (konser)?**	beesakah saya dapat bookoo achara (konser)
Where's the cloakroom?	**Dimanakah tempat penggantungan jas?**	deemanakah t^{e}mpat p^{e}nggantoongan jas

Maaf, semua sudah terjual habis.	I'm sorry, we're sold out.
Masih hanya tinggal beberapa karcis saja di loteng tengah.	There are only a few seats left in the circle (mezzanine).
Bolehkah saya melihat karcis anda?	May I see your ticket?
Inilah tempat duduk anda.	This is your seat.

DAYS OF THE WEEK, see page 151

Ballet—Concert *Balet—Konser*

These are some of the varied cultural entertainments you'll want to experience during your stay:

tarian tradisional (tar**ee**yan tra**dee**seeyonal) — Traditional dance performances are very popular, particularly in Bali, where they tend to be energetic, noisy and exhilarating to watch.

wayang kulit (wayung **koo**lit) — Tales from the Hindu epics, the Mahabaharata and the Ramayana are interpreted by flat, stylized leather puppets projected as shadows on to a screen. Controlling these highly symbolic figures is the *dalang* or puppeteer. Performances are almost always at night.

wayang golek (wayung golay[k]) — These doll puppets are a development from *wayang kulit* and a speciality of West Java. Performances often take place during the day.

wayang topeng (wayung **to**peng) — Masked human performers mime stories.

wayang wong (wayung wong) — Unmasked dancer-actors perform in profile, imitating *wayang kulit.*

gamelan (gam[e]lan) — A gong orchestra, comprised of some 20 instruments, mostly percussion, producing music with a meditative quality that greatly influenced the French composer Claude Debussy.

Innumerable festivals depend on the traditions and religious beliefs in each particular area. Consult the *Calendar of Events* and inquire around.

Can you recommend a(n)…?	**Bisakah anda menyarankan suatu… ?**	bee**sakah** **an**da m[e]**nya**rankan **swa**too
ballet	**balet**	**ba**let
concert	**konser**	**kon**ser
opera	**opera**	opera
traditional dance	**tarian tradisional**	ta**ree**an tra**dee**sional
Where's the opera house/the concert hall?	**Dimana gedung opera/ruang konser?**	dee**ma**na g[e]**doong** opera/ roowung **kon**ser
Who's singing/ dancing?	**Siapa yang menyanyi/menari?**	seeapa yung m[e]**nya**nyee/ m[e]**na**ree
Which orchestra is playing?	**Orkes mana yang main?**	orkes **ma**na yung main
What are they playing?	**Apa yang mereka mainkan?**	apa yung m[e]**ray**ka **main**kan

Nightclubs—Discos *Klub malam—Disko*

Can you recommend a good nightclub?	**Bisakah anda menyarankan suatu klub malam yang baik?**	**bee**sakah **an**da m^{e}**nya**rankan **swa**too klub **ma**lam yung bai^{k}
Is there a floor show?	**Apakah ada acara pertunjukan hiburan di klub malam?**	apakah **a**da **a**cha**ra** p^{e}**rtoon**joo^{k}an **hee**booran dee klub **ma**lam
What time does the show start?	**Jam berapa pertunjukan dimulai?**	jum b^{e}**ra**pa p^{e}**rtoon**joo^{k}an dee**moo**lai
Where can we go dancing?	**Dimana kita bisa pergi untuk berdansa?**	dee**ma**na **kee**ta **bee**sa **p^{e}r**gee **oon**too^{k} b^{e}**rdan**sa
Is there a discotheque in town?	**Apakah ada diskotek di kota?**	apakah **a**da diskotek dee **ko**ta
Would you like to dance?	**Apakah anda ingin berdansa?**	apakah **an**da **ing**in b^{e}**rdan**sa

Sports *Olahraga*

Spectator sports are, as you can well imagine, both varied and extraordinary. On Madura you witness exciting bull races. There's bull fighting in East Java and in West Sumatra at villages near Bukittinggi. Rams butt their heads together in the vicinity of Bandung, West Java. Cock fighting is common in Bali. Flying kites is a favourite activity in many places; there are kite fights as well. Ambon has pioneered *becak* races between locals and visiting Australian yachties.

Mountaineering, trekking and riding are top-rated activities for visitors. Locally-available guides should be able to advise on volcanic activity and suitable clothing as well as supplies for mountaineering and camping in nature reserves. You need permission to enter most conservation areas.

General sports include tennis, table tennis, badminton and bowling. There are several golf courses. Jakarta has horse and greyhound racing.

I'd like to see a bull race.	**Saya ingin lihat kerapan sapi?**	**sa**ya **ing**in **lee**hat k^{e}**ra**pan **sa**pee

basketball	**bola basket**	**bola bask**^e^t
boxing	**bertinju**	b^e^**rtin**joo
car racing	**balap mobil**	**bal**ap **mo**beel
cycling	**naik sepeda**	nai^k^ **spay**da
football (soccer)	**sepakbola**	**say**pa^k^**bo**la
horse racing	**pacuan kuda**	**pa**choo-an **koo**da
horse riding	**naik kuda**	nai^k^ **koo**da
mountaineering	**mendaki gunung**	m^e^**nda**kee **goo**noong
swimming	**berenang**	b^e^r^e^nung
tennis	**main tenis**	main tenis
volleyball	**bola voli**	**bo**la **vo**lee

Can you get me a ticket?	**Bisakah anda mencarikan karcis untuk saya?**	**bee**sakah **an**da m^e^**ncha**reekan **kar**chi**soon**too^k^ **sa**ya
What's the admission charge?	**Berapa harga karcis masuknya?**	b^e^**ra**pa **har**ga **kar**chis **ma**soo^k^nya
Where's the nearest golf course?	**Dimana lapangan golf yang terdekat?**	dee**ma**na **la**pungan golf yung terd^e^kat
Where are the tennis courts?	**Dimana ada lapangan-lapangan tenis?**	dee**ma**na **a**da **la**pungan-**la**pungan tenis
What's the charge per...?	**Berapa ongkos mainnya untuk satu... ?**	b^e^**ra**pa **ong**kos mainnya **oon**too^k^ **sa**too
day/round/hour	**hari/permainan/ jam**	**ha**ree/p^e^rmainan/jum
Can I hire (rent) rackets?	**Apakah saya bisa menyewa raket?**	**a**pakah **sa**ya **bee**sa m^e^**nyay**wa **ra**ket
Where's the race course (track)?	**Dimanakah lapangan?**	dee**ma**nakah **la**pungan
Is there any good fishing/hunting around here?	**Apakah ada kemungkinan baik untuk mengail/ berburu di sekitar sini?**	**a**pakah **a**da k^e^**moong**kinan bai^k^ **oon**too^k^ m^e^**ngail**/ b^e^**rboo**roo dee s^e^**kee**tar **see**nee
Do I need a permit?	**Apakah saya memerlukan izin untuk itu?**	**a**pakah **sa**ya m^e^**m^e^r**lookan izin **oon**too^k^ **ee**too
Where can I get one?	**Dimana saya bisa dapat izin?**	dee**ma**na **sa**ya **bee**sa **da**pat izin
Can one swim in the lake/river?	**Apakah orang boleh berenang di danau/sungai?**	**a**pakah **o**rung **bo**layh b^e^r^e^nug dee **da**now/ **soong**ai
Is there a swimming pool here?	**Apakah ada kolam berenang disini?**	**a**pakah **a**da **ko**lum b^e^r^e^nug dee**see**nee

On the beach *Di pantai*

Major hotels have swimming pools which non-residents can use for a small fee. There are dozens of beaches as well as lakes and rivers. Surfing and scuba diving are exceptional in many places (check on local hazards which may include stinging coral or poisonous stone fish). There's organized boat hire in more developed places, otherwise you can always arrange to rent a boat or go out with locals.

Is it safe to swim here?	**Apakah aman untuk berenang disni?**	apakah **a**man **oon**too^{k} b^{e}r^{e}nung dee**see**nee
Is there a lifeguard?	**Apakah ada pengawal renang?**	apakah **a**da p^{e}ng**a**wal r^{e}nung
Is it safe for children?	**Apakah aman untuk anak-anak?**	apakah **a**man **oon**too^{k} anak-**a**na^{k}
The sea is very calm.	**Lautnya amat tenang.**	**lout**nya **a**mat t^{e}nung
There are some big waves.	**Ada beberapa gelombang besar.**	**a**da b^{e}b^{e}**ra**pa g^{e}**lom**bung b^{e}sar
Are there any dangerous currents?	**Apakah ada arus yang berbahaya?**	apakah **a**da **a**roos yung b^{e}rba**ha**ya
What time is high tide/low tide?	**Jam berapa pasang naik/turun?**	jum b^{e}**ra**pa **pa**sung nayk/ **too**roon
I want to hire (rent) a/an/some...	**Saya ingin menyewa...**	**sa**ya **ing**in m^{e}**nyay**wa
deck chair	**kursi geladak**	**koor**see g^{e}**la**da^{k}
motorboat	**perahu motor**	**pra**hoo **mo**torr
rowing-boat	**perahu dayung**	**pra**hoo da**yoong**
sailing boat	**perahu layar**	**pra**hoo **la**yar
skin-diving equipment	**alat-alat menyelam**	alat-**a**lat m^{e}ny^{e}lam
sunshade (umbrella)	**payung pantai**	**pa**yung **pan**tai
surfboard	**papan luncur**	papan **loon**choor
water-skis	**ski air**	ski **a**yer
windsurfer	**peselancar angin**	p^{e}s^{e}**lan**char **an**gin

PANTAI PRIBADI	PRIVATE BEACH
DILARANG BERENANG	NO SWIMMING

Making friends

Introductions *Memperkenalkan*

Indonesians are eager to meet visitors and practise their English. However, there are a number of important social conventions to adhere to. Rough behaviour and loud voices are shocking to Indonesians, who are naturally a courteous and rather formal race. Public displays of affection are frowned on. Pointing with your finger or your foot (to goods displayed on the ground, for example) is considered a sign of contempt and it is impolite to cross your legs so that someone sees the sole of your foot. Hands on hips is looked on as an aggressive stance.

May I introduce...?	**Bolehkah saya memperkenalkan...?**	bolayhkah saya m^e^mp^e^rk^e^nalkan
John, this is...	**John, ini adalah...**	john eenee adalah
My name is...	**Nama saya adalah...**	nama saya adalah
Pleased to meet you!	**Saya merasa senang berjumpa dengan anda!**	saya m^e^rasa s^e^nung b^e^rjoompa d^e^ngan anda
What's your name?	**Siapa nama anda?**	seeapa nama anda
Where are you going?	**Anda mau pergi ke mana?**	anda mau p^e^rgee k^e^ mana
How are you?	**Bagaimana kabarnya?**	bagai mana kabarnya
Fine, thanks. And you?	**Baik, terima kasih. Dan bagaimana anda?**	bai^k^ treema kasih. dan bagai mana anda

Follow up *Kelanjutannya*

How long have you been here?	**Berapa lama anda sudah ada disini?**	b^e^rapa lama anda soodah ada deeseenee
We've been here a week.	**Kami sudah seminggu ada disini.**	kamee soodah s^e^minggoo ada deeseenee
Is this your first visit?	**Apakah ini kunjungan anda yang pertama?**	apakah eenee koonjoongan anda yung p^e^rtama

No, we came here last year.	**Tidak, tahun yang lalu kami juga datang kemari.**	**tee**da^{k} **ta**hoon yung **la**loo **ka**mee **joo**ga **da**tung k^{e}**ma**ree
Are you enjoying your stay?	**Apakah anda senang dengan kunjungan anda?**	apakah **an**da s^{e}nung d^{e}ngan koon**joong**an **an**da
Yes, I like it very much.	**Ya, saya suka sekali.**	ya **sa**ya **soo**ka **ska**lee
I like the scenery a lot.	**Saya suka sekali pada pemandangannya disini.**	saya **soo**ka **ska**lee **pa**da p^{e}**man**dungannya dee**see**nee
What do you think of the country/people?	**Bagaimana pendapat anda tentang negerinya/rakyatnya?**	**ba**gai **ma**na p^{e}n**da**pat **an**da t^{e}ntung n^{e}**gree**nya/ **rak**yatnya
Where do you come from?	**Anda berasal dari mana?**	**an**da b^{e}**ra**sal **da**ree **ma**na
I'm from...	**Saya dari...**	saya **da**ree
What nationality are you?	**Apakah kebangsaan anda?**	apakah k^{e}**bang**sa-an **an**da
I'm...	**Saya...**	**sa**ya
American	**orang Amerika**	**o**rung amerika
Australian	**orang Australia**	**o**rung au**stra**lia
British	**orang Inggeris**	**o**rung ing-grees
Where are you staying?	**Anda tinggal dimana?**	anda **ting**gal dee**ma**na
Are you on your own?	**Apakah anda sendirian?**	apakah **an**da s^{e}n**dee**ree-an
I'm with my...	**Saya bersama dengan... saya.**	**sa**ya b^{e}r**sa**ma d^{e}ngan... **sa**ya
wife/husband	**isteri/suami**	**ee**stree/**swa**mee
family	**keluarga**	kloo**war**ga
children	**anak-anak**	**a**nak-**a**na^{k}
parents	**orang tua**	**o**rung **too**wa
boyfriend/girlfriend	**pacar**	**pa**char

father/mother	**ayah/ibu**	**a**yah/**ee**boo
son/daughter	**anak laki-laki/anak perempuan**	**a**na^{k} **la**kee-**la**kee/**a**na^{k} p^{e}r^{e}**m**poo-an
brother/sister	**saudara laki-laki/ saudara perempuan**	sau**da**ra **la**kee-**la**kee/ sau**da**ra p^{e}r^{e}**m**poo-an
uncle/aunt	**paman/bibi**	**pa**man/**bee**bee
cousin	**sepupu**	s^{e}**poo**poo

COUNTRIES, see page 146

Are you married/ single?	**Apakah anda sudah kawin/bujang?**	apakah **an**da **soo**dah kawin/**boo**jung
Do you have children?	**Apakah anda punya anak?**	apakah **an**da **poo**nya ana[k]
What do you do?	**Apa pekerjaan anda?**	apa p[e]**k[e]**rja-an **an**da
I'm a student.	**Saya seorang pelajar.**	**sa**ya s[e]-**o**rung p[e]**la**jar
What are you studying?	**Anda belajar apa?**	anda b[e]**la**jar **a**pa
I'm here on a business trip/on holiday.	**Saya disini sedang ada urusan pekerjaan/dalam liburan.**	**sa**ya dee**see**nee s[e]dung ada **oo**roosan p[e]**k[e]**rja-an/ dalum **lee**booran
Do you play cards/ chess?	**Apakah anda main kartu/catur?**	apakah **an**da main **kar**too/ **cha**toor

The weather *Cuaca*

What a lovely day!	**Betapa baiknya cuaca hari ini!**	b[e]**ta**pa bai[k]nya **choo**wacha **ha**ree **ee**nee
What awful weather!	**Betapa buruk cuacanya!**	b[e]**ta**pa **boo**roo[k] **choo**wachanya!
Isn't it cold/hot today?	**Dinginya/panasya hari ini?**	**din**ginya/**pa**nasya **ha**ree **ee**nee
Do you think it's going to ... tomorrow?	**Apakah menurut pendapat anda besok ...**	apakah m[e]**noo**root p[e]ndapat **an**da **bay**so[k]
be a nice day	**akan baik cuacanya**	akan bai[k] **choo**wachanya
rain	**akan hujan**	akan **hoo**jan

cloud	**awan**	awan
dry season	**musim kemarau**	moosim k[e]**ma**rau
fog	**kabut**	**ka**boot
mud	**lumpur**	**loom**poor
ice	**es**	es
lightning	**kilat**	**kee**lat
monsoon/rainy season	**musim hujan**	**moo**sim **hoo**jan
moon	**bulan/rembulan**	**boo**lan/r[e]m**boo**lan
rain	**hujan**	**hoo**jan
sky	**langit**	langit
star	**bintang**	**bin**tung
storm	**badai**	**ba**dai
sun	**matahari**	mata**ha**ree
thunder	**guntur**	**goon**toor
wind	**angin**	angin

Invitations *Undangan*

Would you like to have dinner with us on...?	**Apakah anda suka makan malam dengan kami pada...?**	apakah **an**da **soo**ka **ma**kan **ma**lam d^e^ngan **ka**mee **pa**da
May I invite you to lunch?	**Bolehkah saya mengundang anda untuk makan siang?**	**bo**layhkah **sa**ya m^e^ng**oon**dung **an**da **oon**too^k^ **ma**kan **see**-ung
There's a party. Are you coming?	**Ada pesta. Bisakah anda datang?**	ada pesta. **bee**sakah **an**da **da**tung
That's very kind of you.	**Baik hati sekali anda.**	bai^k^ **ha**tee **ska**lee **an**da
Great. I'd love to come.	**Baik. Saya suka sekali datang.**	bai^k^. **sa**ya **soo**ka **ska**lee **da**tung
What time shall we come?	**Jam berapa kita sebaiknya datang?**	jum b^e^**ra**pa **kee**ta s^e^baiknya **da**tung
May I bring a friend?	**Bolehkah saya membawa seorang teman?**	**bo**layhkah **sa**ya m^e^m**ba**wa s^e^-**o**rung t^e^man
I'm afraid we have to leave now.	**Saya khawatir kita harus pergi sekarang.**	**sa**ya ha**wa**teer **kee**ta **ha**roos **p^e^**rgee s^e^**ka**rung
Thanks for the evening. It was great.	**Terima kasih atas pertemuan malam ini. Sungguh baik sekali.**	**tree**ma **ka**sih **a**tas p^e^**rt^e^**moo-an **ma**lam **ee**nee. **soong**goh bai^k^ **ska**lee

Dating *Berkencan*

Why are you laughing?	**Mengapa anda ketawa?**	m^e^ng**a**pa **an**da k^e^**ta**wa
Is my Indonesian that bad?	**Apakah bahasa Indonesia saya begitu jelek?**	apakah ba**ha**sa indo**nee**sseeya **sa**ya b^e^**gee**too j^e^lay^k^
Do you mind if I sit here?	**Apakah anda keberatan kalau saya duduk disini?**	apakah **an**da k^e^**bra**tan **ka**lau **sa**ya **doo**do^k^ dee**see**nee
Can I get you a drink?	**Bolehkah saya mencari minum untuk anda?**	**bo**layhkah **sa**ya m^e^n**cha**ree minoom **oon**too^k^ **an**da
Are you waiting for someone?	**Apa anda sedang menunggu seseorang?**	apa **an**da s^e^dung m^e^**noong**goo s^e^s^e^-**o**rung
Are you free this evening?	**Apa anda ada waktu malam ini?**	apa **an**da **a**da **wak**too **ma**lam **ee**nee

DAYS OF THE WEEK, see page 151

Would you like to go out with me tonight?	**Apakah anda suka pergi keluar sama saya malam ini?**	apakah **anda sooka** p^{e}rgee kloowar sama **saya malam eenee**
Would you like to go dancing?	**Apakah anda mau pergi keluar untuk berdansa?**	apakah **anda** mau **p^{e}**rgee kloowar **oontoo^{k}** b^{e}**rdansa**
I know a good discotheque.	**Saya tahu suatu diskotek yang baik.**	**saya tahoo swatoo** diskotek yung bai^{k}
Shall we go to the cinema (movies)?	**Sukakah kita pergi ke bioskop?**	**sook**akah **keeta p^{e}**rgee k^{e} **bee**yoskop
Where shall we meet?	**Dimana kita akan bertemu?**	dee**mana keeta** akan b^{e}**rt^{e}**moo
I'll call for you at 8.	**Saya akan datang ke tempat anda jam 8.**	**saya** akan **da**tung k^{e} **t^{e}**mpat **anda** jum 8
May I take you home?	**Bolehkah saya mengantar anda pulang?**	**bolayhkah saya** m^{e}ngantar **anda poolung**
Can I see you again tomorrow?	**Bolehkah saya bertemu lagi dengan anda besok?**	**bolayhkah saya** b^{e}**rt^{e}**moo **lagee** d^{e}ngan **anda bayso^{k}**
I hope we'll meet again.	**Saya harap kita akan bertemu lagi.**	**saya harap keeta akan** b^{e}**rt^{e}**moo **lagee**

... and you might answer:

I'd love to, thank you.	**Ya, saya ingin sekali, terima kasih.**	ya **saya ingin skalee treema kasih**
Thank you, but I'm busy.	**Terima kasih, tetapi saya sibuk.**	**treema kasih** t^{e}**tapee saya seebook**
No, I'm not interested, thank you.	**Maaf, saya tidak tertarik, terima kasih.**	ma-af **saya teeda^{k}** t^{e}**rtari^{k} treema kasih**
Leave me alone, please!	**Biarkanlah saya!**	**bee**-arkanlah **saya**
Thank you, it's been a wonderful evening.	**Terima kasih, sungguh suatu malam yang amat menyenangkan.**	**treema kasih soong**goh **swatoo ma**lam yung amat m^{e}ny^{e}nungkan
I've enjoyed myself.	**Saya sendiri merasa senang sekali.**	**saya** s^{e}ndeeree m^{e}**rasa** s^{e}nung **skalee**

Shopping Guide

This shopping guide is designed to help you find what you want with ease, accuracy and speed. It features:

1. A list of all major shops, stores and services (p.98).
2. Some general expressions required when shopping to allow you to be specific and selective (p.100).
3. Full details of the shops and services most likely to concern you. Here you'll find advice, alphabetical lists of items and conversion charts listed under the headings below.

Shops, stores and services *Toko-toko, toko serba-ada dan kantor-kantor jasa*

City shopping complexes and department stores are open from 8.30 am to 8 pm daily including Sunday. In markets you can bargain, maybe even to half price. Many things are very inexpensive in Indonesia by western standards so restrain your skills with obviously poor, hardworking people like pedicab (*becak*) men.

Where's the nearest...?	**Dimana... yang terdekat?**	dee**ma**na... yung terd^{e}kat
antique shop	**toko barang-barang antik**	toko **ba**rung-**ba**rung anteek
art gallery	**balai/gedung kesenian**	balai/g^{e}**doong** k^{e}s^{e}nee-an
baker's	**toko roti**	toko **ro**tee
bank	**bank**	bank
barber's	**pemangkas rambut**	p^{e}**mung**kas **rum**boot
beauty salon	**salon kecantikan**	salon k^{e}**chan**tikan
bookshop	**toko buku**	toko **boo**koo
butcher's	**toko daging**	toko **da**ging
camera shop	**toko kamera**	toko **kam**^{e}ra
chemist's	**apotek**	apotayk
dentist	**dokter gigi**	dokter **gee**gee
department store	**toko serba-ada**	toko **s**^{e}**r**ba-ada
drugstore	**apotek**	apotayk
dry cleaner's	**binatu kimia**	bina**too** **ki**meeya
electrical goods shop	**toko alat-alat listrik**	toko alat-alat listrik
fishmonger's	**tukang jual ikan**	**too**kung **joo**wal **ee**kan
florist's	**toko bunga**	toko **boon**ga
greengrocer's	**toko penjual sayur-sayuran**	toko p^{e}n**joo**wal **sa**yoor-**sa**yooran
grocer's	**toko bahan makanan**	toko **ba**han **ma**kanan
hairdresser's (ladies/men)	**tempat pemangkas rambut (wanita/pria)**	t^{e}mpat p^{e}**mung**kas **rum**boot (wa**nee**ta/**pree**ya)
hardware store	**toko besi**	toko b^{e}see
health food shop	**toko makanan untuk kesehatan**	toko **ma**kanan **oon**took k^{e}**say**hatan
hospital	**rumah sakit**	**roo**mah **sa**kit
ironmonger's	**tempat pedagang besi**	t^{e}mpat p^{e}**da**gung b^{e}see
jeweller's	**toko mas**	toko mas

LAUNDRY, see page 29/HAIRDRESSER'S, see page 30

launderette	**binatu**	bee**na**too
library	**perpustakaan**	p^{e}rpoo**sta**ka-an
market	**pasar**	**pa**sar
newsstand	**kios**	keeyos
optician	**optik**	**op**tik
pastry shop	**toko kue-kue**	toko kway-kway
photographer	**juru potret**	**joo**roo potret
police station	**kantor polisi**	**kan**tor **po**leesee
post office	**kantor pos**	**kan**tor pos
second-hand shop	**toko barang-barang bekas**	toko **ba**rung-**ba**rung b^{e}kas
shoemaker's (repairs)	**tukang sepatu**	**too**kung s^{e}**pa**too
shoe shop	**toko sepatu**	toko s^{e}**pa**too
shopping centre	**pusat pertokoan**	**poo**sat p^{e}r**to**ko-an
souvenir shop	**toko suvenir**	toko **soo**venir
sporting goods shop	**toko alat-alat olah-raga**	toko **a**lat-alat **o**lah**ra**ga
stationer's	**toko alat tulis menulis**	toko **a**lat **too**lis m^{e}**noo**lis
supermarket	**toko pangan serba-ada**	toko **pung**an **s^{e}r**ba-ada
sweet shop	**toko makanan gula-gula**	toko **ma**kanan **goo**la-**goo**la
tailor's	**tempat tukang jahit**	t^{e}mpat **too**kung **ja**hit
telegraph office	**kantor telegrap**	**kan**tor telegrap
tobacconist's	**toko penjual tem-bakau**	toko p^{e}n**joo**wal t^{e}m**ba**kau
toy shop	**toko mainan kanak-kanak**	toko mainan kana^{k}-kana^{k}
travel agency	**biro perjalanan**	**bee**ro p^{e}r**ja**lanan
vegetable store	**toko sayur-sayuran**	toko **sa**yoor-**sa**yooran
veterinarian	**dokter hewan**	dokter **hay**wan
watchmaker's	**tempat tukang arloji**	**t^{e}m**pat **too**kung ar**lo**jee

JALAN MASUK	ENTRANCE
JALAN KELUAR	EXIT
JALAN DARURAT	EMERGENCY EXIT

General expressions *Pernyataan-pernyataan umum*

Where? *Dimana?*

Where's there a good...?	**Dimana ada... yang baik?**	deemana ada... yung baik
Where can I find a...?	**Dimana saya bisa dapat... ?**	deemana saya beesa dapat
Where's the main shopping area?	**Dimana pusat pertokoan yang utama?**	deemana poosat pertoko-an yung ootama
Is it far from here?	**Apakah jauh dari sini?**	apakah jaooh daree seenee
How do I get there?	**Bagaimana saya bisa pergi kesana?**	bagai mana saya beesa pergee kesana

OBRAL SALE

Service *Pelayanan*

Can you help me?	**Bisakah anda tolong saya?**	beesakah anda tolong saya
I'm just looking.	**Saya hanya melihat-lihat saja.**	saya hanya meleehat-leehat saja
Do you sell...?	**Apakah anda menjual... ?**	apakah anda menjoowal
I'd like to buy...	**Saya ingin beli...**	saya ingin blee
I'd like...	**Saya ingin...**	saya ingin
Do you have any...?	**Apakah anda punya... ?**	apakah anda poonya
Where's the... department?	**Dimanakah bagian... ?**	deemanakah bagee-an
Where is the lift (elevator)/escalator?	**Dimana ada lift/eskalator?**	deemana ada lift/eskalator

That one *Yang itu*

Can you show me...?	**Bisakah anda memperlihatkan saya... ?**	beesakah anda memperleehatkan saya
this/that	**yang ini/yang itu**	yung eenee/yung eetoo
the one in the window/in the display case	**yang ada di jendela/di kotak yang dipamerkan**	yung ada dee jendayla/dee kotak yung deepamayrkan

Defining the article *Menguraikan tentang barang*

I'd like a ... one.	**Saya ingin satu yang ...**	**saya ingin sa**too yung
big	**besar**	besar
cheap	**murah**	**moo**rah
dark	**gelap**	glup
good	**baik**	baik
heavy	**berat**	brat
large	**besar**	besar
light (weight)	**ringan**	ringan
light (colour)	**warna muda**	**warr**na **moo**da
oval	**lonjong**	**lon**jong
rectangular	**empat persegi panjang**	e**mpat** persegee **pan**jung
round	**bundar**	**boon**dar
small	**kecil**	kechil
square	**persegi**	persegee
sturdy	**kokoh**	kokoh
I don't want anything too expensive.	**Saya tidak menginginkan sesuatu yang terlalu mahal.**	**saya teeda**k m**e**ng**ing**inkan s**e**swatoo yung t**e**r**la**loo **ma**hal

Preference *Pilihan*

Can you show me some others?	**Bisakah anda kasih lihat saya yang lain?**	**bee**sakah **an**da **ka**sih **lee**hat **sa**ya yung lain
Don't you have anything ...?	**Apakah anda tidak punya suatu yang ... ?**	apakah **an**da **tee**dak **poo**nya **swa**too yung
cheaper/better	**lebih murah/lebih mahal**	lebih **moo**rah/lebih **ma**hal
larger/smaller	**lebih besar/lebih kecil**	lebih besar/lebih kechil

How much *Berapa*

How much is this?	**Berapa harganya ini?**	b**e**rapa **har**ganya **ee**nee
I don't understand.	**Saya tidak mengerti.**	**sa**ya **tee**dak mengertee
Please write it down.	**Tolong tuliskan.**	**to**long **too**liskan
I don't want to spend more than ... rupiah.	**Saya tidak ingin mengeluarkan lebih dari ... rupiah.**	**saya teeda**k **ingin** meng**eloo**warkan lebih **da**ree ... roo**pee**yah

COLOURS, see page 113

Decision *Keputusan*

It's not quite what I want.	**Bukan ini yang saya inginkan.**	bookan eenee yung saya inginkan
No, I don't like it.	**Tidak, saya tidak suka.**	teeda^{k} saya teeda^{k} sooka
I'll take it.	**Saya akan ambil ini.**	saya akan umbil eenee

Ordering *Memesan*

Can you order it for me?	**Bisakah anda memesannya untuk saya?**	beesakah anda m^{e}m^{e}sannya oontoo^{k} saya
How long will it take?	**Berapa waktu yang diperlukan?**	b^{e}rapa waktoo yung deep^{e}rlookan

Delivery *Penyerahan*

I'll take it with me.	**Saya akan membawanya sendiri.**	saya akan m^{e}mbawanya s^{e}ndeeree
Deliver it to the... Hotel.	**Tolong antarkan barang ini ke Hotel...**	tolong antarkan barung eenee k^{e} hotel
Please send it to this address.	**Tolong mengirimkannya ke alamat ini.**	tolong m^{e}ngeerimkannya k^{e} alamat eenee
Will I have any difficulty with the customs?	**Apakah saya akan mendapat kesulitan dengan bea cukai?**	apakah saya akan m^{e}ndapat k^{e}soolitan d^{e}ngan baya chookai

Paying *Membayar*

How much is it?	**Ini berapa?**	eenee b^{e}rapa
That's very expensive. How about... rupiah?	**Itu mahal sekali. Bagaimana kalau... rupiah?**	etoo mahal s^{e}kalee. bagaimana kalau... roopee-ah
OK, let's say... rupiah.	**OK. Bagaimana kalau... rupiah.**	okay. bagaimana kalau... roopeeyah
Can I pay by traveller's cheque?	**Bolehkah saya membayar dengan cek wisata?**	bolayhkah saya m^{e}mbayar d^{e}ngan chek weesata
Do you accept dollars/pounds?	**Apakah anda menerima dollar/pon?**	apakah anda m^{e}n^{e}reema dollar/pon
Do you accept credit cards?	**Apakah anda menerima kartu kredit?**	apakah anda m^{e}n^{e}reema kartoo kredit
I think there's a mistake in the bill.	**Saya kira ada kesalahan dalam rekening.**	saya keera ada k^{e}salahan dalum rek^{e}ning

Anything else? *Apakah ada yang lain lagi?*

No, thanks, that's all.	**Tidak, terima kasih, itu sudah semua.**	**tee**da^{k} **tree**ma **ka**sih **ee**too **soo**dah s^{e}moowa
Yes, I'd like...	**Ya, saya ingin...**	ya **sa**ya **in**gin
Can you show me...?	**Bisakah anda kasih lihat saya... ?**	**bee**sakah **an**da **ka**sih **lee**hat **sa**ya
May I have a bag, please?	**Bolehkah saya dapat satu kantong?**	**bo**layhkah **sa**ya **da**pat **sa**too **kan**tong
Could you wrap it up for me, please?	**Bisakah anda tolong membungkusnya untuk saya?**	**bee**sakah **an**da **to**long m^{e}m**boong**koosnya **oon**too^{k} **sa**ya
May I have a receipt?	**Bolehkah saya dapat rekeningnya?**	**bo**layhkah **sa**ya **da**pat **rek**^{e}ningnya

Dissatisfied? *Apakah tidak memuaskan?*

Can you exchange this, please?	**Bisakah anda menukar ini?**	**bee**sakah **an**da m^{e}**noo**kar **ee**nee
I want to return this.	**Saya ingin mengembalikan ini.**	**sa**ya **in**gin m^{e}ng^{e}m**ba**leekan **ee**nee
I'd like a refund. Here's the receipt.	**Saya ingin mendapat uang kembali. Ini rekeningnya.**	**sa**ya **in**gin m^{e}n**da**pat wung k^{e}m**ba**lee. **ee**nee **rek**^{e}ningnya

Bisakah saya menolong anda?	Can I help you?
... macam apa yang anda inginkan?	What... would you like?
warna/bentuk/mutu	colour/shape/quality
Maaf, kami tidak mempunyainya.	I'm sorry, we don't have any.
Kami sedang kehabisan persediaan.	We're out of stock.
Apakah saya boleh memesannya untuk anda?	Shall we order it for you?
Apa ada yang lain lagi?	Anything else?
Semua itu jadi... rupiah.	That's... rupiah, please.
Tempat membayar ada disana.	The cash desk is over there.

Bookshop—Stationer's *Toko-buku—Toko alat tulis menulis*

Foreign books, magazines and newspapers can be found at large bookshops and hotels. Several newspapers are published in Indonesia in English.

Where's the nearest…?	**Dimana… yang terdekat?**	dee**ma**na… yung terd^{e}kat
bookshop	**toko buku**	toko **bookoo**
stationer's	**toko alat tulis menulis**	toko alat **too**lis m^{e}**noo**lis
newsstand	**kios**	keeyos
Where can I buy an English-language newspaper?	**Dimana saya bisa beli surat kabar dalam bahasa Inggeris?**	dee**ma**na **sa**ya **bee**sa blee **soo**rat **ka**bar **da**lum **ba**ha**sa** ing-grees
Where's the guidebook section?	**Dimana seksi buku-buku pemandu?**	dee**ma**na seksee **book**oo-**book**oo p^{e}**man**doo
Where do you keep the English books?	**Dimana tempatnya buku-buku dalam bahasa Inggeris?**	dee**ma**na **t**^{e}mpatnya **book**oo-**book**oo **da**lum **ba**hasa ing-grees
Have you any of…'s books in English?	**Apakah anda punya buku dari… dalam bahasa Inggeris?**	apakah **an**da **poo**nya **book**oo **da**ree… **da**lum bahasa ing-grees
Do you have second-hand books?	**Apakah anda punya buku-buku bekas?**	apakah **an**da **poo**nya **book**oo-**book**oo b^{e}kas
I want to buy a/an/some…	**Saya ingin beli…**	**sa**ya **in**gin blee
address book	**buku alamat**	**book**oo **a**lamat
ball-point pen	**pena bolpoin**	**pay**na bolpoin
book	**buku**	**book**oo
calendar	**penanggalan**	p^{e}**nang**galan
carbon paper	**kertas karbon**	**k**^{e}rtas **karr**bon
crayons	**krayon**	krayon
dictionary	**kamus**	**ka**moos
Indonesian-English	**Bahasa Indonesia-Bahasa Inggeris**	bahasa indo**nay**seeya-bahasa ing-grees
pocket	**saku**	**sa**koo
drawing paper	**kertas gambar**	**k**^{e}rtas **gum**bar
drawing pins	**peniti gambar**	p^{e}**nee**tee **gum**bar
envelopes	**amplop**	amplop

eraser	**penghapus**	p^{e}ng**ha**poos
exercise book	**buku latihan**	**boo**koo **la**tihan
fountain pen	**pulpen**	**pull**-pen
glue	**lem/perekat**	lem/p^{e}**r**^{e}kat
grammar book	**buku tatabahasa**	**boo**koo tataba**ha**sa
guidebook	**buku penuntun**	**boo**koo p^{e}**noon**toon
ink	**tinta**	tinta
black/red/blue/	**hitam/merah/ biru**	**hee**tam/**may**rah/**bee**roo
(adhesive) labels	**label (perekat)**	**la**bel (p^{e}**r**^{e}kat)
magazine	**majalah**	ma**ja**lah
map	**peta**	**pay**ta
street map	**peta jalan**	**pay**ta **ja**lan
road map of...	**peta jalan dari...**	**pay**ta **ja**lan **da**ree
mechanical pencil	**pensil mekanis**	pensil me**ka**nis
newspaper	**surat kabar**	surat **ka**bar
English-language	**Inggeris**	ing-grees
notebook	**buku catatan**	**boo**koo chatatan
note paper	**kertas catatan**	**k**^{e}**r**tas chatatan
paintbox	**kotak cat**	**ko**ta^{k} chat
paper	**kertas**	**k**^{e}**r**tas
paperback	**buku bersampul tipis**	**boo**koo b^{e}**rsum**pool teepis
paperclips	**penjepit kertas**	p^{e}nj^{e}pit **k**^{e}**r**tas
paper napkins	**serbet kertas**	serbet **k**^{e}**r**tas
paste	**perekat/lem**	p^{e}**r**^{e}kat/lem
pen	**pena**	**pay**na
pencil	**pensil/potlot**	pensil/potlot
pencil sharpener	**alat pengasah pen- sil**	**a**lat p^{e}ng**a**sah pensil
playing cards	**kartu**	**kar**too
pocket calculator	**kalkulator kecil**	kalkoo**la**tor k^{e}chil
postcard	**kartupos**	**kar**toopos
propelling pencil	**pensil mekanis**	pensil me**ka**nis
refill (for a pen)	**pengisian kembali (untuk pena)**	p^{e}ng**ee**see-an k^{e}m**ba**lee (**oon**too^{k} **pay**na)
rubber	**karet**	**ka**ret
ruler	**penggaris/garisan**	p^{e}ng**ga**ris/**ga**risan
staples	**jeglegan**	jeg**lay**gan
string	**tali/benang**	**ta**lee/b^{e}nung
thumbtacks	**paku jamur**	**pa**koo **ja**moor
travel guide	**penuntun perjala- nan**	p^{e}**noon**toon p^{e}**rja**lanan
typewriter ribbon	**pita mesin tulis**	**pee**ta m^{e}sin **too**lis
typing paper	**kertas tik**	**k**^{e}**r**tas tik
writing pad	**buku catatan**	**boo**koo chatatan

Camping and sports equipment *Alat-alat kemah dan olahraga*

I'd like a/an/some...	**Saya ingin...**	saya **in**gin
I'd like to hire a(n)/ some...	**Saya ingin menyewa...**	saya **in**gin m^{e}**nyay**wa
air bed (mattress)	**tilam angin**	**tee**lum angin
backpack	**ransel**	ransel
butane gas	**gas butan**	gas **boo**tan
campbed	**pelbet**	pelbet
(folding) chair	**kursi (lipat)**	**koor**see (**lee**pat)
charcoal	**arang (kayu)**	arung (**ka**yoo)
compass	**kompas**	kompas
cool box	**kotak pendingin**	**ko**ta^{k} pen**din**gin
fire lighters	**geretan api**	graytan a**pee**
fishing tackle	**alat pancing**	alat **pun**ching
flashlight	**lampu senter**	**lam**poo **sent**^{e}r
groundsheet	**lembaran plastik yang ditaruh dia- tas tanah**	l^{e}mbaran plas**teek** yung deeta**rooh** dee-**atas** **ta**nah
ice pack	**kantong es**	**kan**tong es
insect spray (killer)	**semprotan serangga**	s^{e}mprotan s^{e}**rung**ga
kerosene	**minyak tanah**	minya^{k} **ta**nah
lamp	**lampu**	**lam**poo
mallet	**pemukul**	p^{e}**moo**kool
matches	**korek api**	**ko**re^{k} a**pee**
(foam rubber) mattress	**kasur (karet busa)**	**ka**soor (**ka**ret **boo**sa)
mosquito net	**kelambu nyamuk**	klumboo **nya**moo^{k}
paraffin	**parafin**	parafin
pump	**pompa**	**pom**pa
rope	**tali**	**ta**lee
rucksack	**ransel**	ransel
screwdriver	**obeng**	obeng
skiing equipment	**alat-alat main ski**	alat-**a**lat main ski
sleeping bag	**karung untuk tidur**	**ka**roong **oon**too^{k} **tee**door
(folding) table	**meja lipat**	**may**ja **lee**pat
tent	**tenda**	tenda
tent pegs	**paku tenda**	**pa**koo tenda
tent pole	**tiang tenda**	**tee**yung tenda
torch	**obor**	obor
windsurfer	**peselancar angin**	p^{e}s^{e}**lan**char **an**gin
water flask	**botol air**	**bo**tol ayer

CAMPING, see page 32

Chemist's (drugstore) *Apotek*

Indonesian pharmacies (*apotek*) stock most medicines including American. Many larger hotels have drugstores offering cosmetics as well as medicaments, but to have a doctor's prescription made up you will have to go to an *apotek*. Check the dosage, which may not be the same as you're used to. Drugs are sometimes not made up to the same strengths. If you normally take a particular medicine, bring adequate supplies with you.

Department stores have a full range of cosmetics in internationally-known brands.

General *Umum*

Where's the nearest (all-night) chemist's?	**Dimana apotek terdekat disini (yang buka semalam suntuk)?**	dee**ma**na **a**potayk terd^{e}kat dee**see**nee (yung **boo**ka se**ma**lam **soon**too^{k})
What time does the chemist's open/close?	**Jam berapa apotek buka/tutup?**	jum b^{e}**ra**pa **a**potayk **boo**ka/**too**toop

1—Pharmaceutical *Yang berhubungan dengan farmasi*

I'd like something for...	**Saya ingin sesuatu untuk...**	**sa**ya **in**gin s^{e}**swa**too **oon**too^{k}
a cold/a cough	**pilek/batuk**	**peel**^{e}k/**ba**too^{k}
hay fever	**alergi rumput**	al**er**gee **room**poot
insect bites	**gigitan serangga**	**gee**gitan s^{e}**rung**ga
sunburn	**terbakar sinar matahari**	t^{e}r**ba**kar **see**nar **mata**ha**ree**
travel/altitude sickness	**mabuk/perjalanan ketinggian**	**ma**boo^{k}/p^{e}r**ja**lanan k^{e}**ting**geean
an upset stomach	**perut terganggu**	p^{e}**root** t^{e}r**gung**gu
Can you prepare this prescription for me?	**Dapatkah anda menyiapkan resep ini untuk saya?**	**da**patkah **an**da m^{e}**nyeeap**kan r^{e}sep **ee**nee **oon**too^{k} **sa**ya
Can I get it without a prescription?	**Apakah saya bisa beli ini tanpa resep?**	apakah **sa**ya **bee**sa blee **ee**nee tanpa r^{e}sep
Shall I wait?	**Apakah saya sebaiknya tunggu?**	apakah **sa**ya s^{e}**baik**nya **toong**goo

DOCTOR, see page 137

Can I have a/an/ some ...?	**Bolehkah saya dapat ... ?**	**bo**layhkah **saya dapat**
adhesive plaster	**plester**	plester
analgesic	**obat mematikan rasa sakit**	obat m^{e}**ma**tikan **rasa sakit**
antiseptic cream	**krem penangkal infeksi**	krem p^{e}**nung**kal in**fek**see
aspirin	**aspirin**	aspirin
bandage	**pembalut**	p^{e}mb**a**loot
elastic bandage	**pembalut elastik**	p^{e}mb**a**loot ay**las**teek
Band-Aids®	**plester untuk luka ringan**	plester **oon**too^{k} **loo**ka ringan
condoms	**kondom**	kondom
contraceptives	**alat kontrasepsi**	**a**lat kontra**sep**see
corn plasters	**plester katimumul**	plester kati**moo**mool
cotton wool (absorbent cotton)	**kapas penghisap**	**ka**pas p^{e}ng**hee**sap
cough drops	**permen batuk**	p^{e}rmen **ba**too^{k}
disinfectant	**obat disinfeksi**	obat disinfe^{e}ksee
ear drops	**obat tetes kuping**	obat **te**tes **koo**ping
eye drops	**obat tetes mata**	obat **te**tes **ma**ta
first-aid kit	**kotak pertolongan pertama**	**ko**ta^{k} p^{e}**r**tolongan p^{e}**r**ta**ma**
gauze	**kain kasa**	kain **ka**sa
insect repellent/spray	**semprotan penolak serangga**	s^{e}mprotan p^{e}**no**la^{k} s^{e}**rung**ga
iodine	**yodium**	yodium
laxative	**obat urus-urus**	obat **oo**roos-**oo**roos
mouthwash	**obat kumur**	obat **koo**moor
nose drops	**obat tetes hidung**	obat **te**tes **hee**doong
sleeping pills	**obat tidur**	obat **tee**door
suppositories	**supositoria**	sooposi**to**ree-a
... tablets	**tablet ...**	tablet
tampons	**tampon**	tampon
thermometer	**termometer**	termometer
throat lozenges	**tablet batuk**	tablet **ba**too^{k}
tranquillizers	**obat penenang**	obat p^{e}n^{e}nung
vitamin pills	**pil vitamin**	pil veetamin

RACUN	POISON
OBAT LUAR	FOR EXTERNAL USE ONLY

2—Toiletry *Peranti/alat-alat untuk berhias*

I'd like a/an/some...	**Saya ingin ...**	**sa**ya **ing**in
after-shave lotion	**minyak sesudah-cukur**	minya^k se**soo**dah-**choo**koor
astringent	**astringent**	a**strinj**^{e}nt
bath salts	**garam mandi**	**ga**rum **mun**dee
blusher (rouge)	**pemerah muka**	p^e**may**rah **moo**ka
cream	**krem**	krem
cleansing cream	**krem pembersih**	krem p^{e}m**b**^{e}**r**sih
foundation cream	**krem dasar**	krem **da**sar
moisturizing cream	**krem pelembap**	krem p^{e}l^{e}mbap
night cream	**krem malam**	krem **ma**lam
deodorant	**deodoran**	day**o**doran
emery board	**papan amril**	p**a**pan amril
eyebrow pencil	**pensil alis mata**	pensil alis **ma**ta
eyeliner	**alat untuk membuat penggarisan mata**	**a**lat **oon**too^k m^{e}m**boo**wat p^{e}ng**ga**risan **ma**ta
face powder	**bedak**	b^{e}da^k
foot cream	**krem kaki**	krem **ka**kee
hand cream	**krem tangan**	krem **tung**an
lipsalve	**salep bibir**	**sal**^{e}p **bee**beer
lipstick	**lipstik**	lipstik
make-up remover pads	**alas penghapus rias muka**	**a**las p^{e}ng**ha**poos **ree**yas **moo**ka
mascara	**celak**	ch^{e}la^k
nail brush	**sikat kuku**	**see**kat kookoo
nail clippers	**gunting kuku**	**goon**ting kookoo
nail file	**kikir kuku**	kikir kookoo
nail polish	**cat kuku**	chat kookoo
nail polish remover	**alat penghapus cat kuku**	**a**lat p^{e}ng**ha**poos chat kookoo
nail scissors	**gunting kuku**	**goon**ting kookoo
perfume	**parfum**	parfoom
powder	**bedak**	b^{e}da^k
razor	**pisau cukur**	**pee**sow **choo**koor
razor blades	**silet**	**see**let
rouge	**pemerah pipi**	p^e**may**rah **pee**pee
safety pins	**peniti**	p^e**nee**tee
shaving brush	**sikat cukur**	**see**kat **choo**koor
shaving cream	**sabun cukur**	**sa**boon **choo**koor
soap	**sabun**	**sa**boon
sponge	**spons**	spons
sun-tan cream	**krem warna coke-lat**	krem **war**rna choklat

sun-tan oil	**minyak warna cokelat**	minya^{k} **war**rna choklat
talcum powder	**bedak talk**	b^{e}da^{k} tal^{e}k
tissues	**serbet kertas**	serbet **k^{e}**rtas
toilet paper	**kertas kloset**	**k^{e}**rtas kloset
toilet water	**minyak kelonyo**	minya^{k} k^{e}**lon**yo
toothbrush	**sikat gigi**	**see**kat **gee**gee
toothpaste	**pasta gigi**	pasta **gee**gee
towel	**handuk**	**han**dook
tweezers	**penjepit**	p^{e}**ny^{e}**pit

For your hair *Untuk rambut anda*

bobby pins	**jepitan rambut**	j^{e}pitan **rum**boot
colour shampoo	**langir warna**	lungeer **war**rna
comb	**sisir**	**see**seer
curlers	**alat pengeriting**	alat p^{e}ng^{e}**ri**ting
dry shampoo	**langir kering**	lungeer kring
dye	**celup**	ch^{e}loop
hairbrush	**sikat rambut**	**see**kat **rum**boot
hairgrips	**jepitan rambut kecil dari metal**	j^{e}pitan **rum**boot k^{e}chil **da**ree metal
hair lotion	**pembersih rambut**	p^{e}mb^{e}rsih **rum**boot
hairpins	**jepitan rambut**	j^{e}pitan **rum**boot
hair slide	**peniti rambut untuk mengikat rambut**	p^{e}**nee**tee **rum**boot **oon**too^{k} m^{e}ng**ee**kat **rum**boot
hair spray	**semprot rambut**	**s^{e}m**prot **rum**boot
shampoo	**langir**	**lan**geer
for dry/greasy (oily) hair	**untuk rambut kering/berminyak**	**oon**too^{k} **rum**boot kring/ b^{e}rminya^{k}
tint	**sedikit diwarnai**	s^{e}dikit dee**war**rnai
wig	**rambut palsu**	**rum**boot **pal**soo

For the baby *Untuk bayi*

baby food	**makanan bayi**	**ma**kanan bayee
dummy (pacifier)	**boneka**	**bon**ayka
feeding bottle	**botol makanan**	**bo**tol makanan
nappies (diapers)	**popok**	**po**po^{k}

Clothing *Pakaian*

If you want to buy something specific, prepare yourself in advance. Look at the list of clothing on page 115. Get some idea of the colour, material and size you want. They're all listed on the next few pages.

You'll find western-style clothing, some of it most successfully interpreted in silk or beautiful local *batik* — cloth traditionally decorated by "negative" painting over wax patterns. Long-sleeved *batik* shirts are considered correct semi-formal evening wear for men. A *sarung* length of fabric is a useful acquisition for both men and women, especially as a beach cover-up. Bali boutiques specialize in resort wear.

In towns there are tailors and dressmakers who will run up a garment or do an alteration inexpensively.

General *Umum*

I'd like...	**Saya ingin...**	saya ingin
I'd like something like this.	**Saya ingin sesuatu seperti ini.**	saya ingin s^{e}swatoo s^{e}p^{e}rtee eenee
I like the one in the window.	**Saya ingin yang ada di jendela.**	saya ingin yung ada dee j^{e}ndayla
How much is that per metre?	**Berapa harganya itu setiap meter?**	b^{e}rapa harganya eetoo s^{e}teeyapmayt^{e}r

1 centimetre (cm)	= 0.39 in.	1 inch	= 2.54 cm
1 metre (m)	= 39.37 in.	1 foot	= 30.5 cm
10 metres	= 32.81 ft.	1 yard	= 0.91 m.

Colour *Warna*

I'd like something in...	**Saya ingin sesuatu dalam...**	saya ingin s^{e}swatoo dalum
I'd like a darker/ lighter shade.	**Saya ingin warna yang lebih tua/ muda.**	saya ingin warrna yung l^{e}bih toowa/mooda
I'd like something to match this.	**Saya menginginkan sesuatu yang cocok dengan ini.**	saya m^{e}nginginkan s^{e}swatoo yung chocho^{k} d^{e}ngan eenee

I don't like the colour.	**Saya tidak suka warnanya.**	saya **tee**da^{k} **soo**ka **warr**nanya

black	**hitam**	**hee**tam
blue	**biru**	**bee**roo
brown	**cokelat**	choklat
golden	**keemas-emasan**	k^{e}-^{e}**mas**-masan
green	**hijau**	**hee**jau
grey	**kelabu/abu-abu**	**kla**boo/aboo-aboo
mauve	**lembayung muda**	l^{e}m**ba**yoong **moo**da
orange	**oranye**	**or**any^{e}
pink	**merah muda**	**may**rah **moo**da
purple	**ungu**	**oong**oo
red	**merah**	**may**rah
scarlet	**merah tua**	**may**rah **too**wa
silver	**perak**	**pay**ra^{k}
turquoise	**warna biru-hijau**	**warr**na **bee**roo-**hee**jau
white	**putih**	**poo**tih
yellow	**kuning**	**koo**ning
light...	**... muda**	**... mooda**
dark...	**... tua**	**... toowa**

		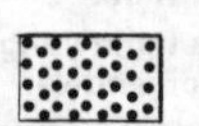		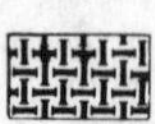
polos (**po**los)	**garis-garis** (**ga**ris-**ga**ris)	**bintik-bintik** (binti^{k}-binti^{k})	**kotak-kotak** (kota^{k}-kota^{k})	**berpola** (b^{e}r**po**la)

Fabric *Kain*

Do you have anything in...?	**Apakah anda punya sesuatu dalam... ?**	apakah **an**da **poo**nya s^{e}**swa**too **da**lum
Is that...?	**Apakah itu... ?**	apakah **ee**too
handmade	**dibuat dengan tangan**	dee**boo**wat d^{e}ngan **tung**an
imported	**diimpor**	dee-**im**por
made here	**dibuat disini**	dee**boo**wat dee**see**nee
I'd like something thinner.	**Saya ingin sesuatu yang lebih tipis.**	saya **in**gin s^{e}**swa**too yung l^{e}bih teepis
Do you have anything of better quality?	**Apakah anda punya sesuatu yang bermutu lebih baik?**	apakah **an**da **poo**nya s^{e}**swa**too yung bermootoo l^{e}bih bai^{k}

What's it made of?	**Ini dibikin dari apa?**	**ee**nee dee**bee**kin **da**ree **a**pa

camel-hair	**bulu unta/kamhar**	**boo**loo **oon**ta/kamhar
corduroy	**beledu/korduroi**	b^{e}l^{e}doo/kordooroy
cotton	**katun**	**ka**toon
denim	**kain kepar/dril**	kain **kay**par/dril
felt	**bulu kempa**	**boo**loo k^{e}mpa
flannel	**pelanel**	**pla**nel
lace	**renda**	rainda
leather	**kulit**	**koo**lit
linen	**linen**	linen
poplin	**poplin**	poplin
satin	**satin**	satin
silk	**sutera**	**soo**tra
suede	**kulit lunak**	**koo**lit **loo**na^{k}
velvet	**beludru**	b^{e}**loo**droo
wool	**wol**	wol

Is it ...?	**Apakah ... ?**	**a**pakah
pure cotton/wool	**katun/wol tulen**	**ka**toon/wol **too**len
synthetic	**sintetis**	**sintetis**
colourfast	**tahan luntur**	**ta**han **loon**toor
crease (wrinkle) resistant	**tahan kusut**	**ta**han **koo**soot
Is it hand washable/ machine washable?	**Apakah ia bisa dicuci dengan tangan/dengan mesin cuci?**	apakah **eea bee**sa dee**choo**chee d^{e}ngan **tung**an/d^{e}ngan m^{e}sin **choo**chee
Will it shrink?	**Apakah ia akan menyusut?**	**a**pakah **ee**a **a**kan m^{e}**nyoo**soot

Size *Ukuran*

I take size 38.	**Saya memakai ukuran 38.**	**sa**ya m^{e}**ma**kai **oo**kooran 38
Could you measure me?	**Bisakah anda mengambil ukuran saya?**	**bee**sakah **an**da m^{e}ng**um**bil **oo**kooran **sa**ya
I don't know the Indonesian sizes.	**Saya tidak mengenal ukuran-ukuran Indonesia.**	**sa**ya **ti**da^{k} m^{e}ng^{e}nal **oo**kooran-**oo**kooran indon**ay**seeya

Tailor—Dressmaker *Penjahit*

I'd like to have a ... made.	**Saya ingin menjahitkan ...**	**sa**ya **in**gin m^{e}**nja**hitkan
dress	**gaun**	gaun
shirt/suit	**kemeja/jas**	k^{e}**may**ja/jas

Can I see some patterns?	**Bisakah saya melihat polanya?**	**bee**sakah **saya** m^{e}**lee**hat **po**lanya
I'd like it the same... as this.	**Saya ingin ... yang sama.**	saya **in**gin ... yung **sa**ma
colour/style	**warna/gaya**	**warr**na/gaya
When can I collect it?	**Kapan bisa saya ambil?**	**ka**pan **bee**sa **sa**ya **am**bil
Will it be ready by Wednesday?	**Apakah bisa selesai hari Rabu?**	apakah **bee**sa sl^{e}sai **ha**ree **ra**boo

Women *Wanita/Perempuan*

Dresses/Suits						
American	8	10	12	14	16	18
British	10	12	14	16	18	20
Continental	36	38	40	42	44	46

Stockings						
American / British	8½	9	9½	10	10½	
Continental	0	1	2	3	4	5

Shoes				
American	6	7	8	9
British	4½	5½	6½	7½
Continental	37	38	40	41

Men *Pria/Laki-laki*

Suits/overcoats						
American / British	36	38	40	42	44	46
Continental	46	48	50	52	54	56

Shirts				
American / British	15	16	17	18
Continental	38	40	42	44

small (S)	**kecil**	k^{e}chil
medium (M)	**sedang**	s^{e}dung
large (L)	**besar**	b^{e}sarr
extra large (XL)	**ekstra besar**	**ek**stra b^{e}sarr
larger/smaller	**lebih besar/lebih kecil**	l^{e}bih b^{e}sarr/l^{e}bih k^{e}chil

A good fit? *Pas benar*

Can I try it on?	**Bolehkah saya mencoba mengenakannya?**	**bo**layhkah **sa**ya m^{e}**ncho**ba m^{e}ng^{e}nakannya
Where's the fitting room?	**Dimana kamarnya untuk mengepas pakaian?**	dee**ma**na **ka**marnya **oon**too^{k} m^{e}ng^{e}**pas** **pa**kayan

NUMBERS, see page 147

Is there a mirror?	**Apakah ada cermin disitu?**	**a**pakah **a**da **ch^{e}r**min dee**see**too
It fits very well.	**Ini pas betul.**	**ee**nee pas b^{e}**tool**
It doesn't fit.	**Ini tidak pas.**	**ee**nee **tee**da^{k} pas
It's too...	**Ini terlalu...**	**ee**nee t^{e}**rla**loo
short/long	**pendek/panjang**	**pen**day^{k}/**pan**jung
tight/loose	**ketat/longgar**	k^{e}tat/**long**gar
How long will it take to alter?	**Berapa lama diperlukan untuk mengubahnya?**	b^{e}**ra**pa **la**ma dee**p^{e}r**lookan **oon**too^{k} m^{e}ng**oo**bahnya

Clothes and accessories *Baju-baju dan tambahan-tambahannya*

I would like a/an/some...	**Saya mengingin-kan...**	**sa**ya m^{e}ng**ing**inkan
bathing cap	**topi mandi**	**to**pee **mun**dee
bathing suit	**baju renang**	**ba**ju r^{e}nung
bathrobe	**mantel mandi**	**mant^{e}l mun**dee
blouse	**blus**	bloos
bow tie	**dasi kupu-kupu**	**da**see **koo**poo-**koo**poo
bra	**beha/kutang**	**bay**ha/**koo**tung
braces	**bingkai penunjang**	**bing**kai p^{e}**noon**jung
cap	**topi**	**to**pee
Indonesian cap	**kopiah**	**ko**peeyah
coat	**jas buka**	jas **boo**ka
dress	**pakaian/gaun**	**pa**kayan/gown
with long sleeves	**dengan lengan panjang**	d^{e}ngan lengan **pan**jung
with short sleeves	**dengan lengan pendek**	d^{e}ngan lengan **pen**day^{k}
sleeveless	**tanpa lengan**	**tan**pa lengan
dressing gown	**daster**	**dast^{e}**r
evening dress (woman's)	**pakaian malam**	**pa**kayan **ma**lam
girdle	**korset**	korset
gloves	**sarung tangan**	**sa**roong **tung**an
handbag	**tas (tangan)**	tas (**tung**an)
handkerchief	**saputangan**	**sa**poo**tung**an
hat	**topi**	**to**pee
jacket	**jaket**	**jak^{e}**t
jeans	**jeans**	jeens
jersey	**baju kaos**	**ba**ju kaus
jumper (Br.)	**baju sweter**	**ba**ju sweter
kneesocks	**kaos lutut**	kaus **loo**toot
nightdress	**pakaian tidur**	**pa**kayan **tee**door
overalls	**pakaian kerja**	**pa**kayan k^{e}rja

pair of...	**sepasang...**	se**pa**sung
panties	**celana dalam**	ch^{e}**la**na **da**lum
pants (Am.)	**celana**	ch^{e}**la**na
panty hose	**celana ketat**	ch^{e}**la**na k^{e}tat
pullover	**pulover**	pullover
polo (turtle)-neck	**leher tinggi**	**lay**her **ting**gi
round-neck	**leher bundar**	**lay**her **boon**dar
without sleeves	**tanpa lengan baju**	**tan**pa l^{e}ngan **ba**joo
pyjamas	**piyama**	pee**ya**ma
raincoat	**jas hujan**	jas **hoo**jan
scarf	**selendang**	s^{e}**len**dung
shirt	**kemeja**	ke**may**ja
shorts	**celana pendek**	ch^{e}**la**na **pen**day^{k}
skirt	**rok**	ro^{k}
slip	**rok dalam**	ro^{k} **da**lum
socks	**kaus kaki**	kaus **ka**kee
stockings	**kaus kaki**	kaus **ka**kee
suit (man's)	**setelan**	**ste**lan
suit (woman's)	**setelan pakaian wanita**	s^{e}t^{e}**lan pa**kayan wa**nee**ta
suspenders (Am.)	**tali selempang**	**ta**lee s^{e}**lem**pung
sweater	**sweter**	sweter
swimming trunks	**celana pendek**	ch^{e}**la**na **pen**day^{k}
swimsuit	**pakaian renang**	**pa**kayan r^{e}nung
T-shirt	**kaos oblong**	kaus oblong
tie	**dasi**	**da**see
tights	**celana ketat**	ch^{e}**la**na k^{e}tat
tracksuit	**baju olahraga**	**ba**ju **o**lah**ra**ga
trousers	**celana**	ch^{e}**la**na
umbrella	**payung**	**pa**yoong
underpants	**celana dalam**	ch^{e}**la**na **da**lum
undershirt	**kaus dalam**	kaus **da**lum
vest (Am.)	**rompi**	**rom**pee
vest (Br.)	**kaos oblong**	kaus oblong
waistcoat	**rompi**	**rom**pee

belt	**ikat pinggang**	**ee**kat pinggung
buckle	**gesper**	gesper
button	**kancing**	**kan**ching
collar	**kerah**	krah
pocket	**saku**	**sa**koo
press stud (snap fastener)	**alat pengancing**	**a**lat p^{e}nganching
zip (zipper)	**kancing tarik**	**kan**ching **ta**ri^{k}

Shoes *Sepatu*

I'd like a pair of...	**Saya ingin sepasang...**	**sa**ya **ing**in se**pa**sung
boots	**sepatu bot**	s^{e}**pa**too bot
moccasins	**sepatu sandal**	s^{e}**pa**too **san**dal
plimsolls (sneakers)	**sepatu karet**	s^{e}**pa**too **ka**ret
sandals	**sandal**	**san**dal
shoes	**sepatu**	s^{e}**pa**too
flat	**rata**	**ra**ta
with a heel	**dengan tumit**	d^{e}ngan **too**mit
with leather soles	**dengan tapak sepatu dari kulit**	d^{e}ngan **ta**pa^{k} s^{e}patoo **da**ree **koo**lit
slippers	**selop**	s^{e}lop
These are too...	**Ini terlalu...**	**ee**nee t^{e}**rla**loo
narrow/wide	**sempit/lebar**	s^{e}mpit/**lay**bar
big/small	**besar/kecil**	b^{e}sar/k^{e}chil
Do you have a larger/smaller size?	**Apakah anda punya yang ukurannya lebih besar/lebih kecil?**	apakah **an**da **poo**nya yung **oo**koorannya l^{e}bih b^{e}sar/l^{e}bih k^{e}chil
Do you have the same in black?	**Apakah anda punya yang berwarna hitam?**	apakah **an**da **poo**nya yung b^{e}**rwarr**na **hee**tam
cloth	**kain**	kain
leather	**kulit**	**koo**lit
rubber	**karet**	**ka**ret
suede	**kulit lunak**	**koo**lit **loo**na^{k}
Is it real leather?	**Apakah ini kulit betul?**	apakah **ee**nee **koo**lit b^{e}**tool**
I need some shoe polish/shoelaces.	**Saya perlu semir sepatu/tali sepatu.**	**sa**ya p^{e}rloo smeer s^{e}**pa**too/**ta**lee s^{e}**pa**too

Shoes worn out? Here's the key to getting them fixed again:

Can you repair these shoes?	**Bisakah anda memperbaiki sepatu ini?**	**bee**sakah **an**da m^{e}mp^{e}r**baik**ee s^{e}**pa**too **ee**nee
Can you stitch this?	**Bisakah anda menjahit ini?**	**bee**sakah **an**da m^{e}n**ja**hit **ee**nee
I want new soles and heels.	**Saya ingin tapak sepatu dan tumit yang baru.**	**sa**ya **ing**in **ta**pa^{k} s^{e}**pa**too dan **too**mit yung **ba**roo
When will they be ready?	**Kapan selesainya?**	**ka**pan sele**sai**nya

COLOURS, see page 113

Electrical appliances *Alat-alat listrik*

Most hotels use 220 volts, 50 cycles and a round, two-pronged slim plug. Some provincial buildings are still on 110 volts. Surabya is considered a good place for buying electronic goods.

What's the voltage?	**Berapa voltasenya?**	b^{e}rapa **volt**as^{e}nya
Do you have a battery for this?	**Apakah anda punya aki untuk ini?**	apakah **an**da **poo**nya **a**kee oontoo^{k} **ee**nee
This is broken. Can you repair it?	**Ini patah. Bisakah anda mereparasinya?**	**ee**nee **pa**tah. **bee**sakah **an**da m^{e}repa**ra**seenya
Can you show me how it works?	**Bisakah anda kasih lihat saya bagaimana caranya bekerja?**	**bee**sakah **an**da **ka**sih **lee**hat **sa**ya bagai**ma**na **ca**ranya b^{e}k^{e}rja
I'd like (to hire) a video cassette.	**Saya ingin (menyewa) satu video kaset.**	**sa**ya **in**gin (m^{e}**nyay**wa) **sa**too video kaset
I'd like a/an/some...	**Saya ingin...**	**sa**ya **in**gin
adaptor	**adaptor**	adap**tor**
amplifier	**amplifier**	ampleefi^{e}r
bulb	**bohlam**	bohlam
CD player	**alat pemain CD**	alat p^{e}main **see**dee
clock-radio	**lonceng-radio**	**lon**cheng-**ra**deeyo
electric toothbrush	**sikat gigi listrik**	**see**kat **gee**gee listrik
extension lead (cord)	**kawat sambungan**	**ka**wat **sam**boongan
hair dryer	**alat pengering rambut**	alat p^{e}ng^{e}ring **rum**boot
headphones	**telepon kepala**	**te**lepon k^{e}**pa**la
(travelling) iron	**setrika**	s^{e}**tri**ka
lamp	**lampu**	**lam**poo
plug	**steker**	**stay**k^{e}r
portable...	**... yang dapat dibawa**	yung **da**pat dee**ba**wa
radio	**radio**	**ra**deeyo
car radio	**radio mobil**	**ra**deeyo **mo**beel
(cassette) recorder	**alat perekam suara (kaset)**	alat p^{e}r^{e}kam **soo**wara (kaset)
record player	**gramofon**	gra**mo**fon
shaver	**alat cukur**	alat **choo**koor
speakers	**alat pengeras suara**	alat p^{e}ng^{e}ras **soo**wara
(colour) television	**televisi (berwarna)**	televeesee (b^{e}r**war**rna)
transformer	**transformator/trafo**	transformator/trafo
video-recorder	**alat perekam video**	alat p^{e}r^{e}kam video

Grocer's *Toko penjual bahan makanan*

Although there are many familiar products, you'll doubtless wish to adjust your shopping list to accommodate more exotic, local goods.

I'd like some bread, please.	**Bolehkah saya dapat roti?**	**bo**layhkah **saya da**pat **ro**tee
What sort of cheese do you have?	**Anda punya keju macam apa?**	**an**da **poo**nya **kay**joo **ma**chum **a**pa
A piece of...	**Sepotong...**	s^e^**po**tong
that one	**yang itu**	yung **ee**too
the one on the shelf	**yang ada di papan rak**	yung **a**da dee **pa**pan rak
I'll have one of those, please.	**Saya ingin beli satu dari yang itu.**	**sa**ya **ing**in blee **sa**too **da**ree yung **ee**too
May I help myself?	**Bolehkah saya mengambil sendiri?**	**bo**layhkah **sa**ya m^e^ng**um**bil s^e^n**dee**ree
I'd like...	**Saya ingin...**	**sa**ya **ing**in
a kilo of apples	**satu kilo buah apel**	**sa**too **kee**lo **boo**wah **a**pel
half a kilo of tomatoes	**setengah kilo buah tomat**	s^e^t^e^ngah **kee**lo **boo**wah tomat
100 grams of butter	**100 gram mentega**	100 gram m^e^n**tay**ga
a litre of milk	**satu liter susu**	**sa**too **leet**^e^r **soo**soo
half a dozen eggs	**setengah lusin telur**	s^e^t^e^ngah **loo**sin t^e^loor
4 slices of ham	**4 iris ham**	4 **ee**ris ham
a packet of tea	**satu bungkus teh**	**sa**too **boong**-koos teh
a jar of jam	**satu botol sele**	**sa**too **bo**tol s^e^lay
a tin (can) of peaches	**satu kaleng persik**	**sa**too **ka**leng **p^e^r**si^k^
a tube of mustard	**satu botol moster**	**sa**too **bo**tol **most**^e^r
a box of chocolates	**satu kotak cokelat**	**sa**too **ko**ta^k^ **chok**lat

1 kilogram or kilo (kg.) = 1000 grams (g.)

100 g. = 3.5 oz. ½ kg. = 1.1 lb.

200 g. = 7.0 oz. 1 kg. = 2.2 lb.

1 oz. = 28.35 g.

1 lb. = 453.60 g.

1 litre (l.) = 0.88 imp. quarts = 1.06 U.S. quarts

1 imp. quart = 1.14 l. 1 U.S. quart = 0.95 l.

1 imp. gallon = 4.55 l. 1 U.S. gallon = 3.8 l.

FOOD, see also page 63

Household articles *Alat-alat rumahtangga*

aluminiumfoil	**kertas aluminium**	k^{e}rtas aloomineeyum
bottle opener	**alat pembuka botol**	alat p^{e}mbooka botol
bucket	**ember**	ember
can opener	**alat pembuka kaleng**	alat p^{e}mbooka kaleng
candles	**lilin**	leelin
dish detergent	**detergen untuk mencuci piring**	dayt^{e}rjen oontoo^{k} m^{e}nchoochee peering
food box	**kotak makanan**	kota^{k} makanan
frying pan	**panci goreng**	panchee goreng
matches	**korek api**	kore^{k} apee
paper napkins	**serbet kertas**	serbet k^{e}rtas
paper towel	**handuk kertas**	handook k^{e}rtas
plastic bags	**tas plastik**	tas plasteek
saucepan	**panci bergagang**	panchee b^{e}rgagung
tin opener	**alat pembuka kaleng**	alat p^{e}mbooka kaleng
vacum flask	**botol pakum**	botol pakoom
washing powder	**deterjen**	dayt^{e}rj^{e}n

... and some useful items

hammer	**palu**	paloo
nails	**paku**	pakoo
penknife	**pisau lipat**	peesow leepat
pliers	**tang/catut**	tung/chatoot
scissors	**gunting**	goonting
screws	**sekerup**	s^{e}kroop
screwdriver	**obeng**	obeng
spanner	**kunci sekerup**	koonchee s^{e}kroop
tools	**alat-alat**	alat-alat

Crockery *Barang-barang tembikar*

cups	**cangkir**	chungkeer
mugs	**mangkuk/mangkok**	mungkoo^{k}/mungko^{k}
plates	**piring**	peering
saucers	**piring cawan**	peering chawan
tumblers	**gelas minum**	glass minoom

Cutlery (flatware) *Alat-alat makan dan masak*

forks	**garpu**	garpoo
knives	**pisau**	peesow
spoons	**sendok**	sendo^{k}
teaspoons	**sendok teh**	sendo^{k} teh

Jeweller's—Watchmaker's *Tempat tukang arloji*

Larger, touristic jewellery and silverware outlets usually have fixed prices (*harga pas*).

Could I see that, please?	**Bolehkah saya lihat itu?**	**bo**layhkah **sa**ya **lee**hat **ee**too
Do you have anything in gold?	**Apakah anda punya sesuatu dari emas?**	apakah **an**da **poo**nya s^{e}**swa**too **da**ree ^{e}mas
How many carats is this?	**Ini berapa karat?**	**ee**nee b^{e}**ra**pa karat
Is this real silver?	**Apa ini perak betul?**	apa **ee**nee **payra**^{k} b^{e}**tool**
Can you repair this watch?	**Bisakah anda memperbaiki arloji ini?**	**bee**sakah **an**da m^{e}mp^{e}**rbaik**ee ar**lo**jee **ee**nee
I'd like a/an/some...	**Saya ingin...**	**sa**ya **ing**in
alarm clock	**beker/weker**	bek^{e}r/wek^{e}r
bangle	**gelang**	glung
battery	**aki**	**a**kee
bracelet	**gelang**	glung
chain bracelet	**gelang rantai**	glung rantai
brooch	**bros/peniti**	bros/p^{e}**nee**tee
chain	**rantai**	rantai
charm	**anting-anting**	**an**ting **an**ting
cigarette case	**kotak rokok**	**ko**ta^{k} **ro**ko^{k}
cigarette lighter	**geretan rokok**	graytan **ro**ko^{k}
clip	**jepitan**	j^{e}pitan
clock	**jam/lonceng**	jum/**lon**cheng
cross	**salib**	**sa**lib
cuckoo clock	**jam kukuk**	jum **koo**koo^{k}
cuff links	**kancing manset**	**kan**ching manset
cutlery	**alat-alat makan dan masak**	alat-**a**lat **ma**kan dan **ma**sak
earrings	**subang**	subang
gem	**permata tulen**	per**ma**ta **too**len
jewel box	**kotak barang-barang perhiasan**	**ko**ta^{k} **ba**rung-**ba**rung p^{e}r**hee**yasan
necklace	**kalung**	**ka**loong
pendant	**anting-anting**	anting-anting
pin	**peniti**	p^{e}**nee**tee
pocket watch	**jam saku**	jum **sa**koo
powder compact	**tempat bedak**	**t**^{e}**m**pat b^{e}da^{k}

ring	**cincin**	chinchin
engagement ring	**cincin pertunangan**	chinchin p^e^**rtoon**ungan
signet ring	**cincin cap**	chinchin chap
wedding ring	**cincin kawin**	chinchin **ka**win
silverware	**barang-barang perak**	**ba**rung-**ba**rung **pay**ra[k]
tie clip	**jepitan dari**	j^e^pitan **da**ree
tie pin	**peniti dasi**	p^e^**nee**tee **da**see
watch	**jam**	jum
automatic	**otomatis**	otomatis
digital	**digital**	digital
quartz	**kuarsa**	**kwar**sa
with a second hand	**dengan jarum detik**	d^e^ngan **ja**room d^e^ti[k]
waterproof	**tahan air**	**ta**han **ay**er
watchstrap	**ikat arloji**	**ee**kat ar**lo**jee
wristwatch	**jam tangan**	jum **tung**an

amber	**ambar**	**am**bar
amethyst	**batu-batuan**	batoo-batooan
chromium	**khrom**	krom
copper	**tembaga**	t^e^mbaga
coral	**batu karang**	batoo **ka**rung
crystal	**kristal**	kristal
diamond	**berlian**	b^e^rleeyan
emerald	**zamrud**	**zam**rood
enamel	**email**	aymail
gold	**emas**	^e^mas
gold plate	**berlapis emas**	b^e^**rla**pis ^e^mas
ivory	**gading**	gading
jade	**batu giok**	**ba**too gyo[k]
pearl	**mutiara**	mootee**ya**ra
platinum	**platina**	pla**tee**na
ruby	**batu delima**	**ba**too d^e^**lee**ma
sapphire	**safir**	**sa**feer
silver	**perak**	**pay**ra[k]
silver plate	**berlapis perak**	b^e^**rla**pis **pay**ra[k]
stainless steel	**baja tahan karat**	**ba**ja **ta**han karat
topaz	**ratna cempaka**	ratna ch^e^**mpa**ka
turquoise	**batu pirus**	**ba**too **pee**roos

Optician *Optik*

I've broken my glasses.	**Kacamata saya patah.**	**ka**cha**ma**ta **sa**ya **pa**tah
Can you repair them for me?	**Bisakah anda memperbaikinya untuk saya?**	**bee**sakah **an**da m^{e}mp^{e}**rbaike**enya **oon**too^{k} **sa**ya
When will they be ready?	**Kapan selesainya?**	**ka**pan s^{e}l^{e}**sai**nya
Can you change the lenses?	**Apakah anda bisa mengganti lensanya?**	apakah **an**da **bee**sa m^{e}ng**gan**tee lensanya
I'd like tinted lenses.	**Saya ingin lensa yang berwarna.**	**sa**ya **ing**in lensa yung b^{e}**rwarr**na
The frame is broken.	**Bingkainya patah.**	**bing**kainya **pa**tah
I'd like a spectacle case.	**Saya ingin tempat kacamata.**	**sa**ya **ing**in **t^{e}m**pat ka**cha**ma**ta
I'd like to have my eyesight checked.	**Saya ingin penglihatan mata saya diperiksa.**	**sa**ya **ing**in p^{e}ng^{e}**lee**hatan **ma**ta **sa**ya dee**priks**a
I'm short-sighted/ long-sighted.	**Saya rabun jauh/ dekat.**	**sa**ya **ra**boon jauh/d^{e}kat
I'd like some contact lenses.	**Saya ingin beberapa lensa kontak.**	**sa**ya **ing**in b^{e}b^{e}**ra**pa lensa kontak
I've lost one of my contact lenses.	**Saya kehilangan salah satu dari lensa-lensa kontak saya.**	**sa**ya ke**hee**lungan **sa**lah **sa**too **da**ree lensa-lensa konta^{k} **sa**ya
Could you give me another one?	**Bisakah anda memberi saya lensa lain?**	**bee**sakah **an**da m^{e}m**bree** **sa**ya lensa lain
I have hard/soft lenses.	**Saya punya lensa keras/lunak.**	**sa**ya **poo**nya lensa krass/ **loo**na^{k}
Do you have any contact-lens fluid?	**Apakah anda punya cairan lensa kontak?**	apakah **an**da **poo**nya **chai**ran lensa kontak
I'd like to buy a pair of sunglasses.	**Saya ingin beli sepasang kacamata hitam.**	**sa**ya **ing**in blee se**pa**sung kacha**ma**ta **hee**tam
May I look in a mirror?	**Bolehkah saya lihat dalam cermin?**	**bo**layhkah **sa**ya **lee**hat **da**lum **ch^{e}r**min
I'd like to buy a pair of binoculars.	**Saya ingin beli sepasang teropong.**	**sa**ya **ing**in blee se**pa**sung **tro**pong

Photography *Fotografi*

You can't be sure of finding all makes of film in out-of-the-way places. Check the date when you buy and keep film in a cool place. Light is best in the early morning and evening. Most people will allow you to photograph them but do ask first.

I'd like a(n) ... camera.	**Saya ingin satu kamera ...**	saya ingin satoo kam^{e}ra
automatic	**otomatis**	otomatis
inexpensive	**yang tidak mahal**	yung teeda^{k} mahal
simple	**yang sederhana**	yung s^{e}d^{e}rhana
Can you show me some ..., please?	**Bolehkah saya melihat bebe-rapa ... ?**	bolayhkah saya m^{e}leehat b^{e}b^{e}rapa
cine (movie) cameras	**kamera film**	kam^{e}ra film
video cameras	**kamera video**	kam^{e}ra video
I'd like to have some passport photos taken.	**Saya ingin punya beberapa foto pas-por.**	saya ingin poonya b^{e}b^{e}rapa foto paspor

Film *Film*

I'd like a film for this camera.	**Saya ingin beli film untuk kamera ini.**	saya ingin blee film oontoo^{k} kam^{e}ra eenee
black and white	**hitam dan putih**	heetam dan pootih
colour	**warna**	warrna
colour negative	**negatif berwarna**	negateef b^{e}rwarrna
colour slide	**slide berwarna**	slaid b^{e}rwarrna
cartridge	**cartridge**	kartrij
disc film	**satu cakra film**	satoo chakra film
roll film	**segulung film**	s^{e}gooloong film
video cassette	**video kaset**	video kaset
24/36 exposures	**pembuatan gambar 24/36**	pemboowatan gumbar 24/36
this size	**ukuran ini**	ookooran eenee
this ASA/DIN number	**nomor ASA/DIN ini**	nomor ASA/DIN eenee
artificial light type	**jenis cahaya bua-tan**	j^{e}nis chahaya boowatan
daylight type	**jenis cahaya siang hari**	j^{e}nis chahaya seeyung haree
fast (high-speed)	**cepat sekali**	ch^{e}pat skalee
fine grain	**jaringan halus**	jaringan haloos

NUMBERS, see page 147

Processing *Pemrosesan*

How much do you charge for processing?	**Berapa ongkosnya memproseskan?**	b^{e}**ra**pa **ong**kosnya m^{e}mpro**ses**kan
I'd like ... prints of each negative.	**Saya ingin ... gambar dari setiap negatif.**	**sa**ya **in**gin ... **gum**bar **da**ree s^{e}**tee**yap negateef
with a matt finish	**dof**	dof
with a glossy finish	**dengan gambar yang mengkilap**	d^{e}ngan **gum**bar yung m^{e}ng**kee**lap
Will you enlarge this, please?	**Bisakah anda memperbesar ini?**	**bee**sakah **an**da m^{e}mp^{e}rb^{e}sar **ee**nee
When will the photos be ready?	**Kapan gambar-gambar itu akan siap?**	**ka**pan **gum**bar-gambar **ee**too **a**kan seeyap

Accessories and repairs *Alat-alat tambahan dan perbaikan-perbaikan*

I'd like a/an/some ...	**Saya ingin ...**	**sa**ya **in**gin
battery	**aki**	akee
camera case	**kotak kamera**	**ko**ta^{k} **kam**^{e}ra
(electronic) flash	**cahaya (elektronik)**	cha**ha**ya (elektronik)
filter	**saringan**	**sa**ringan
for black and white	**untuk hitam dan putih**	**oon**too^{k} **hee**tam dan **poo**tih
for colour	**untuk warna**	**oon**too^{k} **war**rna
lens	**lensa**	lensa
telephoto lens	**lensa telefoto**	lensa telefoto
wide-angle lens	**lensa sudut-luas**	lensa **soo**doot-**loo**was
lens cap	**tutup lensa**	**too**toop lensa
Can you repair this camera?	**Bisakah anda memperbaiki kamera ini?**	**bee**sakah **an**da m^{e}mp^{e}**rbai**kee **kam**^{e}ra **ee**nee
The film is jammed.	**Filmnya macet.**	filmnya **ma**chet
There's something wrong with the ...	**Ada sesuatu yang tidak beres dengan ...**	**a**da s^{e}**swa**too yung **tee**da^{k} **bay**res d^{e}ngan
exposure counter	**alat penghitung pencahayaan**	**a**lat p^{e}ngheetoong p^{e}ncha**ha**yaan
film winder	**alat memutar film**	**a**lat m^{e}**moo**tar film
lens	**lensa**	lensa
light meter	**meteran cahaya**	**mayt**^{e}ran cha**ha**ya
rangefinder	**pengukur jarak**	p^{e}ng**oo**koor **ja**ra^{k}
shutter	**diafragma**	dee-a**frag**ma

Tobacconist's *Toko penjual tembakau, rokok, dsb.*

Western brands of cigarettes are available, along with clove-scented Indonesian *kretek* varieties. Some country markets have tobacco stalls with local plug tobacco.

A packet of cigarettes, please.	**Satu pak rokok.**	satoo pak roko^{k}
Do you have any American/English cigarettes?	**Apakah anda punya rokok Amerika/Inggeris?**	apakah anda poonya roko^{k} am^{e}reeka/ing-grees
I'd like a carton.	**Saya ingin satu slof.**	saya ingin satoo slof
Give me a/some..., please.	**Tolong beri...**	tolong bree
candy	**gula-gula**	goola-goola
chewing gum	**permen karet**	p^{e}rmen karet
chewing tobacco	**tembakau kunyah**	t^{e}mbakau koonyah
chocolate	**cokelat**	choklat
cigarette case	**kotak rokok**	kota^{k} roko^{k}
cigarette holder	**tempat rokok**	t^{e}mpat roko^{k}
cigarettes	**rokok**	roko^{k}
filter-tipped/without filter	**filter/tanpa filter**	filt^{e}r/tanpa filt^{e}r
light/dark tobacco	**tembakau ringan/keras**	t^{e}mbakkau ringan/krass
menthol	**mentol**	mentol
king-size	**ukuran panjang**	ookooran panjung
cigars	**cerutu**	ch^{e}rootoo
lighter	**geretan**	graytan
lighter fluid/gas	**minyak gas**	minya^{k} gas
matches	**korek api**	kore^{k} apee
pipe	**pipa**	peepa
pipe cleaners	**alat membersihkan pipa**	alat m^{e}mb^{e}rsihkan peepa
pipe tobacco	**tembakau pipa**	t^{e}mbakau peepa
pipe tool	**peralatan pipa**	p^{e}ralatan peepa
postcard	**kartupos bergambar**	kartoopos b^{e}rgumbar
snuff	**tembakau sedotan**	t^{e}mbakau s^{e}dotan
stamps	**perangko**	prungko
sweets	**gula-gula**	goola-goola
wick	**sumbu**	soomboo

Miscellaneous *Serbaneka*

Souvenirs *Tandamata*

You're in a shopper's paradise, with an enormous variety of exciting arts, crafts, jewellery and fabrics. For an overall look at it all, visit Sarinah Department Store (fixed prices apply) and Ancol Market in Jakarta. During your travels you'll come across curiosities and treasures including leather and wooden puppets, *batik* cloth of varying qualities, often made in traditional regional colours and patterns, marvellous, hand-loomed silk, expressive carvings, paintings, brassware, and a great range of silver.

Bear in mind the restrictions which may exist in your own country about importing untreated hides, bone and feathers. Note that valuable antiques should be checked and cleared for export. A reputable dealer should assist.

baskets	**keranjang**	k^e**ran**jung
batik	**batik**	**ba**tik
brassware	**kuningan**	**koo**ningan
carvings	**patung**	**pa**toong
fan	**kipas**	**kee**pas
leather goods	**barang-barang kulit**	**ba**rung-**ba**rung **koo**lit
mask	**topeng**	**to**peng
paintings	**lukisan**	**loo**kisan
silk	**sutra**	**soo**tra
silver	**perak**	payra^k
snakeskin shoes	**sepatu kulit ular**	s^e**pa**too **koo**lit **oo**lar
wooden/leather puppets	**wayang golek/kulit**	**wa**yung **go**lek/**koo**lit

Records—Cassettes *Piringan hitam—Kaset*

I'd like a...	**Saya ingin suatu...**	**sa**ya **ing**in **swa**too
cassette	**kaset**	kaset
video cassette	**kaset video**	kaset video
compact disc	**CD**	**see**dee

L.P.(33 rpm)	**Piringan Hitam (Main Lama)**	**pee**ringan **hee**tam (main **la**ma)
E.P.(45 rpm)	**Piringan Hitam (Main Diperluas)**	**pee**ringan **hee**tam (main dee**pe**rlooas)
single	**single**	**sing**gel

Do you have any records by...?	**Apakah anda punya piringan hitam dari... ?**	apakah **an**da **poo**nya **pee**ringan **hee**tam **da**ree
Can I listen to this record?	**Bolehkah saya mendengar piringan hitam ini?**	**bo**layhkah **sa**ya mendengar **pee**ringan **hee**tam **ee**nee
chamber music	**musik kamar**	**moo**seek **ka**mar
classical music	**musik klasik**	**moo**seek klasik
folk music	**musik rakyat**	**moo**seek **rak**yat
folk song	**lagu rakyat**	**la**goo **rak**yat
instrumental music	**musik instrumental**	**moo**seek instrumental
jazz	**jazz**	jazz
light music	**musik ringan**	**moo**seek ringan
orchestral music	**musik orkes**	**moo**seek orkes
pop music	**musik pop**	**moo**seek pop

Toys *Mainan*

I'd like a toy/game...	**Saya ingin satu mainan/permainan...**	**sa**ya **in**gin **sa**too mainan/permainan
for a boy	**untuk anak laki-laki**	**oon**took **a**nak **la**kee-**la**kee
for a 5-year-old girl	**untuk anak perempuan usia 5 tahun**	**oon**took **a**nak perempoo-an **oo**seeya 5 **ta**hoon
bucket and spade (pail and shovel)	**ember dan sekop**	ember dan skop
building blocks (bricks)	**batu**	**ba**too
card game	**permainan kartu**	permainan **kar**too
chess set	**satu set permainan catur**	**sa**too set permainan **cha**toor
doll	**boneka**	**bo**nayka
electronic game	**permainan elektronik**	permainan elektronik
teddy bear	**mainan beruang-beruangan**	mainan **broo**wung-**broo**wungan
toy car	**mobil-mobilan**	**mo**beel-**mo**beelan

Your money: banks—currency

Banks are open from 8 or 8.30 am to noon or 1 pm, Monday to Friday. Money changers, open until later and sometimes at the weekend, often give better rates. You can also change money at major hotels, which offer the lowest rates. Note that rates vary around the country and from bank to bank, so it pays to compare what's available. It's best to travel with U.S. dollar travellers' cheques from a well known company. Other major currencies include pounds sterling, Singapore and Australian dollars. Canadian dollars are more difficult. Remember to present your passport.

Indonesian banks do not like changing worn foreign notes. Don't accept torn *rupiah* bills yourself or you'll have difficulty passing them on. If this occurs, take them to a bank.

If travelling to out-of-the-way places, take plenty of low-denomination notes. Credit cards aren't always accepted outside major touristic establishments.

The national currency unit is the *rupiah* (rp). Banknotes come in denominations of 100, 500, 1 000, 5 000 and 10 000 rp.

Coins, increasingly little used, are 5, 10, 50 and 100 rp.

Where's the nearest bank?	**Dimanakah bank yung terdekat disini?**	dee**ma**nakah bank yung t^{e}rd^{e}**kat** dee**see**nee
Where's the nearest currency exchange office?	**Dimanakah kantor penukaran uang yang terdekat disini?**	dee**ma**nakah **kan**tor p^{e}**noo**karan wung yung t^{e}rd^{e}**kat** dee**see**nee

At the bank *Di bank*

I want to change some dollars/pounds.	**Saya ingin menukar beberapa dollar/pon sterling.**	**sa**ya **ing**in me**noo**kar b^{e}b^{e}**ra**pa **do**lar/pon st^{e}**rling**

I want to cash a traveller's cheque.	**Saya ingin menukar cek wisata.**	**saya ingin** menookar chek weesata
What's the exchange rate?	**Berapakah nilai tukarnya?**	b^{e}**ra**pakah **nee**lai too**kar**nya
How much commission do you charge?	**Anda minta komisi berapa?**	anda **min**ta **ko**meesee b^{e}**ra**pa
Can you cash a personal cheque?	**Dapatkah anda menukar cek pribadi?**	**da**patkah **an**da me**noo**kar chek pree**ba**dee
Can you telex my bank in London?	**Bisakah anda menghubungi bank saya di London melalui teleks?**	**bee**sakah **an**da m^{e}ng**hoo**boongee bank **sa**ya dee **lon**don m^{e}**la**looee **te**leks
I have a...	**Saya punya...**	**saya poo**nya
credit card	**kartu kredit**	**kar**too **kre**deet
letter of credit	**surat kredit**	**soo**rat **kre**deet
I'm expecting some money from New York. Has it arrived?	**Saya sedang menunggu pengiriman uang dari New York. Apakah sudah datang?**	**sa**ya s^{e}**dung** m^{e}**noong**goo p^{e}ng**ee**riman wung **da**ree noo york. apakah **soo**dah **da**tung
Please give me... notes (bills) and some small change.	**Bolehkah saya dapat... uang kertas dan beberapa uang kecil.**	**bo**laykah **sa**ya **da**pat... wung k^{e}**rtas** dan b^{e}b^{e}**ra**pa wung k^{e}**cheel**
Give me... large notes and the rest in small notes.	**Berikan saya... uang kertas besar dan selebihnya dalam uang kertas kecil.**	b^{e}**ree**kan **sa**ya... wung k^{e}rtas b^{e}**sar** dan sel^{e}**bay**hnya **da**lam wung k^{e}**rtas** k^{e}**cheel**

Deposits—Withdrawals *Deposito—Penarikan uang*

I want to...	**Saya ingin...**	**saya ingin**
open an account	**membuka rekening**	m^{e}m**boo**ka **rek**^{e}ning
withdraw... rupiah	**menarik... rupiah**	m^{e}**nari**^{k}... roo**pee**yah
Where should I sign?	**Dimana saya mesti tanda tangan?**	dee**ma**na **sa**ya m^{e}stee **tan**da **tan**gan
I'd like to pay this into my account.	**Saya ingin masukkan ini dalam rekening saya.**	**sa**ya **in**gin **ma**sookan **ee**nee **da**lam **rek**^{e}ning **sa**ya

NUMBERS, see page 147

Business terms *Syarat-syarat bisnis*

My name is…	**Nama saya adalah…**	**na**ma **sa**ya **a**dalah
Here's my card.	**Ini kartu saya.**	**ee**nee **kar**too **sa**ya
I have an appointment with…	**Saya punya janji dengan…**	**sa**ya **poo**nya **jan**jee d^e^n**gan**
Can you give me an estimate of the cost?	**Dapatkah anda memberi saya suatu perkiraan dari ongkosnya?**	**da**patkah **an**da m^e^m**bree** **sa**ya **swa**too p^e^r**keera**-an **da**ree **ong**kosnya
What's the rate of inflation?	**Barapakah tingkat inflasi?**	bara**pa**kah **ting**kat in**fla**see
Can you provide me with a/an…?	**Dapatkah anda mengusahakan untuk saya…?**	**da**patkah **an**da m^e^ng**oos**ahakan **oon**to^k^ **sa**ya
interpreter	**seorang juru bahasa**	s^e^**o**rung **joo**roo ba**ha**sa
a personal computer	**sebuah komputer**	s^e^**boo**ha kom**pyoo**t^e^r
a secretary	**seorang sekretaris**	s^e^**o**rung sekr^e^**ta**ris
Where can I make photocopies?	**Dimana saya bisa membuat fotokopi?**	dee**ma**na **sa**ya **bee**sa m^e^m**boo**at foto**kop**pee

amount	**jumlah**	**joom**lah
balance	**neraca**	n^e^**ra**cha
capital	**modal**	**mo**dal
cheque	**cek**	chek
contract	**kontrak**	**kon**trak
discount	**potongan/diskonto**	**po**tongan/dis**kon**to
expenses	**pengeluaran**	p^e^ng^e^**loo**aran
interest	**bunga**	**boon**ga
investment	**investasi**	inves**ta**see
invoice	**faktur**	**fak**toor
loss	**kerugian**	k^e^**roo**gee-an
mortgage	**hipotek**	**hee**potek
payment	**pembayaran**	p^e^m**ba**yaran
percentage	**persentase**	p^e^rsen**ta**say
profit	**keuntungan**	k^e^-**oon**toongan
purchase	**pembelian**	p^e^mb^e^**lee**an
sale	**penjualan/obral**	p^e^n**joo**walan/**ob**ral
share	**saham**	**sa**ham
transfer	**pemindahan/transfer**	p^e^**min**dahan/**trans**f^e^r
value	**nilai**	**nee**lai

At the post office

Post offices are crowded and involve long, slow queues and a good deal of frustration. It's much easier to use the services of large hotels which will efficiently take care of your mail even if you're not a guest there. Make sure all important outgoing and incoming mail is registered. Ask your correspondents to write your surname in capital letters and underline it to avoid confusion. If you're sending parcels from a post office, don't wrap them since the contents may have to be inspected. There's an express service for domestic mail. Post offices sell blue envelopes marked *kilat* for airmail and yellow ones, *kilat khusus* for express airmail.

If you decide to try the post office experience, take your own glue for stamp-sticking.

Where's the nearest post office?	**Dimanakah kantor pos yang terdekat disini?**	dee**ma**nakah **kan**tor pos yung t^{e}rd^{e}**kat** dee**see**nee
What time does the post office open/close?	**Jam berapa kantor pos buka/tutup?**	jum b^{e}**ra**pa **kan**tor pos **boo**ka/**too**toop
A stamp for this letter/postcard, please.	**Bolehkah beli satu perangko untuk surat/kartupos ini.**	**bo**laykah blee **sa**too **prang**ko **oon**to^{k} **soo**rat/**kar**toopos eenee
A . . .-rupiah stamp, please.	**Perangko . . . -rupiah.**	**prang**ko . . . roo**pee**yah
What's the postage for a letter to London?	**Berapa ongkos perangko untuk satu surat ke London?**	b^{e}**ra**pa **ong**kos **prang**ko **oon**to^{k} **sa**too **soo**rat k^{e} **lon**don
What's the postage for a postcard to Los Angeles?	**Berapa ongkos perangko untuk satu kartupos ke Los Angeles?**	b^{e}**ra**pa **ong**kos **prang**ko **oon**to^{k} **sa**too **kar**toopos k^{e} los **ang**^{e}l^{e}s
Where's the letter box (mailbox)?	**Dimanakah bis surat?**	dee**ma**nakah bis **soo**rat

I want to send this parcel.	**Saya ingin kirim paket ini.**	**sa**ya **ing**in **kee**rim **pa**ket **ee**nee
I'd like to send this (by)...	**Saya ingin kirim ini melalui...**	**sa**ya **ing**in **kee**rim eenee m^{e}**la**looee
airmail	**pos udara**	pos oo**da**ra
express (special delivery)	**pos kilat**	pos **kee**lat
registered mail	**pos tercatat**	pos t^{e}r**cha**tat
At which counter can I cash an international money order?	**Di loket mana saya bisa menarik satu poswesel internasional?**	dee **lock**et **ma**na **sa**ya **bee**sa m^{e}**na**ri^{k} **sa**too **pos**wesel inter**na**seeyonal
Where's the poste restante (general delivery)?	**Dimana pos restante?**	dee**ma**na pos restante
Is there any post (mail) for me? My name is...	**Apakah ada surat untuk saya? Nama saya adalah...**	apakah **a**da **soo**rat **oon**to^{k} **sa**ya. **na**ma **sa**ya **a**dalah

PERANGKO-PERANGKO	STAMPS
PAKET-PAKET	PARCELS
POSWESEL	MONEY ORDERS

Telegrams—Telex—Fax *Telegram—Teleks—Faks*

Major hotels will be able to deal with faxes, telexes and telegrams.

I'd like to send a telegram/telex.	**Saya ingin kirim telegram/teleks.**	**sa**ya **ing**in **kee**rim telay**gram**/**te**leks
May I have a form, please?	**Bolehkah saya dapat formulir?**	**bo**laykah **sa**ya **da**pat **for**mooleer
How much is it per word?	**Berapa ongkosnya untuk satu kata?**	b^{e}**ra**pa **ong**kosnya **oon**to^{k} **sa**too **ka**ta
How long will a cable to Boston take?	**Dalam waktu berapa lama kawat ke Boston akan sampai?**	**da**lam **wak**too b^{e}**ra**pa **la**ma **ka**wat k^{e} **bos**ton **a**kan **sam**pai
How much will this fax cost?	**Berapa ongkosnya faks ini?**	b^{e}**ra**pa **ong**kosnya faks **ee**nee

Telephoning *Menelepon*

Indonesia has direct dialling for domestic and overseas calls. It is simplest to put calls through your hotel.

Where's the telephone?	**Dimana ada telepon?**	dee**ma**na **ada tele**pon
I'd like a telephone token.	**Saya ingin ketipan untuk telepon.**	**saya ing**in **k**^{e}tipan **oonto**^{k} **tele**pon
Where's the nearest telephone booth?	**Dimana telepon umum terdekat?**	dee**ma**na **tele**pon **oo**moom t^{e}rd^{e}**kat**
May I use your phone?	**Bolehkah saya pakai telepon anda?**	**bo**laykah **saya pakai tele**pon **an**da
Do you have a telephone directory for Bandung?	**Apakah anda punya buku petunjuk telepon untuk Bandung?**	apakah **an**da **poo**nya **boo**koo p^{e}**toon**joo^{k} **tele**pon **oon**to^{k} **ban**doong
I'd like to call ... in England.	**Saya ingin menelepon ... di Inggeris.**	**saya ing**in m^{e}**nele**pon ... dee **ing**grees
What's the dialling (area) code for ...?	**Apakah kode wilayah untuk ...?**	apakah **kode** wee**la**yah **oon**to^{k}
How do I get the international operator?	**Bagaimana saya bisa dapat operator internasional?**	**ba**gaimana **saya bee**sa **da**pat op^{e}**ra**tor inter**na**seeyonal

Operator *Penghubung/Operator*

I'd like Surabaya 23 45 67.	**Saya ingin bicara dengan Surabaya 23 45 67.**	**saya ing**in bee**cha**ra d^{e}ngan soora**ba**ya 23 45 67
Can you help me get this number?	**Bisakah anda tolong mendapatkan nomor ini?**	**bee**sakah **an**da **to**long m^{e}n**da**patkan **no**mor eenee
I'd like to place a personal (person-to-person) call.	**Saya ingin bicara telepon pribadi.**	**saya ing**in bi**cha**ra **tele**pon pree**ba**dee
I'd like to reverse the charges (call collect).	**Saya ingin membalikkan ongkos telepon.**	**saya ing**in m^{e}m**ba**likan **ong**kos **tele**pon

NUMBERS, see page 147

Speaking *Bicara*

Hello. This is...	**Halo. Disini...**	**ha**lo. dee**see**nee
I'd like to speak to...	**Saya ingin bicara dengan...**	**sa**ya **ing**in bi**cha**ra d^e^ngan
Extension...	**Pesawat...**	p^e^**sa**wat
Speak louder/more slowly, please.	**Silahkan bicara lebih keras/lebih pelan-pelan.**	**see**lahkan bi**cha**ra l^e^bih kras/l^e^bih plan-plan

Bad luck *Sial*

Would you try again later, please?	**Apakah mau coba lagi kemudian?**	**a**pakah mau **cho**ba **la**gee k^e^**moo**deean
Operator, you gave me the wrong number.	**Operator, anda memberi saya nomor yang salah.**	**op**^e^raytor **an**da m^e^m**bree** saya **no**mor yung **sa**lah
Operator, we were cut off.	**Operator, kami ter-putus.**	**op**^e^raytor **ka**mee t^e^r**poo**toos

Telephone alphabet *Abjad telepon*

If you need to spell something over the phone, the standard alphabet in English will be understood.

A	Alpha	**H**	Hotel	**O**	Oscar	**U**	Ultra
B	Beta	**I**	India	**P**	Papa	**V**	Volvo
C	Charlie	**J**	Juliet	**Q**	Quebec	**W**	Whisky
D	Delta	**K**	Kilo	**R**	Romeo	**X**	X-ray
E	Echo	**L**	Lima	**S**	Sierra	**Y**	Yankee
F	Foxtrot	**M**	Mike	**T**	Tango	**Z**	Zulu
G	Golf	**N**	November				

Not there *Tidak ada ditempat*

When will he/she be back?	**Kapan dia kembali?**	**ka**pan deeya k^e^m**ba**lee

Will you tell him/her I called?	**Bisakah anda memberitahu kepadanya bahwa saya telah menelepon?**	**bee**sakah **an**da m^e^mbree**ta**hoo k^e^**pa**danya **bah**wa **sa**ya t^e^lah m^e^**ne**lepon
My name is...	**Nama saya adalah...**	**na**ma **sa**ya **a**dalah
Would you ask him/her to call me?	**Bisakah anda tolong minta dia untuk menelepon saya?**	**bee**sakah **an**da **to**long **min**ta deeya **oon**to^k^ m^e^**ne**lepon **sa**ya
My number is...	**Nomor saya adalah...**	**no**mor **sa**ya **a**dalah
Would you take a message, please	**Dapatkah anda menerima pesan.**	**da**patkah **an**da m^e^n^e^**ree**ma p^e^**san**

Charges *Ongkos-ongkos*

What was the cost of that call?	**Berapa ongkosnya telepon itu?**	b^e^**ra**pa **ong**kosnya **te**lepon **ee**too
I want to pay for the call.	**Saya ingin bayar ongkos telepon.**	**sa**ya **in**gin **ba**yar **ong**kos **te**lepon

Ada telepon untuk anda.	There's a telephone call for you.
Anda menelepon nomor berapa?	What number are you calling?
Salurannya sedang dipakai.	The line's engaged.
Tidak ada jawaban.	There's no answer.
Anda salah sambung.	You've got the wrong number.
Teleponnya sedang rusak.	The phone is out of order.
Tunggu sebentar.	Just a moment.
Tunggu dulu.	Hold on, please.
Dia sekarang sedang pergi.	He's/She's out at the moment.

Doctor

It is wise to take out travel health insurance in your country of origin. Provided you have suitable immunizations before you arrive, allow yourself to adjust slowly to the climate and pay attention to food and personal hygiene, you shouldn't expect to experience anything more than mild stomach upsets. Remember to take your malaria pills as prescribed, to drink plenty of fluids and keep your salt intake up.

Indonesians themselves often prefer the *dukun* or folk doctor to western-style medicine. They are knowledgeable about herbal remedies, called *jamu*.

General *Umum*

I need a doctor, quickly.	**Saya perlu dokter, cepat.**	saya p^e^rloo dokt^e^r ch^e^pat
Where can I find a doctor who speaks English?	**Dimana saya bisa dapat dokter yang bisa bicara bahasa Inggeris?**	deemana saya beesa dapat dokt^e^r yung beesa bichara bahasa inggrees
Where's the surgery (doctor's office)?	**Dimana kantor praktek dokter?**	deemana kantor prakek^e^ dokt^e^r
What are the surgery (office) hours?	**Kapankah jam-jam kerja praktek dokter?**	kapankah jum-jum k^e^rja praktek dokt^e^r
Could the doctor come to see me here?	**Apakah dokter bisa datang memeriksa saya disni?**	apakah dokt^e^r beesa datung m^e^m^e^riksa saya deeseenee
What time can the doctor come?	**Jam berapa dokter bisa datang?**	jum b^e^rapa dokt^e^r beesa datung
Can you recommend a/an...?	**Dapatkah anda memberi nasehat tentang...**	dapatkah anda m^e^mbree nasayhat t^e^ntung
general practitioner	**dokter umum**	dokt^e^r oomoom
children's doctor	**dokter anak-anak**	dokt^e^r ana^k^-ana^k^
eye specialist	**dokter mata**	dokt^e^r mata
gynaecologist	**seorang ginekolog**	s^e^orung geenaykolog
Can I have an appointment...?	**Bisakah saya bikin janji...?**	beesakah saya beekin janjee
tomorrow	**untuk besok**	oonto^k^ bayso^k^
as soon as possible	**untuk secepat-cepatnya**	oonto^k^ s^e^chepat-chepatnya

CHEMIST'S, see page 108

Parts of the body *Bagian-bagian tubuh*

appendix	**usus buntu**	oosoos **boon**too
arm	**lengan**	l^{e}**ngan**
back	**punggung**	**poong**goong
bladder	**kandung kemih**	**kan**doong **ke**mih
bone	**tulang**	**too**lung
bowel	**isi perut**	**ee**see p^{e}**root**
breast	**buah dada**	**boo**ah **da**da
chest	**dada**	**da**da
ear	**kuping**	**koo**ping
eye(s)	**mata**	**ma**ta
face	**muka**	**moo**ka
finger	**jari**	**ja**ree
foot	**kaki**	**ka**kee
genitals	**alat kelamin**	alat k^{e}**la**min
gland	**kelenjar**	k^{e}l^{e}**njar**
hand	**tangan**	**tan**gan
head	**kepala**	k^{e}**pa**la
heart	**jantung**	**jan**toong
jaw	**rahang**	**ra**hung
joint	**tulang sendi**	**too**lung s^{e}**ndee**
kidney	**ginjal**	**gin**jal
knee	**lutut**	**loo**toot
leg	**kaki**	**ka**kee
ligament	**ikatan sendi tulang**	**i**katan s^{e}**ndee too**lung
lip	**bibir**	**bee**beer
liver	**hati**	**ha**tee
lung	**paru-paru**	**pa**roo-**pa**roo
mouth	**mulut**	**moo**loot
muscle	**otot**	**o**tot
neck	**leher**	**lay**her
nerve	**urat syaraf**	**oo**rat **sha**raf
nose	**hidung**	**hee**doong
rib	**tulang rusuk**	**too**lung **roo**soo^{k}
shoulder	**bahu**	**ba**hoo
skin	**kulit**	**koo**lit
spine	**tulang belakang**	**too**lung be**la**kang
stomach	**perut**	p^{e}**root**
tendon	**urat daging**	**oo**rat **da**ging
thigh	**paha**	**pa**ha
throat	**tenggorokan**	t^{e}ngg**o**rokan
thumb	**ibu jari**	**ee**boo **ja**ree
toe	**jari kaki**	**ja**ree **ka**kee
tongue	**lidah**	**lee**dah
tonsils	**amandel**	a**man**del
vein	**nadi**	**na**dee

Accident—Injury *Kecelakaan—Luka-luka*

There's been an accident.	**Telah terjadi kecelakaan.**	telah t^{e}rjadee k^{e}ch^{e}laka-an
My child has had a fall.	**Anak saya telah jatuh.**	ana^{k} saya t^{e}lah jatooh
He/She has hurt his/her head.	**Kepalanya telah luka.**	k^{e}palanya t^{e}lah looka
He's/She's unconscious.	**Ia jatuh pingsang.**	eea jatooh pingsang
He's/She's bleeding (heavily).	**Ia berdarah (berat).**	eea b^{e}rdarah (brat)
He's/She's (seriously) injured.	**Ia luka (berat).**	eea looka (brat)
His/Her arm is broken.	**Lengannya patah.**	l^{e}ngannya patah
His/Her ankle is swollen.	**Pergelangan kakinya bengkak.**	p^{e}rg^{e}lungan kakeenya b^{e}ngka^{k}
I've been stung.	**Saya telah tersengat.**	saya t^{e}lah t^{e}rs^{e}ngat
I've got something in my eye.	**Mata saya kemasukan sesuatu.**	mata saya k^{e}masookan seswatoo
I've got a/an...	**Saya punya...**	saya poonya
blister	**lepuh**	l^{e}pooh
boil	**bisul**	beesool
bruise	**luka memar**	looka m^{e}mar
burn	**luka bakar**	looka bakar
cut	**luka**	looka
graze	**luka keserempet**	looka k^{e}s^{e}rempet
insect bite	**gigitan serangga**	geegitan s^{e}rangga
lump	**gumpalan**	goompalan
rash	**ruam**	roowam
sting	**sengatan**	s^{e}ngatan
swelling	**bengkak**	b^{e}ngka^{k}
wound	**luka**	looka
Could you have a look at it?	**Bisakah anda memeriksa ini?**	beesakah anda m^{e}m^{e}riksa eenee
I can't move my...	**Saya tidak bisa menggerakkan... saya.**	saya teeda^{k} beesa m^{e}ngg^{e}rakkan... saya
It hurts.	**Sakit.**	sakit

Dimana sakitnya?	Where does it hurt?
Sakitnya bagaimana?	What kind of pain is it?
tumpul/tajam/denyut	dull/sharp/throbbing
konstan/sekali-sekali	constant/on and off
Adalah . . .	It's . . .
patah/keseleo	broken/sprained
tergelincir/terrobek	dislocated/torn
Saya ingin supaya anda mendapat sinar-X.	I'd like you to have an X-ray.
Kita akan terpaksa membalutnya dalam gips.	We'll have to put it in plaster.
Ia telah kena infeksi.	It's infected.
Apakah anda sudah divaksin terhadap tetanus?	Have you been vaccinated against tetanus?
Saya akan beri anda penawar rasa sakit.	I'll give you a painkiller.

Illness *Keadaan sakit*

I'm not feeling well.	**Saya tidak merasa sehat.**	saya **tee**da^k merasa **say**hat
I'm ill.	**Saya sakit.**	saya **sa**kit
I feel . . .	**Saya merasa . . .**	saya merasa
dizzy	**pusing**	**poo**sing
nauseous	**mual**	**moo**wal
shivery	**menggigil**	m^{e}ngg**i**gil
I have a temperature (fever).	**Saya merasa demam.**	saya merasa d^{e}mam
My temperature is 38 degrees.	**Panas saya 38 derajat.**	**pa**nas **sa**ya **tee**gapoolooh d^e**la**pan d^e**ra**jat
I've been vomiting.	**Saya telah muntah-muntah.**	saya t^{e}lah **moon**tah-**moon**tah
I'm constipated/I've got diarrhoea.	**Saya sembelit/ Saya murus.**	saya s^{e}mblit/**sa**ya **moo**roos
My . . . hurt(s).	**. . . saya sakit.**	. . . **sa**ya **sa**kit
I've got (a/an) . . .	**Saya punya . . .**	saya **poo**nya
asthma	**sakit bengek**	sakit b^e**nge**^{k}
backache	**sakit punggung**	sakit **poong**goong
cold	**masuk angin**	**ma**soo^k angin

cough	**sakit batuk**	sakit **ba**too^{k}
cramps	**kejang**	**k^{e}**jang
earache	**sakit telinga**	sakit t^{e}**ling**a
hay fever	**alergi rumput**	al**er**gee **room**poot
headache	**sakit kepala**	sakit k^{e}**pa**la
indigestion	**salah cerna**	salah **ch^{e}r**na
nosebleed	**mimisan**	**mee**misan
palpitations	**jantung berdebar-debar**	**jan**toong b^{e}**rd^{e}**bar-**d^{e}**bar
rheumatism	**encok**	encho^{k}
sore throat	**sakit tenggorokan**	sakit t^{e}ng**gor**okan
stiff neck	**leher kaku**	**lay**her **ka**koo
stomach ache	**sakit perut**	sakit p^{e}**root**
sunstroke	**kelengar matahari**	k^{e}l^{e}ngar **mataha**ree
I have difficulties breathing.	**Saya sulit bernapas.**	saya **soo**lit b^{e}**rna**pas
I have chest pains.	**Saya sakit di dada.**	saya **sa**kit dee **da**da
I had a heart attack... years ago.	**Saya dapat serangan jantung... tahun yang lalu.**	saya **da**pat s^{e}**rang**an **jan**toong... tahoon yung **la**loo
My blood pressure is too high/too low.	**Tekanan darah saya terlalu tinggi/rendah.**	t^{e}**ka**nan **da**rah **sa**ya t^{e}**rla**loo **ting**gee/**r^{e}**ndah
I'm allergic to...	**Saya peka sekali terhadap...**	saya **pay**ka s^{e}**ka**lee t^{e}**rha**dap
I'm diabetic.	**Saya punya penyakit kencing manis.**	saya **poo**nya p^{e}**nya**kit **k^{e}n**ching **ma**nis

Women's section *Seksi wanita*

I have period pains.	**Saya selalu sakit kalau datang bulan.**	saya sel**a**loo **sakit ka**lau datung **boo**lan
I have a vaginal infection.	**Saya kena infeksi di liang peranakan.**	saya k^{e}na in**fek**see dee **lee**ang p^{e}ranakan
I'm on the pill.	**Saya sedang makan pel pencegah kehamilan.**	saya s^{e}**dung ma**kan pel p^{e}**nch^{e}**gah k^{e}**ha**milan
I haven't had a period for 2 months.	**Saya sudah 2 bulan tidak mengalami masa haid.**	saya **soo**dah **doo**wa **boo**lan **tee**da^{k} m^{e}ngalami **ma**sa haid
I'm (3 months) pregnant.	**Saya sudah (3 bulan) hamil.**	saya **soo**dah (3 **boo**lan) **ha**mil

Sudah berapa lama anda merasa begini?	How long have you been feeling like this?
Apakah ini pertama kali anda mengalami demikian ini?	Is this the first time you've had this?
Saya akan mengambil panas badan/tekanan darah anda.	I'll take your temperature/ blood pressure.
Harap menyingsingkan lengan baju anda.	Roll up your sleeve, please.
Harap lepas baju (sampai di pinggang).	Please undress (down to the waist).
Silahkan berbaring disana.	Please lie down over here.
Harap buka mulut anda.	Open your mouth.
Silahkan ambil napas panjang.	Breathe deeply.
Batuklah.	Cough, please.
Dimana yang sakit?	Where does it hurt?
Anda punya . . .	You've got (a/an) . . .
radang usus buntu	appendicitis
radang kandung kemih	cystitis
radang lambung perut	gastritis
influensa	flu
radang pada . . .	inflammation of . . .
peracunan makanan	food poisoning
penyakit kuning	jaundice
penyakit kelamin	venereal disease
radang paru-paru	pneumonia
campak	measles
Ia (tidak) menular.	It's (not) contagious.
Ini suatu alergi.	It's an allergy.
Saya akan berikan anda suntikan.	I'll give you an injection.
Saya ingin mendapat contoh dari darah/berak/air kencing anda.	I want a specimen of your blood/stools/urine.
Anda harus tetap berbaring di tempat tidur untuk . . . hari.	You must stay in bed for . . . days.
Saya ingin anda pergi ke seorang spesialis.	I want you to see a specialist.
Saya ingin anda pergi ke rumah sakit untuk menjalani pemeriksaan umum badan.	I want you to go to the hospital for a general check-up.

Prescription—Treatment *Resep—Perawatan*

This is my usual medicine.	**Ini adalah obat biasa saya.**	eenee **a**dalah **o**bat beeasa **sa**ya
Can you give me a prescription for this?	**Dapatkah anda memberi saya resep untuk ini?**	**da**patkah **an**da m^{e}m**bree** saya **ray**sep **oon**to^{k} eenee
Can you prescribe a/an/some...?	**Dapatkah anda memberi saya resep untuk...?**	**da**patkah **an**da m^{e}m**bree** saya **ray**sep **oon**to^{k}
antidepressant	**obat anti-depresi**	**o**bat **an**tee-de**press**ee
sleeping pills	**obat tidur**	**o**bat **tee**door
tranquillizer	**obat penenang**	**o**bat p^{e}**n**^{e}nung
Are you using a sterilized needle?	**Apakah jarumnya steril?**	apakah **ja**roomnya st^{e}**reel**
I'm allergic to certain antibiotics/penicillin.	**Saya peka sekali terhadap antibiotika/penisilin tertentu.**	**sa**ya **pay**ka s^{e}**ka**lee t^{e}r**ha**dap **an**teebee**yo**teeka/ pen**ee**seelin t^{e}rtentu
How many times a day should I take it?	**Berapa kali sehari saya harus makan ini?**	b^{e}**ra**pa **ka**lee s^{e}**ha**ree **sa**ya **ha**roos **ma**kan eenee

Anda sedang mendapat perawatan apa?	What treatment are you having?
Anda makan obat apa?	What medicine are you taking?
Dengan disuntikkan atau dimakan?	By injection or orally?
Makan obat ini... sendok teh.	Take... teaspoons of this medicine.
Makan satu pel dengan satu gelas air...	Take one pill with a glass of water...
setiap... jam	every... hours
... kali sehari	... times a day
sebelum/sesudah makan	before/after each meal
pagi hari/malam hari	in the morning/at night
jika ada yang sakit	if there is any pain
untuk... hari	for... days

CHEMIST'S, see page 108

Fee *Ongkos*

How much do I owe you?	**Berapa saya berhutang pada anda?**	b^{e}**rapa** **sa**ya b^{e}**rhoot**ung pada **an**da
May I have a receipt for my health insurance?	**Bolehkah saya mendapat tanda terima untuk asuransi kesehatan saya?**	**bo**laykah **sa**ya m^{e}**nda**pat **tan**da t^{e}rima **oon**to^{k} asoo**ran**see k^{e}**say**hatan saya
Can I have a medical certificate?	**Bolehkah saya mendapat surat keterangan dokter?**	**bo**laykah **sa**ya m^{e}**nda**pat **soo**rat k^{e}t^{e}**rung**an **dok**t^{e}r
Would you fill in this health insurance form, please?	**Bisakah anda tolong mengisi formulir asuransi kesehatan ini?**	**bee**sakah **an**da **to**long m^{e}ng**ee**see **for**mooleer asoo**ran**see k^{e}**say**hatan eenee

Hospital *Rumah sakit*

Please notify my family.	**Tolong beritahu keluarga saya.**	**to**long b^{e}ree**ta**hoo k^{e}loo-arga **sa**ya
What are the visiting hours?	**Bilamanakah jam-jam kunjungan?**	**bee**lama**na**kah jum-jum **koon**joongan
When can I get up?	**Kapan saya boleh bangun?**	**ka**pan **sa**ya **bo**layh **ban**goon
When will the doctor come?	**Kapan dokter datang?**	**ka**pan **dok**t^{e}r **da**tung
I'm in pain.	**Saya kesakitan.**	**sa**ya k^{e}**sa**kitan
I can't eat/sleep.	**Saya tak bisa makan/tidur.**	**sa**ya ta^{k} **bee**sa **ma**kan/ **tee**door
Where is the bell?	**Dimana belnya?**	deemana belnya

nurse	**jururawat**	**joo**roorawat
patient	**pasien**	**pa**seeyen
anaesthetic	**obat bius**	obat **bee**yoos
blood transfusion	**transfusi darah**	**trans**foosee **da**rah
injection	**suntikan**	**soon**tikan
operation	**operasi**	**o**perasee
bed	**tempat tidur**	**t**^{e}**m**pat **tee**door
bedpan	**bejana sorong**	b^{e}**ja**na **so**rong
thermometer	**termometer**	t^{e}**rmom**ayter

Dentist *Dokter gigi*

Can you recommend a good dentist?	**Bisakah anda menganjurkan seorang dokter gigi yang baik?**	**bee**sakah **an**da m^{e}ng**an**joorkan s^{e}**o**rung **dokt**^{e}r **gee**gee yung bai^{k}
Can I make an appoint ment to see Dr...?	**Bolehkah saya membuat janji untuk berjumpa dengan Dr....?**	**bo**laykah **sa**ya m^{e}m**boo**at **jan**jee **oon**to^{k} b^{e}r**joom**pa d^{e}ngan **dokt**^{e}r
Couldn't you make it earlier?	**Bisakah anda membikinnya lebih pagi?**	**bee**sakah **an**da mem**bee**kinnya l^{e}bih **pa**gee
I have a broken tooth.	**Saya punya gigi patah.**	**sa**ya **poo**nya **gee**gee **pa**tah
I have toothache.	**Saya sakit gigi.**	**sa**ya **sa**kit **gee**gee
I have an abscess.	**Saya punya bisul bernanah.**	**sa**ya **poo**nya **bee**sool b^{e}r**na**nah
This tooth hurts.	**Gigi ini sakit.**	**gee**gee eenee **sa**kit
at the top	**di atas**	dee atas
at the bottom	**di bawah**	dee **ba**wah
at the front	**di depan**	dee d^{e}pan
at the back	**di belakang**	dee **bla**kang
Can you fix it temporarily?	**Bisakah anda memasangnya untuk sementara waktu?**	**bee**sakah **an**da m^{e}**ma**sungnya **oon**to^{k} s^{e}m^{e}n**ta**ra **wak**too
I don't want it pulled out.	**Saya tidak ingin ia dicabut.**	**sa**ya **tee**da^{k} **ing**in eea dee**cha**boot
Could you give me an anaesthetic?	**Dapatkah anda memberi saya obat bius?**	**da**patkah **an**da m^{e}m**bree** **sa**ya **o**bat **bee**yoos
I've lost a filling.	**Saya kehilangan tambalan gigi.**	**sa**ya k^{e}**hee**lungan tambalan **gee**gee
My gums...	**Gusi saya...**	**goo**see **sa**ya
are very sore	**sakit sekali**	**sa**kit s^{e}**ka**lee
are bleeding	**berdarah**	b^{e}r**da**rah
I've broken my dentures.	**Gigi palsu saya patah.**	**gee**gee **pal**soo **sa**ya **pa**tah
Can you repair my dentures?	**Bisakah anda memperbaiki gigi palsu saya?**	**bee**sakah **an**da m^{e}mp^{e}r **ba**-ikee **gee**gee **pal**soo **sa**ya
When will they be ready?	**Kapan ia akan siap?**	**ka**pan eea **a**kan seeap

Reference section

Where do you come from? *Anda datang dari mana?*

Africa	**Afrika**	af**ree**ka
Asia	**Asia**	**a**seeya
Australia	**Australia**	aus**tra**lee-a
Europe	**Eropa**	^{e}**ro**pa
North America	**Amerika Utara**	am**e**reeka oo**ta**ra
South America	**Amerika Selatan**	am**e**reeka **sla**tan
Austria	**Austria**	**aus**treeya
Belgium	**Belgia**	**bel**geeya
Canada	**Kanada**	ka**na**da
China	**Cina**	**chee**na
Denmark	**Denmark**	denmark
England	**Inggeris**	**ing**grees
Finland	**Finlandia**	fin**lan**deeya
France	**Perancis**	p^{e}**ran**chis
Germany	**Jerman**	j^{e}**rman**
Great Britain	**Britannia Raya**	bri**tan**neeya **ra**ya
Greece	**Yunani**	yoo**na**nee
Indonesia	**Indonesia**	indo**nay**seeya
India	**India**	**in**deeya
Ireland	**Irlandia**	ir**lan**deeya
Israel	**Israel**	**is**rael
Italy	**Italia**	ee**ta**leeya
Japan	**Jepang**	j^{e}**pung**
Kampuchea	**Kamboja**	kam**bo**ja
Laos	**Laos**	**la**os
Myanmar (Burma)	**Myanmar**	**myan**mar
Netherlands	**Negeri Belanda**	n^{e}**gree** be**lan**da
New Zealand	**New Zealand**	new **zee**land
Norway	**Norwegia**	nor**way**geeya
Philippines	**Filipina**	feelee**pee**na
Portugal	**Portugal**	por**too**gal
Russia	**Rusia**	**roo**seeya
Scotland	**Skotlandia**	skot**lan**deeya
South Africa	**Afrika Selatan**	af**ree**ka **sla**tan
Spain	**Spanyol**	**span**yol
Sweden	**Swedia**	**sway**deeya
Switzerland	**Negeri Swis**	n^{e}**gree** swis
Thailand	**Thailand**	**tai**land
United States	**Amerika Serikat**	am^{e}**ree**ka s^{e}**ree**kat
Vietnam	**Vietnam**	vee^{e}**tnam**
Wales	**Wales**	wayls

Numbers *Nomor*

0	**nol**	nol
1	**satu**	**sa**too
2	**dua**	**doo**wa
3	**tiga**	**tee**ga
4	**empat**	^{e}mpat
5	**lima**	**lee**ma
6	**enam**	^{e}nam
7	**tujuh**	**too**jooh
8	**delapan**	d^{e}**la**pan
9	**sembilan**	s^{e}m**bee**lan
10	**sepuluh**	s^{e}**poo**looh
11	**sebelas**	s^{e}blas
12	**duabelas**	**doo**wablas
13	**tigabelas**	**tee**gablas
14	**empatbelas**	^{e}mpatblas
15	**limabelas**	**lee**mablas
16	**enambelas**	^{e}namblas
17	**tujuhbelas**	**too**joohblas
18	**delapanbelas**	d^{e}**la**panblas
19	**sembilanbelas**	s^{e}m**bee**lanblas
20	**duapuluh**	**doo**wapoolooh
21	**duapuluh satu**	**doo**wapoolooh **sa**too
22	**duapuluh dua**	**doo**wapoolooh **doo**wa
23	**duapuluh tiga**	**doo**wapoolooh **tee**ga
24	**duapuluh empat**	**doo**wapoolooh ^{e}mpat
25	**duapuluh lima**	**doo**wapoolooh **lee**ma
26	**duapuluh enam**	**doo**wapoolooh ^{e}nam
27	**duapuluh tujuh**	**doo**wapoolooh **too**jooh
28	**duapuluh delapan**	**doo**wapoolooh d^{e}**la**pan
29	**duapuluh sembilan**	**doo**wapoolooh s^{e}m**bee**lan
30	**tigapuluh**	**tee**gapoolooh
31	**tigapuluh satu**	**tee**gapoolooh **sa**too
32	**tigapuluh dua**	**tee**gapoolooh **doo**wa
33	**tigapuluh tiga**	**tee**gapoolooh **tee**ga
40	**empatpuluh**	^{e}mpatpoolooh
41	**empatpuluh satu**	^{e}mpatpoolooh **sa**too
42	**empatpuluh dua**	^{e}mpatpoolooh **doo**wa
43	**empatpuluh tiga**	^{e}mpatpoolooh **tee**ga
50	**limapuluh**	**lee**mapoolooh
51	**limapuluh satu**	**lee**mapoolooh **sa**too
52	**limapuluh dua**	**lee**mapoolooh **doo**wa
53	**limapuluh tiga**	**lee**mapoolooh **tee**ga
60	**enampuluh**	^{e}nampoolooh
61	**enampuluh satu**	^{e}nampoolooh **sa**too
62	**enampuluh dua**	^{e}nampoolooh **doo**wa
63	**enampuluh tiga**	^{e}nampoolooh **tee**ga

70	**tujuhpuluh**	**too**joohpoolooh
71	**tujuhpuluh satu**	**too**joohpoolooh **sa**too
72	**tujuhpuluh dua**	**too**joohpoolooh **doo**wa
73	**tujuhpuluh tiga**	**too**joohpoolooh **tee**ga
80	**delapanpuluh**	d^{e}**la**panpoolooh
81	**delapanpuluh satu**	d^{e}**la**panpoolooh **sa**too
82	**delapanpuluh dua**	d^{e}**la**panpoolooh **doo**wa
83	**delapanpuluh tiga**	d^{e}**la**panpoolooh **tee**ga
90	**sembilanpuluh**	sem**bee**lanpoolooh
91	**sembilanpuluh satu**	sem**bee**lanpoolooh **sa**too
92	**sembilanpuluh dua**	sem**bee**lanpoolooh **doo**wa
93	**sembilanpuluh tiga**	sem**bee**lanpoolooh **tee**ga
100	**seratus**	s^{e}**ra**toos
101	**seratus satu**	s^{e}**ra**toos **sa**too
102	**seratus dua**	s^{e}**ra**toos **doo**wa
110	**seratus sepuluh**	s^{e}**ra**toos s^{e}**poo**looh
120	**seratus duapuluh**	s^{e}**ra**toos **doo**wapoolooh
130	**seratus tigapuluh**	s^{e}**ra**toos **tee**gapoolooh
140	**seratus empatpuluh**	s^{e}**ra**toos ^{e}mpatpoolooh
150	**seratus limapuluh**	s^{e}**ra**toos **lee**mapoolooh
160	**seratus enampuluh**	s^{e}**ra**toos ^{e}nampoolooh
170	**seratus tujuhpuluh**	s^{e}**ra**toos **too**joohpoolooh
180	**seratus delapanpuluh**	s^{e}**ra**toos d^{e}**la**panpoolooh
190	**seratus sembilanpuluh**	s^{e}**ra**toos sem**bee**lanpoolooh
200	**dua ratus**	**doo**wa **ra**toos
300	**tiga ratus**	**tee**ga **ra**toos
400	**empat ratus**	^{e}mpat **ra**toos
500	**lima ratus**	**lee**ma **ra**toos
600	**enam ratus**	^{e}nam **ra**toos
700	**tujuh ratus**	**too**jooh **ra**toos
800	**delapan ratus**	d^{e}**la**pan **ra**toos
900	**sembilan ratus**	sem**bee**lan **ra**toos
1000	**seribu**	s^{e}**ree**boo
1100	**seribu seratus**	s^{e}**ree**boo s^{e}**ra**toos
1200	**seribu dua ratus**	s^{e}**ree**boo **doo**wa **ra**toos
2000	**dua ribu**	**doo**wa **ree**boo
5000	**lima ribu**	**lee**ma **ree**boo
10,000	**sepuluh ribu**	s^{e}**poo**looh **ree**boo
50,000	**limapuluh ribu**	**lee**mapoolooh **ree**boo
100,000	**seratus ribu**	s^{e}**ra**toos **ree**boo
1,000,000	**satu juta**	**sa**too **joo**ta
1,000,000,000	**seribu juta**	**sa**too mil**yar**

first	**pertama**	p^{e}**rta**ma
second	**kedua**	k^{e}**doo**wa
third	**ketiga**	k^{e}**tee**ga
fourth	**keempat**	k^{e}-^{e}mpat
fifth	**kelima**	k^{e}**lee**ma
sixth	**keenam**	k^{e}-^{e}nam
seventh	**ketujuh**	k^{e}**too**jooh
eighth	**kedelapan**	k^{e}d^{e}**la**pan
ninth	**kesembilan**	k^{e}sem**bee**lan
tenth	**kesepuluh**	k^{e}s^{e}**poo**looh
once/twice	**satu kali/dua kali**	**sa**too **ka**lee/**doo**wa **ka**lee
three times	**tiga kali**	**tee**ga **ka**lee
a half	**setengah**	st^{e}ngah
half a...	**setengah...**	st^{e}ngah
half of...	**setengah dari...**	st^{e}ngah **da**ree
half (adj.)	**setengah**	st^{e}ngah
a quarter/one third	**seperempat/ sepertiga**	s^{e}p^{e}r^{e}mpat/s^{e}p^{e}r**tee**ga
a pair of	**sepasang**	s^{e}**pa**sung
a dozen	**satu lusin**	**sa**too **loo**sin
one per cent	**satu persen**	**sa**too **p^{e}r**sen
3.4%	**3,4 (tiga koma empat) persen**	**tee**ga koma ^{e}mpat p^{e}**rsen**

Year and age *Tahun dan usia/umur*

1981	**seribu sembilan ratus delapan-puluh satu**	s^{e}**ree**boo sem**bee**lan **ra**toos d^{e}**la**panpoolooh **sa**too
1993	**seribu sembilan ratus sembilan-puluh tiga**	s^{e}**ree**boo sem**bee**lan **ra**toos sem**bee**lan-poolooh **tee**ga
2005	**dua ribu lima**	**doo**wa **ree**boo **lee**ma
year	**tahun**	tahoon
leap year	**tahun kabisat**	tahoon ka**bee**sat
decade	**dekade**	de**kad**^{e}
century	**abad**	**a**bad
this year	**tahun ini**	tahoon eenee
last year	**tahun lalu**	tahoon **la**loo
next year	**tahun depan**	tahoon d^{e}pan
each year	**tiap tahun**	teeap tahoon
2 years ago	**2 tahun yang lalu**	dua tahoon yung **la**loo
in one year	**dalam satu tahun**	**da**lam **sa**too tahoon
in the eighties	**di tahun delapanpuluhan**	dee tahoon d^{e}**la**panpooloohan
the 16th century	**abad ke-16**	**a**bad k^{e}-^{e}namblas
in the 20th century	**dalam abad ke-20**	**da**lam **a**bad k^{e}-duapoolooh

How old are you?	**Berapa usia anda?**	b^{e}rapa oosya anda
I'm 30 years old.	**Umur saya 30 tahun.**	oomoor saya 30 tahoon
He/She was born in 1960.	**Ia dilahirkan di tahun 1960.**	eea deelaheerkan dee tahoon 1960
What is his/her age?	**Berapakah umur-nya?**	b^{e}rapakah oomoornya
Children under 16 are not admitted.	**Anak-anak diba-wah 16 tidak diper-bolehkan masuk.**	ana^{k}-ana^{k} deebawah 16 teeda^{k} deep^{e}rbolayhkan masoo^{k}

Seasons *Musim*

spring/summer	**musim semi/ musim panas**	moosim s^{e}mee/moosim panas
autumn/winter	**musim gugur/ musim dingin**	moosim googoor/moosim dingin
in spring	**di musim semi**	dee moosim s^{e}mee
during the summer	**selama musim panas**	selama moosim panas
in autumn	**di musim gugur**	dee moosim googoor
during the winter	**selama musim dingin**	selama moosim dingin
high season	**musim ramai**	moosim ramai
low season	**musim sepi**	moosim s^{e}pee

Months *bulan*

January	**Januari**	janoowaree
February	**Pebruari**	pebroowaree
March	**Maret**	mar^{e}t
April	**April**	april
May	**Mei**	mei
June	**Juni**	joonee
July	**Juli**	joolee
August	**Agustus**	agoostoos
September	**September**	septemb^{e}r
October	**Oktober**	oktob^{e}r
November	**Nopember**	nopemb^{e}r
December	**Desember**	daysemb^{e}r
in September	**di bulan September**	dee boolan septemb^{e}r
since October	**sejak Oktober**	s^{e}ja^{k} oktob^{e}r
the beginning of January	**permulaan Januari**	p^{e}rmoola-an janoowaree
the middle of February	**di pertengahan Pebruari**	dee p^{e}rt^{e}ngahan pebroowaree
the end of March	**pada akhir Maret**	pada aheer mar^{e}t

Days and Date *Hari dan Tanggal*

What day is it today?	**Hari ini hari apa?**	**har**ee eenee **har**ee **a**pa
Sunday	**Minggu**	**ming**goo
Monday	**Senin**	s^e^nin
Tuesday	**Selasa**	s^e^**la**sa
Wednesday	**Rabu**	raboo
Thursday	**Kamis**	**ka**mees
Friday	**Jumat**	**joo**mat
Saturday	**Sabtu**	**sab**too
It's...	**Sekarang adalah...**	s^e^**ka**rung **a**dalah
July 1	**tanggal 1 Juli**	**tang**gal 1 **joo**lee
March 10	**tanggal 10 Maret**	**tang**gal 10 **mar**^e^t
in the morning	**di pagi hari**	dee **pa**gee **ha**ree
during the day	**selama siang hari**	sel**a**ma seeyung **ha**ree
in the afternoon	**di sore hari**	dee **so**ray **ha**ree
in the evening	**di malam hari**	dee **ma**lam **ha**ree
at night	**pada waktu malam**	**pa**da **wak**too **ma**lam
the day before yesterday	**kemarin dulu**	k^e^**ma**rin **doo**loo
yesterday	**kemarin**	k^e^**ma**rin
today	**hari ini**	**ha**ree **ee**nee
tomorrow	**besok/esok hari**	bayso^k^/ayso^k^ **ha**ree
the day after tomorrow	**lusa**	**loo**sa
the day before	**hari sebelumnya**	**ha**ree s^e^**bloom**nya
the next day	**hari berikutnya**	**ha**ree b^e^**ree**kootnya
two days ago	**dua hari yang lalu**	**doo**wa **ha**ree yung **la**loo
in three days' time	**dalam waktu tiga hari**	**da**lam **wak**too **tee**ga **ha**ree
last week	**minggu yang lalu**	**ming**-goo yung **la**loo
next week	**minggu depan**	**ming**goo d^e^pan
for a fortnight (two weeks)	**selama dua minggu**	**sla**ma **doo**wa **ming**goo
birthday	**hari ulang tahun**	**ha**ree **oo**lung tahoon
day off	**satu hari libur**	**sa**too **ha**ree **lee**boor
holiday	**hari besar**	**ha**ree b^e^**sar**
holidays/vacation	**liburan**	**lee**booran
week	**minggu/pekan**	**ming**goo/p^e^kan
weekend	**akhir pekan**	**a**heer p^e^kan
working day	**hari kerja**	**ha**ree k^e^rja

Public holidays *Hari raya umum*

Although Indonesia follows our Gregorian calendar, many festivals are held according to the applicable religious calendar. Muslim holidays are calculated on the lunar principle; two calendars co-exist on Bali.

January 1	**Tahun Baru**	New Year's Day
April 21	**Hari Kartini**	Kartini Day
August 17	**Hari Kemerdekaan**	Independence Day
December 25	**Natal**	Christmas

Moveable days:

Lebaran	two-day public holiday at end of the fasting month of Ramadan
Idul Adha	recalling Abraham's dutiful acceptance of sacrificing Isaac
Maulaud Nabi Mohammed	Mohammed's birthday
Isra Miraj Nabi Mohhamed	commemorating Mohammed's ascension

Greetings and wishes *Salam dan harapan*

Merry Christmas!	**Selamat Hari Natal!**	**sla**mat **ha**ree **na**tal
Happy New Year!	**Selamat Tahun Baru!**	**sla**mat tahoon **ba**roo
Happy Easter!	**Selamat Paskah!**	**sla**mat **pas**kah
Happy birthday!	**Selamat Hari Ulang Tahun!**	**sla**mat **ha**ree **oo**lung tahoon
Best wishes!	**Harapan-harapan terbaik!**	harapan-**ha**rapan t^{e}**rbai**^{k}
Congratulations!	**Kami ucapkan selamat!**	**ka**mee **oo**chapkan **sla**mat
Have a good trip!	**Selamat jalan!**	**sla**mat **ja**lan
Best regards from…	**Salam dari…**	salam **da**ree
My regards to…	**Salamku kepada…**	salamku k^{e}**pa**da

What time is it? *Sekarang jam berapa?*

The country has three official time zones: West Indonesia Standard Time (GMT 7 hours) applies to Sumatra, Java, Madura and Bali; Central Indonesia Standard Time (GMT 8) is valid in Kalimantan, Sulawesi and Nusa Tenggara; East Indonesia Standard Time (GMT 9) relates to Maluku and Irian Jaya.

There are two attitudes to time-keeping in Indonesia; fairly punctual for businesses and tourist schedules for visitors—and flexible for everything else. Learn to accept the latter, aptly described locally as *jam karet* (rubber time).

Excuse me. Can you tell me the time?	**Bisakah anda kasih tahu saya jam berapa sekarang?**	**bee**sakah **an**da **ka**sih tahoo **sa**ya jum b^e^**ra**pa s^e^**ka**rung
It's...	**Sekarang...**	s^e^**ka**rung
five past one	**jam satu lewat lima**	jum **sa**too laywat **lee**ma
ten past two	**jam dua lewat sepuluh**	jum **doo**wa laywat s^e^**poo**looh
a quarter past three	**jam tiga lewat seperempat**	jum **tee**ga laywat s^e^p^e^r^e^mpat
twenty past four	**jam empat lewat duapuluh**	jum ^e^mpat laywat **doo**wapoolooh
twenty-five past five	**jam lima lewat duapuluh lima**	jum **lee**ma laywat **doo**wapoolooh **lee**ma
half past six	**setengah tujuh**	st^e^ngah **too**jooh
twenty-five to seven	**jam tujuh kurang duapuluh lima**	jum **too**jooh **koo**rung **doo**wapoolooh **lee**ma
twenty to eight	**jam delapan kurang duapuluh**	jum d^e^**la**pan **koo**rung **doo**wapoolooh
a quarter to nine	**jam sembilan kurang seperempat**	jum s^e^m**bee**lan **koo**rung s^e^p^e^r^e^mpat
ten to ten	**jam sepuluh kurang sepuluh**	jum s^e^**poo**looh **koo**rung s^e^**poo**looh
five to eleven	**jam sebelas kurang lima**	jum s^e^blas **koo**rung **lee**ma
twelve o'clock (noon/ midnight)	**jam duabelas (tengah hari/ tengah malam)**	jum **doo**wablas (t^e^ngah **ha**ree/t^e^ngah **ma**lam)
in the morning	**di pagi hari**	dee **pa**gee **ha**ree
in the afternoon	**di sore hari**	dee **so**ray **ha**ree
in the evening	**di malam hari**	dee **ma**lam **ha**ree
in a quarter of an hour	**dalam waktu seperempat jam**	**da**lam **wak**too s^e^p^e^r^e^mpat jum
half an hour ago	**setengah jam yang lalu**	st^e^ngah jum yung **la**loo
about two hours	**kira-kira dua jam**	**kee**ra-**kee**ra **doo**wa jum
more than 10 minutes	**lebih dari 10 menit**	**l**^e^bih **da**ree 10 m^e^nit
less than 30 seconds	**kurang dari 30 detik**	**koo**rung **da**ree 30 d^e^ti^k^

Common abbreviations *Singkatan-singkatan yang umum*

ABRI	**Angkatan Bersenjata Republik Indonesia**	Indonesian Armed Forces
ASEAN		Association of South East Asian Nations
Bappenas	**Badan Perencanaan Pembangunan Nasional**	National Development Planning Board
BPEN	**Badan Pengembangan Ekspor Nasional**	National Agency for Export Development
Bpk.	**Bapak**	Mr., Mrs.
DKI Jakarta	**Daerah Khusus Ibukota Jakarta**	Special Region of Jakarta
DIY	**Daerah Istimewa Yogyakarta**	Special Region of Yogyakarta
dkk	**dan kawan-kawan**	et al
dll	**dan lain-lain**	etc.
drs	**doctorandus**	degree in humanities
Gg	**Gang**	lane
IPTN	**Industri Pesawat Terbang Nusantara**	state aircraft industry
Ir.	**Insinyur**	degree in engineering
Jl.	**Jalan**	Street, Road
LIPI	**Lembaga Ilmu Pengetuhuan Indonesia**	Indonesian Institute of Science
KTP	**Kartu Tanda Penduduk**	ID card
PT	**Perseroan Terbatas**	limited liablility company
p.p.	**pulang pergi**	return/round trip
Perumka	**Perusahaan Umum Kereta Api**	State Railway Company
K.A.	**Kereta-api**	train
Polri	**Polisis Republik Indonesia**	Indonesian police force
PPN	**Pajak Pertambahan Nilai**	sales tax, VAT
TURI	**Televisi Republik Indonesia**	Indonesian state television
RRI	**Radio Republik Indonesia**	Indonesian state radio
UI	**Universitas Indonesia**	state university in Jakarta
WIB	**Waktu Indonesia Barat**	Western Indonesian Time
WITA	**Waktu Indonesia Tangah**	Central Indonesian Time
WIT	**Waktu Indonesia Timur**	Eastern Indonesian Time
WNA	**Warga Negara Asing**	foreign national
WNI	**Warga Negara Indonesia**	Indonesian national

Signs and notices *Tanda-tanda dan pemberitahuan-pemberitahuan*

Awas anjing	Beware of the dog
Bahaya (kematian)	Danger (of death)
Bebas masuk	Free admittance
Buka	Open
Cat basah	Wet paint
Dilarang buang sampah	No littering
Dilarang . . .	. . . forbidden
Dilarang masuk	No admittance
Dilarang merokok	No smoking
Dingin	Cold
Disewakan	To let
Doronglah	Push
Harap tunggu	Please wait
Hati-hati	Caution
Informasi/Keterangan	Information
Jalan keluar darurat	Emergency exit
Jalan keluar	Exit
Jalan masuk	Entrance
Jalan pribadi	Private road
Jangan mengganggu	Do not disturb
Jangan menyentuh	Do not touch
Jangan merintangi jalan masuk	Do not block entrance
Keatas	Up
Kebawah	Down
Keterangan	Information
Kosong	Vacant
Laki-Laki	Gentlemen
Lift	Lift
loket kasir	Cash desk
Masuk tanpa mengetok pintu	Enter without knocking
Panas	Hot
Penjualan	Sale
Perempuan	Ladies
Pria	Gentlemen
Sedang dipakai	Occupied
Sedang rusak	Out of order
Silahkan mengebel	Please ring
Tariklah	Pull
Telah dipesan	Reserved
Terjual habis	Sold out
Tidak ada lowongan	No vacancies
Untuk dijual	For sale
Untuk disewakan	For hire
Wanita/Perempuan	Ladies

Emergency *Darurat*

However little you have, you have more than most Indonesians. Don't provoke envy by revealing a wallet full of notes or wearing tempting jewellery. Keep valuables in the hotel strongbox. Carry the day's cash in a belt or a bag with a strap which goes around or across the body.

Call the police	**Panggil polisi**	punggil poleesee
Consulate	**Konsulat**	konsoolat
DANGER	**BAHAYA**	bahaya
Embassy	**Kedutaan besar**	k^{e}doota-an b^{e}sar
FIRE	**KEBAKARAN**	k^{e}bakaran
Gas	**Gas**	gas
Get a doctor	**Panggil dokter**	punggil dokt^{e}r
Go away	**Pergilah**	p^{e}rgeelah
HELP	**TOLONG**	tolong
Get help quickly	**Cepat cari pertolongan**	ch^{e}pat charee pertolongan
I'm ill	**Saya sakit**	saya sakit
I'm lost	**Saya bingung/Saya kehilangan jalan**	saya bingoong/saya k^{e}heelungan jalan
Leave me alone	**Biarkanlah saya**	bee-arkanlah saya
LOOK OUT	**AWAS!**	awas
Poison	**Racun**	rachoon
POLICE	**POLISI**	poleesee
Stop that man/woman	**Hentikan laki-laki/perempuan itu**	h^{e}nteekan lakee-lakee/p^{e}r^{e}mpooan eetoo
STOP THIEF	**TANGKAP PENCURI**	tungkap p^{e}nchooree

Lost property—Theft *Barang-barang hilang—Pencurian*

Where's the...?	**Dimana...**	deemana
lost property (lost and found) office	**kantor barang-barang hilang**	kantor barung-barung heelung
police station	**kantor polisi**	kantor poleesee
I want to report a theft.	**Saya ingin melaporkan suatu pencurian.**	saya ingin m^{e}laporkan swatoo p^{e}nchooree-an
My... has been stolen.	**... saya telah dicuri.**	... saya t^{e}lah deechooree
I've lost my...	**Saya kehilangan... saya.**	saya k^{e}heelungan... saya
handbag	**tas tangan**	tas tungan
passport	**paspor**	paspor
wallet	**dompet**	dompet

CAR ACCIDENTS, see page 78

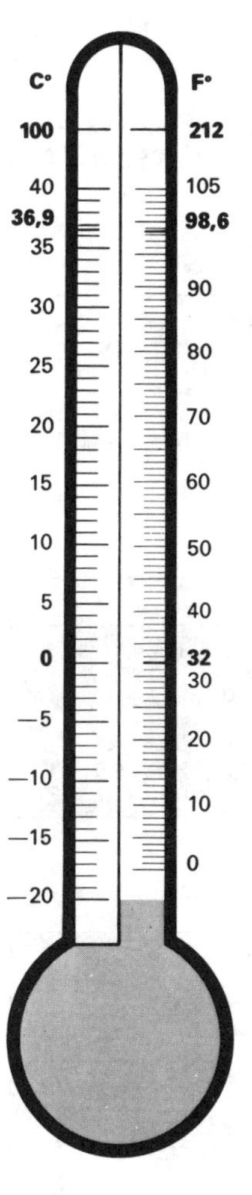

Conversion tables

Centimetres and inches

To change centimetres into inches, multiply by .39.

To change inches into centimetres, multiply by 2.54.

	in.	feet	yards
1 mm	0.039	0.003	0.001
1 cm	0.39	0.03	0.01
1 dm	3.94	0.32	0.10
1 m	39.40	3.28	1.09

	mm	cm	m
1 in.	25.4	2.54	0.025
1 ft.	304.8	30.48	0.304
1 yd.	914.4	91.44	0.914

(32 metres = 35 yards)

Temperature

To convert Centigrade into degrees Fahrenheit, multiply Centigrade by 1.8 and add 32.

To convert degrees Fahrenheit into Centigrade, subtract 32 from Fahrenheit and divide by 1.8.

Kilometres into miles

1 kilometre (km.) = 0.62 miles

km.	10	20	30	40	50	60	70	80	90	100	110	120	130
miles	6	12	19	25	31	37	44	50	56	62	68	75	81

Miles into kilometres

1 mile = 1.609 kilometres (km.)

miles	10	20	30	40	50	60	70	80	90	100
km.	16	32	48	64	80	97	113	129	145	161

Fluid measures

1 litre (l.) = 0.88 imp. quart or 1.06 U.S. quart
1 imp. quart = 1.14 l. 1 U.S. quart = 0.95 l.
1 imp. gallon = 4.55 l. 1 U.S. gallon = 3.8 l.

litres	5	10	15	20	25	30	35	40	45	50
imp. gal.	1.1	2.2	3.3	4.4	5.5	6.6	7.7	8.8	9.9	11.0
U.S. gal.	1.3	2.6	3.9	5.2	6.5	7.8	9.1	10.4	11.7	13.0

Weights and measures

1 kilogram or kilo (kg.) = 1000 grams (g.)

100 g. = 3.5 oz. ½ kg. = 1.1 lb.
200 g. = 7.0 oz. 1 kg. = 2.2 lb.
1 oz. = 28.35 g.
1 lb. = 453.60 g.

Grammar

Although Indonesian grammar is complex, everyday Indonesian can be used with a knowledge of just a few simple rules.

Nouns

Indonesian has no articles (corresponding to "a" and "the" in English) and there is usually no difference between the singular and plural of the noun. For example, the word **hari** can mean both "day" and "days".

If you need to specify the number, the following words can be used, preceding the nouns they qualify:

singular	***satu*** **kamar**	*one* room
plural	***berapa*** **kamar** ***banyak*** **kamar** ***dua/tiga*** **kamar**	*some* rooms *many* rooms *two/three* rooms

In addition, plural meaning is sometimes conveyed by doubling the noun, particularly in writing.

pernangko-perangko stamps   **anak-anak** children

1. Acronyms

When words or compounds are unwieldy, Indonesians often turn them into acronyms (that is, taking a syllable from each word to form a new word).

Jawa Barat (West Java) becomes **Jabar**
Sumatera Selatan (South Sumatra) **Sumsel**
Polisi Lalu Lintas (Traffic Police) **Polantas**

2. Loan words

Many Indonesian words are foreign loan-words spelt phonetically. These can often be recognized without difficulty:

botani	botany	**oksigen**	oxygen
menejemen	management		

Words with the English ending "-tion" often appear with the Indonesian **-si**; while words ending with "-ty" in English sometimes take **-as** in Indonesian:

administrasi	administration	**situasi**	situation
konfrontasi	confrontation	**permisi**	permission
kwalitas	quality	**universitas**	university

You will also notice a common sound change when "f" in a foreign loan-word becomes "p" in Indonesian.

kopi	coffee	**sopir**	chauffeur, driver

Adjectives

In Indonesian, the adjective follows the noun.

kota city	**besar** large	**kota besar** large city
orang person	**jutan** forest	**orang hutan** orang utang (literally forest person)

To attribute two adjectives, separate them by **yang** (which). Note that some terms in Indonesian already contain an adjective, such as **tempat tidur** (bed, literally sleeping place).

kota besar *yang* berisik	(the) large, noisy city
tempat tidur *yang* kecil	(a) small bed

The comparative is formed by adding **lebih** (more) and the superlative with **yang paling** (which most).

baik good	**lebih baik** better	**yang paling baik** best

Personal pronouns

I	**saya**	
you (sing.)	**anda** **saudara** **bapak** **ibu**	(a general word, suiting most purposes) (more formal than **anda**) (polite form of addressing an older man) (polite form of addressing an older woman)
he, she, it	**dia**	
we	**kami** **kita**	(includes person being addressed) (excludes person being addressed)
you (plur.)	**kamu sekalian**	(means "all of you")
they	**mereka**	

Possessive adjectives

The same words as personal pronouns are used for possessive adjectives, but, like other adjectives, they follow the noun.

bapak *saya* *my* father **ibu *anda*** *your* mother

However, note that **dia** (he, she, it) changes to **-nya** (his, her, its) and is attached to the end of the noun.

botol*nya* *his* bottle, *her* bottle, *its* bottle

Verbs

1. To be

The verb "to be" has no exact equivalent in Indonesian and is often not required.

Nama saya Marta.	My name (is) Marta.
Kamar makan besar.	(The) dining room (is) big.

Ini (this/these) and **itu** (that/those) are used when referring to objects or people. **Ada** (to exist) can have the meaning “there is”.

***Ini* terlalu asin.**	*This is* too salty.
***Ini* karta saya.**	*Here's* my card.
***Itu* kameranya.**	*That is* his/her camera.
***Ada* kereta-api ke Jakarta.**	*There is* a train to Jakarta.

2. Tenses

Verbs does not have different forms for the past, present and future. For example, **datang** can mean “came”, “come” or “will come”. To refer specifically to the past, present or future, auxiliary words need to be added. The most frequently used are **sudah** (past), **sedang** (present) and **akan** (future).

Kami *sudah* seminggu ada disini.	We've been here a week.
Saya *sedang* mencari ...	I am looking for ...
Saya *akan* pergi ...	I will leave ...

3. Singular and plural

Verbs also do not change between singular and plural subject.

Bolehkah saya minta ...?	Can I have ...?
Bolehkah kami minta ...?	Can we have ...?

Negation

There are two words in Indonesian meaning “no’ or “not”. **Tidak** is used to negate verbs and adjectives, **bukan** is used to negate nouns.

***Tidak* ada air panas.**	There is *no* hot water.
Ini *bukan* yang saya pesan.	This is *not* what I ordered.

Both can be used to say “no’ in answer to questions.

Affixes

A feature of Indonesian is its use of affixation. A large number of verbs, nouns and adjectives take affixes. While the root word is understood and often used in colloquial speech, affixes are often added in formal speech and written communication. For example:

affix	root word	meaning	
be(r)–	**bicara**	***ber*bicara**	to speak
	kerja	***be*kerja**	to work
me(m/n)–	**bantu**	***mem*bantu**	to help
	jual	***men*jual**	to buy

Affixation can also extend the meaning of the root verb. Here are a couple of examples with the prefix **ter**:

dapat to get, find	***ter*dapat** to be situated, find oneself
baik good	***ter*baik** best

Only a rudimentary outline of this subject is possible within the confines of this phrase book. However, it is helpful to remember that, when faced with new, unfamiliar words, you may recognize the root words within the affixes. The table below provides some more common affixes to look out for:

prefixes:		suffixes:	
	di–		**–an**
	ke– –an		**–i**
	memper–		**–kan**
	pe–		**–mu**
	se–		**–wan**

Dictionary
and alphabetical index

English-Indonesian

appointment janji 131, 137, 145
apricot aprikot 55
April April 150
archaeology arkeologi 83
architect arsitek 83
area code kode wilayah 134
arm lengan 138, 139
around *(approximately)* kira-kira 31
arrival kedatangan 16
arrive, to tiba 66; datang 68, 130
art seni 83
art gallery balai ksesnian 81, 98
artificial buatan 124
artificial light cahaya buatan 124
artist seniman 83
ashtray asbak 37
Asia Asia 146
ask for, to meminta 25, 61, 136
asparagus asparagus 52
aspirin aspirin 108
asthma sakit bengek 140
astringent astringent 109
at di 15
aubergine terong 52
August Agustus 150
aunt bibi 93
Australia Australia 146
Austria Austria 146
automatic otomatis 20, 122, 124
autumn musim gugur 150
awful mengerikan 84; buruk 94

B

baby bayi 110
baby food makanan bayi 110
babysitter penjaga anak 27
back punggung 138
back, to be/to get kembali 21, 80, 135
backache sakit punggung 140
backpack ransel 106
bacon bacon 40
bacon and eggs bacon dan telur 40
bad buruk 14; jelek 95
bag tas 18; kantong 103
baggage *(luggage)* barang 18, 26, 31; bagasi 71
baggage cart kereta bagasi 18, 71
baggage check mendaftarkan barang 71
baggage locker lemari bagasi 71
baked dikukus 44; dimasak 47
baker's toko roti 98
balance *(finance)* neraca 131
balcony balkon 23
ball-point pen pena bolpoin 104
ballet balet 88
banana pisang 55, 64
banana fritters pisang goreng 57
Band-Aid® plester untuk luka ringan 108
bandage pembalut 108
bangle gelang 121
bangs poni 30
bank *(finance)* bank 98, 129
banknote uang kertas 130
barber's pemangkas rambut 30, 98
basil kemangi 54
basketball bola basket 90
bath mandi 23, 25, 27
bath salts garam mandi 109
bath towel handuk mandi 27
bathing cap topi mandi 115
bathing suit baju renang 115
bathrobe mantel mandi 115
bathroom kamar mandi 28
battery aki 75, 78, 119, 121, 125
beach pantai 91
bean kacang 52
beard jenggot 31
beautiful cantik 14, 84
beauty salon salon kecantikan 98
bed tempat tidur 23, 24, 29, 142, 144
bed and breakfast penginapan dan makan pagi 24
bedpan bejana sorong 144
beef daging sapi 46
beer bir 58, 64
before *(time)* sebelum 15
begin, to memulai 86
beginning permulaan 150
behind di belakang 15, 77
Belgium Belgia 146
bell *(electric)* bel 144
below dibawah 15
belt ikat pinggang 116
bend *(road)* belokan 79
berth tempat tidur 69, 70, 71
better lebih baik 14, 25
between antara 15
bicycle sepeda 74
big besar 14, 101
bill rekening 28, 31, 62, 102
bill *(banknote)* uang kertas 130

billion *(Am.)* seribu juta 148
binoculars teropong 123
bird burung 85
birth kelahiran 26
birthday hari ulang tahun 151, 152
biscuit *(Br.)* biskuit 64
bitter pahit 61
black hitam 112
black and white *(film)* hitam dan putih 124, 125
black coffee kopi hitam 41, 61
bladder kandung kemih 138
blanket selimut 27
bleed, to berdarah 139, 145
blind *(window shade)* gorden 29
blister lepuh 139
blocked tersumbat 29
blood darah 142
blood pressure tekanan darah 141, 142
blood transfusion transfusi darah 144
blouse blus 115
blow-dry diblow 30
blue biru 112
blusher pemerah muka 109
boat kapal, perahu 74
bobby pin jepitan rambut 110
body tubuh 138
boil bisul 139
boiled egg telur rebus 40
bone tulang 138
book buku 12, 104
booking office kantor mesanan 19, 67
bookshop toko buku 98, 104
boot sepatu bot 117
born dilahirkan 150
botanical gardens kebun raya 81
botany botani 83
bottle botol 17, 58, 59
bottle-opener pembuka botol 120
bottom bawah 145
bow tie dasi kupu-kupu 115
bowel isi perut 138
box kotak 119
boxing bertinju 90
boy anak laki-laki 128
boyfriend pacar 93
bra kutang, beha 115
bracelet gelang 121
braces *(suspenders)* bingkai penunjang 115
brake rem 78
brake fluid oli rem 75
bread roti 37, 41, 64
break down, to rusak 78
break, to merusak 29
breakdown kerusakan 78
breakdown van mobil gerbong kerusakan 79
breakfast makan pagi 24, 27, 34, 40
breast buah dada 138
breathe, to bernapas 141, 142
bridge jembatan 85
bring, to mengambilikan 13, 59
British *(person)* orang Inggeris 93
broken patah 118, 123, 139, 140
brooch bros, peniti 121
brother saudara laki-laki 93
brown cokelat 112
bruise luka memar 139
brush sikat 110
bucket ember 120, 128
buckle gesper 116
buffalo kerbau 85
build, to membangun 83
building gedung 81, 83
building blocks/bricks batu-batu 128
bulb *(light)* bola lampu 29, 76, 119
burn luka bakar 139
burn out, to *(bulb)* mati 29
bus bis 18, 19, 66, 71, 72, 80
bus stop setasiun bis 73
bus stop pemberhentian bis 73
business bisnis 131
business class kelas busnis 65
business district daerah bisnis 81
busy sibuk 96
but tetapi 15
butane gas gas butan 32, 106
butcher's toko daging 98
butter mentega 37, 41, 64
button kancing 116
buy, to membeli 83, 100, 104, 123

C

cabbage kubis, kol 52
cabin *(ship)* kamar di kapal 74
cable lama kawat 133
café warung 33
cake kue 38, 64
calculator kalkulator 105
calendar penanggalan 104

call *(phone)* telepon 136
call, to *(give name)* menamakan 11
call, to *(phone)* menelepon 134, 136
call, to *(summon)* panggilkan 79, 156
calm tenang 91
camel-hair bulu unta, kamhar 113
camera kamera 124, 125
camera case kotak kamera 125
camera shop toko kamera 98
camp site tempat berkemah 32
camp, to berkemah 32
campbed pelbet 106
camping berkemah 32
camping equipment alat-alat kemah 106
can *(be able to)* bisa 12; dapat 13
can *(container)* kaleng 119
can opener alat pembuka kaleng 120
Canada Kanada 146
cancel, to membatalkan 66
candle lilin 120
candy gula-gula 126
cap topi 115
capital *(finance)* modal 131
car mobil 19, 20, 32, 75,
car hire sewa mobil 20
car mechanic montir 78
car park parkir 78
car racing balapan mobil 90
car radio radio mobil 118
car rental sewa mobil 20
carafe karaf 59
carat karat 121
caravan kereta gandengan 32
caraway jintan, jemuju 54
carbon paper kertas karbon 104
carbonated *(fizzy)* membuih 60
carburettor karburator 78
card kartu 94, 131
card game permainan kartu 128
carp karper 44
carrot wortel 53
cart kereta 18
carton (of cigarettes) slof (rokok) 17, 126
cartridge *(camera)* cartridge 124
case tempat 123; kotak 125
cash desk tempat membayar 103; loket kasir 155
cash, to menukar 130; menarik 133
cassette kaset 118, 127
cassette recorder perekam suara kaset 118
castle kastil 81
catacombs kuburan dibawah tanah 81
catalogue katalog 82
Catholic Katolik 84
cauliflower kol kembang 52
caution hati-hati 79, 155
cave gua 81
celery seledri 53
cemetery kuburan 81
centre pusat 21, 76, 81; tenga-tenga 17
century abad 149
ceramics keramik 84
cereal hasil biji-bijian 40
certificate surat keterangan 144
chain *(jewellery)* rantai 121
chain bracelet gelang rantai 121
chair kursi 108
chamber music musik kamar 128
change *(money)* uang kembali 63, 77; uang kecil 130
change, to mengganti 68, 72, 76, 123; menukar 61; merobah 65
change, to *(money)* menukar 18, 129
chapel kapel 81
charcoal arang (kayu) 106
charge ongkos 20, 32, 78, 90
charge, to minta 130
charm *(trinket)* anting-anting 121
cheap murah 14, 24, 25, 101
check cek 130, 131
check-up *(medical)* pemeriksaan 142
check *(restaurant)* rekening 62
check in, to *(airport)* mendaftarkan diri 65
check out, to meninggalkan 31
check, to periksa 75, 123
check, to *(luggage)* mendarftarkan 71
cheers! sorak sorai 56
cheese keju 55, 64
chemist's apotek 98, 107
cheque cek 130, 131
cherry buah ceri 55
chess catur 93
chess set set permainan catur 128
chest dada 138, 141
chestnut kastanye 55

chewing gum permen karet 126
chewing tobacco tembakau kunyah 126
chicken ayam 49
child anak 61, 82, 93, 139, 150
children's doctor dokter anak-anak 137
chilli cabe rawit 52
China Cina 146
chips keripik 64
chives lokio 54
chocolate cokelat 64, 119, 126
chocolate (hot) cokelat (panas) 41, 61
chocolate bar sebatang cokelat 64
chop *(meat)* potongan 46
Christmas Natal 152
chromium khrom 122
church gereja 81, 85
cigar cerutu 126
cigarette rokok 17, 126
cigarette case kotak rokok 121, 126
cigarette holder tempat rokok 126
cigarette lighter geretan 121, 126
cine camera kamera film 124
cinema bioskop 86, 96
cinnamon kayu manis 54
city kota 81
city centre pusat kota 81
classical klasik 128
clean bersih 62
clean, to mencuci 29; membersihkan 76
cleansing cream krem pembersihan 109
cliff jurang 85
clip jepitan 121
cloakroom tempat penggantungan jas 87
clock jam 121; lonceng 121
clock-radio lonceng-radio 118
close, to tutup 11, 82, 108, 132
cloth kain 117
clothes baju 29, 115
clothing pakaian 111
cloud awan 94
clove cengkeh 54
coach *(bus)* bis jarak-juah 72
coat jas buka 115
coconut kelapa 56
coffee kopi 41, 61, 64
coin uang logam 84
cold dingin 14, 25, 62, 94, 155
cold *(illness)* pilek 107; masuk angin 140
collar kerah 116
colour warna 103, 112, 124, 125
colour rinse bilasan warna 30
colour shampoo langir warna 110
colour slide slide berwarna 124
colourfast tahan luntur 113
comb sisir 110
come, to datang 36, 93, 95, 137, 144, 146
comedy komedi 86
commission *(fee)* komisi 130
common *(frequent)* umum 154
compact disc CD 127
compartment *(train)* compartemen 70
compass kompas 106
complaint pengaduan 61
concert konser 88
concert hall ruangan konser 81, 88
condom kondom 108
conference room kamar konperensi 24
confirm, to menegaskan 66
confirmation penegasan 23
congratulation ucapan selamat 152
connection *(transport)* sambungan 65, 68
constipation sembelit 140
contact lens lensa kontak 123
contagious menular 142
contain, to mengandung 38
contraceptive alat kontrasepsi 108
contract kontrak 131
control pemeriksaan 16
cookie kue 64
cool box kotak pendingin 106
copper tembaga 122
coral karang 122
corduroy beledu, korduroi 113
coriander ketumbar 54
corn *(Am.)* jagung 52
corn plaster katimumul 108
corner sudut 21, 77; pojok 36
cost ongkos 131, 136
cost, to harganya 11
cot tempat tidur untuk bayi 24
cotton katun 113
cotton wool kapas penghisap 108
cough batuk 107, 141
cough drops permen batuk 108
cough, to batuk 142

counter loket 133
country negeri 93
countryside daerah luar kota 85
court house gedung pengadilan 81
cousin sepupu 93
cover charge ongkos tambahan 62
crab kepiting 44
cramp kejang 140
crayon krayon 104
cream kepala susu 61
cream *(toiletry)* krem 109
crease resistant tahan kusut 113
credit kredit 130
credit card kartu kredit 20, 31, 62, 102, 130
crisps kering, garing 62
crockery barang-barang tembikar 120
crocodile buaya 85
cross salib 121
crossing *(maritime)* penyeberangan 73
crossroads persimpangan jalan 77
cruise pelayaran 74
crystal kristal 122
cucumber ketimun 52
cuff link kancing manset 121
cuisine masakan 35
cup cangkir 37, 61, 143
curler alat pengeriting 110
currency mata uang 129
currency exchange office kantor penukaran uang 18, 67, 129
current arus 91
curtain gorden 29
customs pabean 16; bea cukai 102
cut *(wound)* luka 139
cut off, to *(interrupt)* terputus 135
cut, to *(with scissors)* potong 31
cutlery alat-alat masak dan makan 120, 121
cutlet potongan 46
cycling naik sepeda 90
cystitis radang kandung kemih 142

D

dance tari 88
dance, to menari 88; berdansa 96
danger bahaya 155, 156
dangerous berbahaya 91
dark gelap 25, 101; tua 111, 112
date *(appointment)* berkencan 95
date *(day)* tanggal 26, 151
date *(fruit)* kurma 55
daughter anak perempuan 93
day hari 20, 24, 32, 80, 94, 151
day off hari libur 151
daylight siang hari 124
decade dekade 149
decaffeinated tanpa kafeina 41, 61
December Desember 150
decision keputusan 25, 102
deck *(ship)* geladak 74
deck chair kursi geladak 91
declare, to *(customs)* melaporkan 17
degree *(temperature)* derajat 140
delay kelambatan 69
delicious lezat 63
deliver, to mengantarkan 102
delivery penyerahan 102
denim kain kepar, dril 113
Denmark Denmark 146
dentist dokter gigi 98, 145
denture gigi palsu 145
deodorant deodoran 109
department store toko serba-ada 98
departure keberangkatan 66
deposit *(down payment)* deposito 20
dessert kue-kue 38, 57
detour *(traffic)* pengalihan lalu-lintas 79
diabetic penyakit gula 37; penyakit kencing manis 141
dialling code kode petunjuk 134
diamond berlian 122
diaper popok 110
diarrhoea murus 140
dictionary kamus 104
diesel solar 75
diet diet 38
difficult sulit 14
difficulty kesulitan 28, 102
digital digital 122
dine, to makan malam 95
dining room kamar makan 28
dinner makan malam 34, 95
direct langsung 65
direct, to menunjukkan 13
direction petunjuk 76
director *(theatre)* sutradara 86
directory *(phone)* buku petunjuk 134

disabled cacat 82
discotheque diskotek 89, 96
discount potongan 131
disease penyakit 142
dishwashing detergent detergen untuk cuci piring 120
disinfectant obat disinfeksi 108
dislocated tergelincir 140
display case kotak yang dipamerkan 100
dissatisfied tidak memuaskan 103
district *(of town)* daerah 81
disturb, to mengganggu 155
diversion *(traffic)* pengalihan lalu lintas 79
dizzy pusing 140
doctor dokter 79, 137, 144, 145
doctor's office kantor dokter 137
dog anjing 155
doll boneka 128
dollar dolar 18, 102, 129
double bed tempat tidur untuk dua orang 23
double room kamar untuk dua orang 19, 23
down ke bawah 15
downtown daerah perdagangan 81
dozen lusin 149
drawing paper kertas gambar 104
drawing pins peniti gambar 104
dress gaun, pakaian 115
dressing gown daster 115
drink minuman 58, 59, 60
drink, to minum 37
drinking water air minum 32
drip, to menetes 29
drive, to mengendarai 76
driving (driver's) licence surat izin mengendarai *(SIM)* 20, 79
drop *(liquid)* tetes 108
drugstore apotek 98, 107
dry kering 59, 110
dry cleaner's binatu kimia 29, 98
dry shampoo langir kering 110
duck bebek 49
dummy *(baby's)* boneka 110
during selama 15, 150, 151
duty-free shop toko bebas cukai 19
duty *(customs)* cukai 17
dye celup 30, 110

E

each tiap 149
ear kuping 138
ear drops obat tetes kuping 108
earache sakit kuping 141
early pagi 14, 31
earring subang 121
east timur 77
Easter Paskah 152
easy mudah 14
eat, to makan 37, 144
eel belut 44
egg telor, telur 40, 41, 43
eggplant terong 52
eight delapan 147
eighteen delapanbelas 147
eighth kedelapan 149
eighty delapanpuluh 148
elastic elastik 108
elastic bandage pembalut elastik 108
electric(al) listrik 118
electrical appliance alat-alat listrik 118
electrical goods shop toko barang-barang listrik 98
electricity listrik 32
electronic elektronik 128
elevator lift 28, 100
eleven sebelas 147
embarkation point tempat embarkasi 73
embassy kedutaan besar 156
emerald zamrud 122
emergency darurat 156
emergency exit jalan keluar darurat 28; pintu darurat 99
emery board papan amril 109
empty kosong 14
enamel email 122
end akhir 150
engaged *(phone)* sedang dipakai 136
engagement ring cincin pertunangan 122
engine *(car)* mesin 78
England Inggeris 134, 146
English Inggeris 11, 126; *(language)* bahasa Inggeris 16, 80, 82, 104, 137
enjoyable menyenangkan 31
enlarge, to memperbesar 125
enough cukup 14, 68

entrance jalan masuk 67, 99, 155
entrance fee karcis masuk 82
envelope amplop 104
equipment alat-alat 91, 106
eraser penghapus 105
escalator eskalator 100
estimate *(cost)* perkiraan 79
Eurocheque Eurocek 130
Europe Eropa 146
evening malam 95, 96
evening dress *(woman's)* pakaian malam 115
evening, in the di malam hari 151, 153
every setiap 143
exchange rate nilai tukar 18, 130
exchange, to menukar 103
excuse, to memaafkan 11
exercise book buku latihan 105
exhaust pipe knalpot 78
exhibition pameran 81
exit jalan keluar 67, 99, 155
expect, to menunggu 130
expenses pengeluaran 131
expensive mahal 14, 19, 24, 101
exposure counter penghitung pencahayaan 125
exposure *(photography)* pembuatan gambar 124
express pos kilat 133
expression ekspresi 10; pernyataan 100
expressway jalan tol 76
extension *(phone)* pasawat 135
extension cord/lead kawat sambungan 118
extra tambahan 27
eye mata 138, 139
eye drops obat tetes mata 108
eye specialist dokter mata 137
eyebrow pencil penghitam alis mata 109
eyesight penglihatan 123

F

fabric *(cloth)* kain 112
face muka 138
face pack perawatan muka 30
face powder bedak 109
factory paberik 81
fair pasar malam 81
fall *(autumn)* musim gugur 150
fall, to jatuh 139
family keluarga 93, 144
fan kipas 127
fan belt tali kipas 76
far jauh 14, 100
fare *(ticket)* harga 68, 72
farm tanah pertanian 85
fast cepat 124
fat *(meat)* lemak 38
father ayah 93
faucet keran 29
fax faks 133
February Pebruari 150
feeding bottle botol makanan 110
feel, to *(physical state)* merasa 140, 142
felt bulu kempa 113
ferry ferry 74
fever demam 140
few sedikit 14
field lapangan 85
fifteen limabelas 147
fifth kelima 149
fifty limapuluh 147
file *(tool)* kikir 109
fill in, to mengisi 26, 144
filling *(tooth)* tambalan 145
filling station pompa bensin 75
film film 86, 124, 125
film winder alat memutar film 125
filter saringan 125
filter-tipped filter 126
find, to mendapat 11, 100; menemukan 76
fine *(OK)* baik 10, 25, 92
fine arts kesenian murni 84
finger jari 138
Finland Finlandia 146
fire kebakaran 156
first pertama 68, 72, 149
first-aid kit kotak pertolongan pertama 108
first class kelas satu 69
first name nama pertama 26
fish ikan 44
fishing mengail 90
fishing tackle alat pancing 106
fishmonger's tempat jual ikan 98
fit, to pas 114
fitting room kamar mengepas 114
five lima 147
fix, to memasang 145
fizzy *(mineral water)* membuih 60

flannel pelanel 113
flash *(photography)* cahaya 125
flashlight lampu senter 106
flat *(shoe)* rata 117
flat tyre ban kempes 78
flea market pasar loak 81
flight penerbangan 65
floor lantai 27
floor show acara hiburan di klab malam 89
florist's toko bunga 98
flour tepung 38
flower bunga 85
flu influensa 142
fluid cairan 123
foam rubber mattress kasur busa karet 106
fog kabut 94
folding chair kursi lipat 106
folding table meja lipat 106
folk music musik rakyat 128
follow, to mengikuti 77
food makanan 38, 62
food box kotak makanan 120
food poisoning keracunan makanan 142
foot kaki 138
foot cream krem kaki 109
football sepakbola 90
for untuk 15
forbidden dilarang 155
forest hutan 85
forget, to lupa 62
fork garpu 37, 61, 120
form *(document)* formulir 26, 133, 144
fortnight dua minggu 151
fortress benteng 81
forty empatpuluh 147
foundation cream krem dasar 109
fountain air mancur 81
fountain pen pulpen 105
four empat 147
fourteen empatbelas 147
fourth keempat 149
frame *(glasses)* bingkai 123
France Perancis 146
free kosong 14, 70; bebas 80, 83, 155
fresh segar 62
Friday Jumat 151
fried digoreng 45, 47
fried egg telor mata sapi 41
friend teman 95
fringe poni 30
from dari 15
front depan 75
fruit buah-buahan 55
fruit cocktail koktail buah-buahan 55
fruit juice sari buah 41, 60
frying pan panci goreng 120
full penuh 14
full board penginapan lengkap dengan makanan 24
full insurance asuransi penuh 20
furniture mebel 84

G

gallery balai kesenian 81, 98
game permainan 128
game *(food)* binatang buruan 49
garage garasi 26; bengkel mobil 78
garden kebun 85
gardens kebun 81
garlic bawang putih 54
gas gas 156
gasoline bensin 75, 78
gastritis radang perut 142
gauze kain kasa 108
gem permata tulen, mutiara 121
general umum 27, 100, 137
general delivery pos restante 133
general practitioner dokter umum 137
genitals alat kelamin 138
gentleman pria 155
geology geologi 84
Germany Jerman 146
get off, to turun 73
get past, to melewati 70
get to, to pergi ke 19, 76
get up, to bangun 144
get, to *(find)* mendapatkan 11, 19, 21, 32
gift hadiah 17
gin jenewer 60
gin and tonic gin dan tonic 60
ginger jahe 54
girdle korset 115
girl anak perempuan 128
girlfriend pacar 93
give, to memberi 13, 63, 123, 126, 135
gland kelenjar 138

glass gelas 37, 59, 143
glasses kacamata 123
gloomy muram 84
glove sarung tangan 115
glue lem, perekat 105
go away! pergilah! 156
go back, to kembali 77
go out, to pergi keluar 96
go, to pergi 72, 77, 96
gold emas 121, 122
gold plated berlapis emas 122
golden keemas-emasan 112
golf golf 90
golf course lapangan golf 90
good baik 14, 86, 101
good afternoon selamat siang 10
good evening selamat malam 10
good morning selamat pagi 10
good night selamat tidur 10
good-bye selamat tinggal 10
goose angsa 49
gooseberry frambus 55
gram gram 119
grammar tata bahasa 159
grammar book buku tatabahasa 105
grape buah anggur 55, 64
grapefruit jeruk besar 55
grapefruit juice sari jeruk besar 41, 60
gray abu-abu, kelabu 112
graze luka keserempet 139
greasy berminyak 110
great *(excellent)* baik 95
Great Britain Britannia Raya 146
Greece Yunani 146
green hijau 112
green grocer's toko penjual sayur-sayuran 98
greeting salam 10, 152
grey abu-abu, kelabu 112
grilled dipanggang 44; dibakar 47
grocer's toko bahan makanan 98, 119
groundsheet lembaran plastik yang ditaruh diatas tanah 106
group rombongan 82
guesthouse wisma tamu 19, 22
guide pengantar 80
guidebook buku tuntunam 82; buku penuntun 104, 105
guinea fowl ayam mutiara 49
gum *(teeth)* gusi 145
gynaecologist ginekolog 137

H

hair rambut 30, 110
hair dryer pengering rambut 118
hair gel hair gel 30
hair lotion pembersih rambut 110
hair spray semprot rambut 110
hairbrush sikat rambut 110
haircut pangkas rambut 30
hairdresser penata rambut 30
hairgrip jepitan rambut 110
hairpin jepitan rambut 110
half setengah 149
half an hour setengah jam 153
half price setengah harga 69
hall *(large room)* ruangan 81, 88
hall porter portir ruangan 27
ham ham 63
hammer palu 120
hand tangan 138
hand cream krem tangan 109
handbag tas tangan 115, 156
handicrafts kerajinan tangan 84
handkerchief saputangan 115
handmade dibuat dengan tangan 112
handwashable bisa dicuci dengan tangan 113
hanger gantungan 28
harbour pelabuhan 74, 81
hard keras 123
hard-boiled egg telur rebus matang 40
hardware store toko besi 98
hare kelinci 49
hat topi 115
have to, to *(must)* harus 17, 68, 69, 77, 95
hay fever alergi rumput 107, 141
hazelnut buah kemiri 55
he dia 160
head kepala 138, 139
head waiter pelayan kepala 62
headache sakit kepala 141
headphones telepon kepala 118
health food shop toko makanan untuk kesehatan 98
health insurance (company) asuransi kesehatan 144
health insurance form formulir asuransi kesehatan 144

heart jantung 138
heart attack serangan jantung 141
heating pemanasan 28
heavy berat 14, 101, 139
heel tumit 117
hello halo 10, 135
help pertolongan 156
help! tolong! 156
help, to tolong 13, 71, 100, 134
help, to *(oneself)* mengambil (sendiri) 119
her dia 160
herb tea teh jamu 60
here disini 14
hi halo 10
high tinggi 141; haik 91
high season musim ramai 150
high tide pasang naik 91
hill bukit 85
hire sewa 20, 74
hire, to menyewa 19, 20, 74, 90, 91, 118
his dia 161
history sejarah 84
hitchhike, to menggonceng 74
hold on! *(phone)* tunggu dulu 136
hole lobang 30
holiday hari besar 151
holidays libur 16, 151
home pulang 96
home town tempat tinggal 26
honey madu 41
hope, to mengharap 96
horse racing pacuan kuda 90
horseback riding naik kuda 90
horseradish tanaman lobak 54
hospital rumah sakit 99, 142, 144
hot *(warm)* panas 14, 25, 93
hot water air panas 24, 28
hot-water bottle botol air panas 28
hotel hotel 19, 21, 22, 26, 80, 102
hotel directory/guide buku petunjuk hotel 19
hotel reservation pesanan tempat di hotel 19
hour jam 80, 143, 153
house rumah 83, 85
household article alat rumahtangga 120
how bagaimana 11
how far berapa jauh 11, 76, 85
how long *(distance)* berapa panjang 11; *(time)* berapa lama 11, 25, 115
how many berapa banyak 11
how much berapa banyak 11; *(price)* berapa ongkosnya 24, 85, 133
hundred seratus 148
hungry lapar 13, 36
hunting berburu 90
hurry, to be in a terburu-buru 21
hurt (to be) lukai 139
hurt, to melukai 139; sakit 140, 142, 145
husband suami 93
hydrofoil hidrofoil 74

I

I saya 160
ice es 94
ice cream eskrim 57
ice cube es batu 28
ice pack kantong es 106
iced tea teh es 61
if jika 143
ill sakit 140
illness keadaan sakit 140
important penting 13
imported diimpor 112
impressive mengesankan 84
in di 15
include, to termasuk 24
included tergantung 20; termasuk 62
India India 146
indigestion salah cerna 141
Indonesia Indonesia 146
Indonesian Indonesia 113; *(language)* Indonesia 12, 95
inexpensive tidak mahal 36, 124
infected kena infeksi 140
infection infeksi 141
inflammation radang 142
inflation inflasi 131
inflation rate tingkat inflasi 131
influenza influensa 142
information informasi, keterangan 67, 155
injection suntikan 142, 144
injure, to melukai 139
injured terluka 139
injury luka-luka 139
ink tinta 105
inquiry keterangan 68

insect bite gigitan serangga 107, 139
insect repellent penolak serangga 108
insect spray semprotan 106
inside didalam 15
instead of sebagai pengganti 38
insurance asuransi 20, 144
insurance company perusahaan asuransi 79
interest *(finance)* bunga 131
interested, to be tertarik 96
interesting interesan 84
international internasional 133, 134
interpreter juru bahasa 131
intersection persimpangan 77
introduce, to memperkenalkan 92
introduction *(social)* merkenalkan 92
investment investasi 131
invitation undangan 95
invite, to mengundang 95
invoice faktur 131
iodine yodium 108
Ireland Irlandia 146
iron *(for laundry)* seterika 118
iron, to diseterikan 29
Israel Israel 146
it dia 161
Italy Italia 146
its -nya 161
ivory gading 122

J

jacket jaket 115
jade batu giok 122
jam *(preserves)* selai 41
jam, to macet 29, 125
January Januari 150
Japan Jepang 146
jar *(container)* botol 119
jaundice penyakit kuning 142
jaw rahang 138
jazz jazz 128
jeans jeans 115
jersey baju kaos 115
jewel box kotak perhiasan 121
jeweller's toko mas 98
joint tulang sendi 138
journey perjalanan 72
juice sari buah 38, 60
July Juli 150
jumper baju sweter 115
June Juni 150
just *(only)* saja 37, 100

K

Kampuchea Kamboja 146
kerosene minyak tanah 106
key kunci 27
kidney ginjal 138
kilo*(gram)* kilo(gram) 119
kilometre kilometer 20, 79
kind baik hati 95
kind *(type)* macam 85
knee lutut 138
kneesocks kaos lutut 115
knife pisau 37, 67, 120
know, to tahu 16, 25, 96, 114

L

label label 105
lace renda 113
lady wanita 155
lake danau, telaga 81, 85, 90
lamb *(meat)* daging kambing 46
lamp lampu 29, 106, 118
language bahasa 104
Laos Laos 146
large besar 20, 101, 130
last terakhir 14, 68, 73; lalu 149, 151
last name nama 26
late terlambat 14
later kemudian 135
laugh, to ketawa 95
launderette penatu 99
laundry *(clothes)* cucian 30
laundry *(place)* binatu 29, 99
laundry service pelayanan binatu 24
laxative obat urus-urus 108
lead *(metal)* timah 75
lead *(theatre)* main peranan 86
leap year tahun kabisat 149
leather kulit 113, 117
leave, to pergi 31, 95; berangkat 68
leave, to *(deposit)* disimpan 26
leave, to *(leave behind)* meninggalkan 20; menitipkan 71
leeks bawang perai 52
left kiri 21, 77
left-luggage office kantor penitipan koper 67
leg kaki 138

lemon jeruk sitrun 37, 41, 55, 60
lemonade limun, limonade 60
lens *(glasses)* lensa 123; *(camera)* lensa 125
lentils miju-miju 52
less lebih kurang 14
let, to *(hire out)* disewakan 155
letter surat 132
letter box bis surat 132
letter of credit surat kredit 130
lettuce selada 52
library perpustakaan 81, 99
licence *(driver's)* surat 20
lie down, to berbaring 142
life belt rompi pelampung 74
life boat sekoci penolong 74
life guard *(beach)* pengawal renang 91
lift *(elevator)* lift 28, 100
light cahaya 28, 124
light *(weight)* ringan 14, 57, 101; *(colour)* muda 101, 112
light meter meteran cahaya 125
lighter geretan 126
lighter fluid/gas minyak gas 126
lightning kilat 94
like seperti 111
like, to ingin 13, 20, 23, 61, 103, 122
like, to *(please)* suka 25, 93, 102
linen *(cloth)* linen 113
lip bibir 138
lipsalve salep bibir 109
lipstick lipstik 109
liqueur liqueur 60
listen, to mendengarkan 128
litre liter 75, 119
little *(a little)* sedikit 14
live, to hidup 83
liver hati 138
lobster udang karang 44
long panjang 115
long-sighted rabun dekat 123
look for, to mencari 13
look out! awas! 156
look, to melihat 100; 123; *(examine)* memeriksa 139
loose *(clothes)* longgar 115
lose, to kehilangan 123, 156
loss kerugian 131
lost tersesat 13
lost and found office/lost property office kantor barang-barang hilang 67, 156
lot *(a lot)* banyak 14
loud *(voice)* keras 135
lovely baik 94
low rendah 141
low season musim sepi 150
low tide pasang turun 91
lower bawah 69, 70
luggage barang 18, 21, 26, 31; bagasi 71
luggage locker lemari bagasi 71
luggage trolley kereta bagasi 18, 71
lump *(bump)* gumpalan 139
lunch makan siang 34, 95
lung paru-paru 138

M

machine washable bisa dicuci dengan mesin 113
magazine majalah 105
magnificent bagus sekali 84
maid pembantu wanita 27
mail pos 28, 133
mail, to masukkan dalam pos 28
mailbox bis surat 132
main utama 100
make-up remover pad alas penghapus dandanan 109
make up, to *(prepare)* membereskan 29, 71
make, to membuat 131, 162
mallet pemukul 106
man pria 114
manager manajer 27
mango mangga 56
manicure perawatan tangan dan kuku 30
many banyak 14
map peta 77, 105
March Maret 150
marinated diasinkan 45
market pasar 81, 99
marmalade sele jeruk 41
married kawin 94
mask topeng 127
match *(matchstick)* korek api 106, 126
matinée pertunjukkan siang 87
matt *(finish)* dof 125
mattress kasur 106
May Mei 150
may *(can)* boleh 12
meadow padang rumput 85

meal makanan 24, 34, 143
mean, to berarti 11, 26
means alat 74
measles campak 142
measure, to mengambil 113
meat daging 38, 46, 47, 61
meatball bakso 46
mechanic montir 78
mechanical pencil pensil mekanis 105
medical certificate surat kesehatan dokter 144
medicine ilmu kedokteran 84; *(drug)* obat 143
medium-sized ukuran sedang 20
medium *(meat)* setengah matang 47
meet, to bertemu 96
melon semangka 55
memorial tanda peringatan 81
mend, to menambal 75
mend, to *(clothes)* memperbaiki 30
menthol *(cigarettes)* mentol 126
menu menu 37, 40; daftar makanan 39
message pesan 28, 136
metre meter 111
middle tengah 69, 150
midnight tengah malam 153
milk susu 41, 61, 64
milkshake milkshake 60
milliard seribu juta 148
million juta 148
mineral water air mineral 60
mint permen 54
minute menit 21, 69, 153
mirror cermin 114, 123
miscellaneous serbaneka 127
Miss Nona 10
miss, to kehilangan 18, 29, 61
mistake kesalahan 31, 61, 62, 102
moccasin sepatu sandal 117
moisturizing cream krem pelembap 109
moment tenggu sebentar 12, 136
monastery biara 81
Monday Senin 151
money uang 18, 130
money order poswesel 133
monkey monyet 85
monsoon musim hujan 94
month bulan 16, 150
monument monumen 81
moon bulan, rembulan 94
moped sepeda kumbang 74
more lebih banyak 15
morning, in the di pagi hari 143, 151, 153
mortgage hipotek 131
mosque mesjid 85
mosquito net kelambu nyamuk 106
mother ibu 93
motor way jalan tol 76
motorbike sepeda motor 74
motorboat perahu motor 91
mountain gunung 85
mountaineering mendaki gunung 90
moustache kumis 31
mouth mulut 138, 142
mouthwash obat kumur 108
move, to menggerakkan 139
movie bioskop 86
movie camera kamera film 124
movies bioskop 86, 96
Mr. Tuan 10
Mrs. Nyonya 10
much banyak 12, 14
mug mangkuk 120
muscle otot 138
museum museum 81
mushroom jamur, candawan 52
music musik 84, 128
musical komedi musik 86
mussel remis 44
must *(have to)* harus 142
my saya 161
Myanmar (Burma) Myanmar 146
myself saya sendiri 119

N

nail *(human)* kuku 109
nail brush sikat kuku 109
nail clippers gunting kuku 109
nail file kikir kuku 109
nail polish cat kuku 109
nail polish remover alat penghapus cat kuku 109
nail scissors gunting kuku 109
name nama 23, 26, 79, 92, 131, 136
napkin serbet 37, 105, 120
nappy popok 110
narrow sempit 117
nationality kebangsaan 26, 93
natural history ilmu pengetahuan

alam 84
nausea mual 140
near dekat 14, 15
nearby didekat sini 78
nearest yang terdekat 75, 78, 98
neat *(drink)* murni 60
neck leher 31, 138
necklace kalung 121
need, to memerlukan 29, 90
needle jarum 28
needle *(medical)* jarum 143
negative negatif 124, 125
nerve urat syaraf 138
Netherlands Negeri Belanda 146
never tidak pernah 15
new baru 14
New Year Tahun Baru 152
New Zealand New Zealand 146
newspaper surat kabar 104, 105
newsstand kios 99
newsstand kios 19, 67, 99, 104
next berikut 14, 65, 68, 73, 76; depan 149, 151
next to berikut 15; di sebelah 77
night malam 151; tidur 10
night cream krem malam 109
night, at pada watku malam 151
nightclub klab malam 89
nightdress/gown pakaian tidur 115
nine sembilan 147
nineteen sembilanbelas 147
ninety sembilanpuluh 148
ninth kesembilan 149
no tidak 10
noisy berisik 25
nonalcoholic tanpa alkohol 60
none tidak ada 15
nonsmoker tidak merokok 36
noodle mi 50
noon tengah hari 31, 153
north utara 77
North America Amerika Utara 146
Norway Norwegia 146
nose hidung 138
nose drops obat tetes hidung 108
nosebleed mimisan 141
not tidak 15
note *(banknote)* uang kertas 130
note paper kertas catatan 105
notebook buku catatan 105
nothing tidak ada 15, 17
notice *(sign)* pemberitahuan 155
notify, to memberitahukan 144
November Nopember 150
now sekarang 15
number nomor 26, 66, 135, 136, 147
nurse jururawat 144
nutmeg pala 54

O

o'clock jam 153
occupation *(profession)* pekerjaan 26
occupied terisi 14; sedang dipakai 155
October Oktober 150
octopus ikan gurita 44
office kantor 19, 67, 80, 99, 132, 133, 156
oil minyak 37, 64
oily *(greasy)* berminyak 110
old lama; *(person)* tua 14
old town kota lama 81
olive buah zaitun 41
on pada 15
on foot jalan kaki 76
on request atas permintaan 73
on time tepat pada waktunya 68
once satu kali 149
one satu 147
one-way (traffic) jalan satu jurusan 77
one-way ticket karcis satu jalan 65, 69
onion bawang 52
only hanya 15, 25, 80, 87
open buka 14, 82, 155
open, to membuka 11, 17, 82, 107, 130, 132, 142
opera opera 88
operation operasi 144
operator operator 134
opposite di seberang 77
optician optik 99, 123
or untuk 15
orange jeruk manis 55, 64
orange *(colour)* oranye 112
orange juice jeruk manis 41, 60
orangeade air jeruk 60
orchestra orkes 88
order, to *(goods, meal)* pesan 61; memesan 102
ornithology ilmu burung 84
other lain 74, 101
out of order sedang rusak 136, 155

photo foto 124; gambar 125
photocopy fotokopi 131
photographer juru potret 99
photography fotografi 124
phrase ucapan 12
pick up, to *(person)* menjemput 80
picnic piknik 63
picture *(painting)* lukisan 83
pig babi 46
pill pil 141, 143
pillow bantal 28
pin peniti 109, 121
pineapple nanas 55
pink merah muda 112
pipe pipa 126
pipe cleaner pembersih pipa 126
pipe tobacco tembakau pipa 126
pipe tool peralatan pipa 126
pisang banana 57
place tempat 26, 77
place of birth tempat lahir 26
plain *(colour)* polos 112
plane pesawat terbang 65
planetarium planetarium 82
plaster gips 140
plastic plastik 120
plastic bag tas plastik 120
plate piring 37, 61, 120
platform *(station)* peron 67, 68, 69
platinum platina 122
play *(theatre)* sandiwara 86
play, to pertunjukkan 86; memainkan 88; bermain 94
playground tempat bermain 32
playing card main kartu 105, 128
please silahkan 10
plimsolls sepatu karet 117
plug *(electric)* steker 29, 118
plum buah prem 55
pneumonia radang paru-paru 142
poached direbus 44
pocket saku 116
pocket calculator kalkulator kecil 105
pocket watch jam saku 121
point of interest *(sight)* wisata yang menarik 80
point, to menunjuk 12
poison racun 108, 156
poisoning peracunan 142
pole *(tent)* tiang 106
police polisi 79, 156
police station kantor polisi 99, 156
pond kolam 85
poplin poplin 113
pork daging babi 46
port pelabuhan 74
portable dapat dibawa 118
porter porter 18; kuli 71
portion porsi 61
Portugal Portugal 146
possible, (as soon as) secepat-cepatnya 137
post *(mail)* pos 28, 133
post office kantor pos 99, 132
post, to masukkan dalam pos 28
postage ongkos perangko 132
postage stamp perangko 28, 126, 132, 133
postcard *(picture)* kartupos (bergambar) 105, 126, 132
poste restante pos restante 133
potato kentang 54
pottery barang tembikar 84
poultry unggas 49
pound pon 18, 102, 129
powder bedak 109
powder compact tempat bedak 121
prawn udang 45
pregnant hamil 141
premium *(gasoline)* bensin premium 75
prescribe, to memberi resep 143
prescription resep 107, 143
present hadiah 17
press stud pengancing 116
press, to *(iron)* diseterika 29
pressure tekanan 75, 141
pretty molek 84
price harga 24
print *(photo)* gambar 125
private pribadi 24, 81, 91, 155
processing *(photo)* pemrosesan 125
profit keuntungan 131
programme acara 87
pronounce, to mengucapkan 12
pronunciation pengucapan 6
propelling pencil pensil mekanis 105
Protestant Protestan 85
provide, to mengusahakan 131
public holiday hari raya 152
pull, to menarik 155
pull, to *(tooth)* dicabut 145
pullover pulover 116

rib tulang rusuk 138
ribbon pita 105
rice nasi 50
right *(correct)* benar 14
right *(direction)* kanan 21, 77
ring *(jewellery)* cincin 122
ring, to *(door bell)* mengebel 155
river sungai 85, 90
river trip pelabuhan pelayaran sungai 74
road jalan 76, 77, 85
road assistance pertolongan jalan 78
road map peta jalan 105
road sign tanda jalan 79
roasted panggang 47
roll roti kadet 41, 64
roll film segulung film 124
room kamar 19, 23, 24, 25, 27, 28
room *(space)* ruang 32
room number nomor kamar 26
room service pelayanan kamar 24,
rope tali 106
rouge pemerah pipi 109
round bundar 101
round-neck leher bundar 116
round-trip ticket karcis pulang pergi 65, 69
round *(golf)* permainan 90
round up, to bulatkan menjadi 62
rowing boat perahu dayung 91
royal kerajaan 82
rubber *(eraser)* karet 105
rubber *(material)* karet 117
ruby batu delima 122
rucksack ransel 106
ruin puing 82
ruler *(for measuring)* penggaris 105
rum rum 60
running water air leding 23
rupiah rupiah 21, 101, 130, 132
Russia Rusia 146

S

safe lemari 27
safe *(free from danger)* aman 91
safety pin peniti 109
saffron kunyit 54
sailing boat perahu layar 91
salad selada 52
sale penjualan 131
sale *(bargains)* obral 100
salt garam 37, 41, 64
salty asin 61
sandal sandal 117
sandwich sandwich 63
sapphire safir 122
sardine sarden 44
satin satin 113
Saturday Saptu 151
sauce sosis 51
saucepan panci bergagang 120
saucer piring cawan 120
sausage sosis 46, 64
scarf selendang 116
scarlet merah tua 112
scenery pemandangan 93
scissors gunting 109, 120
scooter sekuter 74
Scotland Skotlandia 146
scrambled eggs telor aduk goreng 41
screen *(mesh)* kasan 29
screwdriver obeng 106, 120
sculptor pemahat 83
sculpture patung 84
sea laut 85, 91
seafood makanan hasil laut 44
season musim 150
seasoning bumbu 37
seat tempat duduk 65, 69, 70, 87
second kedua 149; detik 153
second-hand shop toko barang-barang bekas 99
second class kelas dua 69
second hand jarum detik 122
secretary sekretaris 27, 131
section seksi 104
see, to melihat 25, 26, 87, 90, 121
sell, to menjual 100
send, to mengirim 78, 102; kirim 133
sentence kalimat 12
separately sendiri-sendiri 62
September September 150
seriously berat 139
service pelayanan 24, 62, 100
service *(church)* kebaktian 84
serviette serbet 37
set *(hair)* letak rambut 30
set menu menu khusus 37
setting lotion pembersih penataan rambut 30
seven tujuh 147
seventeen tujuhbelas 147

seventh yang ketujuh 149
seventy tujuhpuluh 148
shampoo sampoo 30; langir 110
shampoo and set sampo dan set 30
shape bentuk 103
share *(finance)* saham 131
sharp *(pain)* tajam 140
shave cukur 31
shaver alat cukur 27, 118
shaving brush sikat cukur 109
shaving cream sabun cukur 109
she dia 161
shelf papan rak 119
ship kapal 74
shirt kemeja 116
shivery menggigil 140
shoe sepatu 117
shoe polish semir sepatu 117
shoe shop toko sepatu 99
shoelace tali sepatu 117
shoemaker's tukang sepatu 99
shop toko 98
shop window jendela 100, 111
shopping berbelanja 97
shopping area daerah pertokoan 82, 100
shopping centre pusat pertokoan 99
shopping facilities fasilitas berbelanja 32
short pendek 30, 115
short-sighted rabun jauh 123
shorts celana pendek 116
shoulder bahu 138
shovel sekop 128
show pertunjukkan 86, 89
show, to memperlihatkan 100, 101, 103, 119, 124; menunjukkan 13
shower mandi dus 23, 32
shrink, to menyusut 113
shut tertutup 14
shutter *(camera)* diafragma 125
shutter *(window)* daun penutup jendela 29
sick *(ill)* sakit 140
side sisi 31
sideboards/burns cambang 31
sightseeing tamasya 80
sightseeing tour perjalanan tamasya 80
sign *(notice)* tanda 77, 79, 155
sign, to tanda tangan 26, 130
signature tanda tangan 26
signet ring cincin cap 122
silk sutera 113
silver perak 121, 122; *(colour)* perak 112
silver plated berlapis perak 122
silverware barang-barang perak 122
simple sederhana 124
since sejak 15, 150
sing, to menyanyi 88
single *(ticket)* satu jalan (karcis) 65, 69
single *(unmarried)* bujangan 94
single cabin kamar (di kapal) untuk seorang 74
single room kamar untuk seorang 19, 23
sister saudara perempuan 93
sit down, to duduk 95
six enam 147
sixteen enambelas 147
sixth keenam 149
sixty enampuluh 148
size *(clothes, shoes)* ukuran 113, 117, 124
skin kulit 138
skin-diving menyelam 91
skin-diving equipment alat-alat menyelam 91, 106
skipjack cakalan 44
skirt rok 116
sky langit 94
sleep, to tidur 144
sleeping bag karung untuk tidur 106
sleeping car kereta tidur 69; gerbong tidur 70
sleeping pill obat tidur 108, 143
sleeve lengan 115, 142
sleeveless tanpa lengan 115
slice iris 119
slide *(photo)* slide 124
slip *(underwear)* rok dalam 116
slipper selop 117
slow(ly) lambat 14, 21; pelan 135
small kecil 14, 20, 25, 101, 117, 130
smoked diasap 44
smoker perokok 70
snack makanan kecil 63
snack bar warung makanan kecil 67
snake ular 85
snap fastener pengancing 116
snuff tembakau sedotan 126

soap sabun 27, 109
soccer sepakbola 90
sock kaus kaki 116
socket *(electric)* stopkontak 27
soft lunak 123
soft-boiled (egg) (telur) rebus setengah 40
soft drink minuman tanpa alkohol 64
sold out terjual habis 87
sole *(shoe)* tapak sepatu 117
some beberapa 14
something sesuatu 30, 57, 107, 111, 112, 125, 139
somewhere kira-kira 87
son anak laki-laki 93
song lagu 128
soon segera 15
sore *(painful)* sakit 145
sore throat sakit tenggorokan 141
sorry maaf 11, 16, 87, 103
sort *(kind)* macam 119
soup sup 42
south selatan 77
South Africa Afrika Selatan 146
South America Amerika Selatan 146
souvenir tandamata 127
souvenir shop toko suvenir 99
spade sekop 128
Spain Spanyol 146
spare tyre ban serep 75
spark(ing) plug busi 76
speak, to bicara 11, 12, 16, 135
speaker *(loudspeaker)* pengeras suara 118
special istimewa 20
special delivery pos kilat 133
specialist spesialis 142
specimen *(medical)* contoh 142
spectacle case tempat kacamata 123
spell, to mengeja 12
spend, to mengeluarkan 101
spices rempah-rempah 54
spicy pedas 54
spinach bayam 52
spine tulang belakang 138
sponge spons 109
spoon sendok 37, 61, 120
sport olahraga 90
sporting goods shop toko alat-alat olahraga 99
sprained keseleo 140
spray menyemprot 29
spring *(season)* musim semi 150
spring *(water)* mata air 85
square persegi 101
square *(town)* alun-alun 82
squid cumi-cumi 44
stadium stadion 82
staff *(personnel)* staf 26
stain noda 30
stainless steel baja tahan karat 122
stamp *(postage)* perangko 28, 126, 132, 133
staple jeglegan 105
star bintang 94
starfruit belimbing 56
start, to memulai 80, 89
starter *(meal)* pengantar 41
station *(railway)* setasiun 19, 21, 67, 70
stationer's toko alat tulis menulis 99, 104
statue patung 82
stay tinggal 31; kunjungan 92
stay, to tinggal 16, 24, 26, 142
stay, to *(reside)* tinggal 93
steak bistik 46
steal, to mencuri 156
steamed didukus 44
sterilized steril 143
stewed direbus 47
stiff neck leher kaku 141
sting sengatan 139
sting, to tersengat 139
stitch, to setik 30; menjahit 117
stock exchange bursa saham 82
stocking kaus kaki 116
stomach perut 138
stomach ache sakit perut 141
stools darah 142
stop *(bus)* pemberhentian 73
stop thief! tangkap pencuri! 156
stop! hentikan 156
stop, to berhenti 21, 68, 70, 72
store *(shop)* toko 98
straight *(drink)* murni 60
straight ahead lurus 21, 77
strange aneh 84
strawberry arbei 55
street jalan 26, 77
street map peta jalan 19, 105
string tali 105
student pelajar 82, 94

study, to belajar 93
sturdy kokoh 101
suede kulit lunak 113, 117
sugar gula 37, 64
suit *(man's)* setelan 116
suit *(woman's)* setelan pakaian wanita 116
suitcase koper 18
summer musim panas 150
sun matahari 94
sun-tan cream krem warna cokelat 109
sun-tan oil minyak warna cokelat 110
sunburn terbakar sinar matahari 107
Sunday Minggu 151
sunglasses kacamata hitam 123
sunshade *(beach)* kere penghalang sinar matahari 91
sunstroke kelengar matahari 141
super *(petrol)* bensin premium 75
superb hebat 84
supermarket toko pangan serba-ada 99
suppository supositoria 108
surgery *(consulting room)* kantor praktek dokter 137
suspenders *(Am.)* tali selempang 116
sweater sweter 116
Sweden Swedia 146
sweet manis 59, 61
sweet *(confectionery)* gula-gula 126
sweet shop toko makanan gula-gula 99
sweetcorn jagung manis 52
sweetener bahan pemanis 37
swelling bengkak 139
swim, to berenang 90
swimming berenang 89, 91
swimming pool kolam renang 32, 90
swimming trunks celana pendek 116
swimsuit pakaian renang 116
switch *(electric)* sakelar 29
switchboard operator operator 27
Switzerland Negeri Swis 146
swollen bengkak 139
swordfish ikan todak 44
synthetic sintetis 113

T
T-shirt kaus oblong 116
table meja 36, 106
tablet *(medical)* tablet 108
tailor's tempat tukang jahit 99
take, to mengambil 18, 102
take away, to dibawa pulang 63, 102
take to, to bawalah 21, 67
taken *(occupied)* sudah mengambil 70
talcum powder bedak talk 110
tamarind asam 54
tampon tampon 108
tap *(water)* keran 29
taxi taksi 19, 21, 31, 67
taxi rank/stand pangkalan taksi 21
tea teh 41, 61, 64
teaspoon sendok teh 120
telegram telegram 133
telegraph office kantor telegrap 99
telephone telepon 28, 78, 79, 134
telephone call telepon 136
telephone directory buku petunjuk telepon 134
telephone number nomor telepon 135, 136, 156
telephone, to *(call)* menelepon 134
telephoto lens lensa telefoto 125
television televisi 24, 28, 118
telex teleks 133
telex, to melalui teleks 130
tell, to memberitahu 13, 73, 76, 136, 153
temperature panas 90, 140, 142
temple candi 85
temporary sementara 145
ten sepuluh 147
tendon urat daging 138
tennis main tennis 90
tennis court lapangan tenis 90
tennis racket raket tenis 90
tent tenda 32, 106
tent peg paku tenda 106
tent pole tiang tenda 106
tenth kesepuluh 149
terrace teras 36
terrifying menakutkan 84
tetanus tetanus 140
Thailand Thailand 146
than dari 14
thank you terima kasih 10, 96
that ini 11; itu 100

theatre sandiwara 82; teater 86
theft pencurian 156
then lalu 15
there disana 14
thermometer termometer 108, 144
these ini 163
they mereka 161
thief pencuri 156
thigh paha 138
thin tipis 112
think, to *(believe)* pikir 31; menurut 94
third ketiga 149
thirsty, to be haus 13, 36
thirteen tigabelas 147
thirty tigapuluh 147
this ini 11, 100, 162
thousand seribu 148
thread benang 28
three tiga 147
throat tenggorokan 138, 141
throat lozenge tablet batuk 108
through melalui 15
thumb ibu jari 138
thumbtack paku jamur 105
thunder guntur 94
Thursday Kamis 151
ticket karcis 65, 69, 87, 89
ticket office tempat penjualan karcis 68
tide pasang 91
tie dasi 116
tie clip jepitan dasi 122
tie pin peniti dasi 122
tight *(close-fitting)* ketat 115
tights celana ketat 116
time *(occasion)* kali 142, 143
timetable *(trains)* daftar perjalanan 68
tin *(container)* kaleng 119
tin opener pembuka kaleng 120
tint sedikit diwarnai 110
tinted berwarna 123
tire ban 75, 76
tired lelah 13
tissue *(handkerchief)* serbet kertas 110
to ke 15
to get *(fetch)* carikan 137
to get *(go)* pergi 100
to get *(obtain)* mendapat 11, 90, 134
toast roti panggang 41
tobacco tembakau 126
tobacconist's toko penjual tembakau 99, 126
today hari ini 29, 151
toe jari kaki 138
toilet paper kertas kloset 110
toilet water minyak kelonyo 110
toiletry alat-alat kecantikan 110
toilets kamar kecil 24, 28, 32, 38, 68
tomato buah tomat 52
tomato juice sari tomat 60
tomb makam 82
tomorrow besok 29, 96, 151
tongue lidah 138
tonic water tonikum 60
tonight malam ini 30, 86, 87, 96
tonsils amandel 138
too terlalu 14
too *(also)* juga 15
too much terlalu banyak 14
tools alat-alat 120
tooth gigi 145
toothache sakit gigi 145
toothbrush sikat gigi 110, 118
toothpaste pasta gigi 110
top, at the atas 31, 145
torch *(flashlight)* obor 106
torn terrobek 140
touch, to menyentuh 155
tough *(meat)* liat 61
tour perjalanan keliling 74, 80
tourist office kantor turis 19, 80
tow truck mobil gerbong kerusakan 79
towards terhadap 15
towel handuk 27, 110
tower menara 82
town kota 19, 76, 89
town centre pusat kota 21, 72, 76
town hall balai kota 82
toy mainan 128
toy shop toko mainan 99
tracksuit baju olahraga 116
traffic light lampu lalu-lintas 77
trailer kereta gandengan 32
train kereta-api 68, 69, 70
tranquillizer obat penenang 108, 143
transfer *(finance)* pemindahan 131
transformer transformator, trafo 118
translate, to menterjemahkan 12
transport, means of alat

pengangkutan 74
travel agency biro perjalanan 99
travel guide petunjuk perjalanan 105
travel sickness mabuk perjalanan 107
traveller's cheque cek wisata 18, 62, 102, 130
travelling bag tas perjalanan 18
treatment perawatan 143
tree pohon 85
trim, to *(a beard)* potong sedikit 31
trip perjalanan 72, 152; pekerjaan 94
trolley kereta 18, 71
trousers celana 116
try on, to mencoba mengenakan 114
Tuesday Selasa 151
tumbler gelas minum 120
tuna ikan tongkol 44
turkey kalkun 49
turn, to *(change direction)* membelok 21, 77
turnip lobak cina 52
turquoise *(colour)* warna biru-hjau 112
turquoise batu pirus 122
turtle-neck leher tinggi 115
tweezers penjepit 110
twelve duabelas 147
twenty duapuluh 147
twice dua kali 149
twin beds dua tempat tidur 23
two dua 147
typewriter mesin tik 27
typing paper kertas tik 105
tyre ban 75, 76

U

ugly jelek 14, 84
umbrella payung 116; *(beach)* payung pantai 91
uncle paman 93
unconscious pingsan 139
under dibawah 15
underdone *(meat)* matang 47
underpants celana dalam 116
undershirt kaus dalam 116
understand, to mengerti 12, 16
undress, to lepas baju 142
United States Amerika Serikat (A.S.) 146
university universitas 82
unleaded tidak mengandung timah 75
until sampai 15
up keatas 15
upper atas 69
upset stomach perut terganggu 107
upstairs naik keatas 15
urgent mendesak 13
urine air kencing 142
useful berguna 15

V

vacancy kamar kosong 23
vacant kosong 14, 155
vacation liburan 151
vaccinated, to be sudah divaksin 140
vacuum flask botol pakum 120
vaginal infection infeksi di liang peranakan 141
valley lembah 85
value nilai 131
value-added tax pajak pertambahan nilai 24
vanilla panili 54
veal daging anak sapi 46
vegetable sayur-mayur 52
vegetable store toko sayur-sayuran 99
vegetarian *(food)* vegetaris 37
vein nadi 138
velvet beludru 113
venereal disease penyakit kelamin 142
venison menjangan 49
vermouth vermouth 60
very sekali 15
vest baju kaos 116
vest *(Am.)* rompi 116
veterinarian dokter hewan 99
video camera kamera video 124
video cassette kaset video 118, 124, 127
video recorder perekam video 118
Vietnam Vietnam 146
view *(panorama)* pemandangan 23, 25
village desa 76, 85
vinegar cuka 37

visit kunjungan 92
visiting hours jam-jam kunjungan 144
vitamin pill pil vitamin 108
vodka vodka 60
volleyball bola voli 90
voltage voltase 118
vomit, to memuntahkan 140

W
waist pinggang 142
waistcoat rompi 116
wait, to menunggu 21
waiter pelayan (pria) 27, 37
waiting room ruang tunggu 68
waitress pelayan wanita 26
wake, to membangunkan 27, 71
Wales Wales 146
walk, to berjalan kaki 74, 85
wall tembok 85
wallet dompet 156
walnut kenari 55
want, to ingin 13, 101, 102
wash, to mencuci 29, 113
washable bisa dicuci 113
washbasin wastafel 29
washing powder deterjen 120
watch arloji 121, 122
watchmaker's tempat tukang arloji 99, 121
watchstrap ikat arloji 122
water air 24, 28, 32, 41, 60, 75
water-skis ski air 91
water buffalo kerbau 46
water flask botol air 106
watercress seledri air 52
waterfall air terjun 85
watermelon semangka 55
waterproof tahan air 122
wave gelombang 91
way jalan 76
we kami, kita 161
weather cuaca 94
wedding ring cincin kawin 122
Wednesday Rabu 151
week minggu 16, 20, 25, 80, 92, 151
well baik 10; sehat 140
well-done *(meat)* dimasak matang-matang 47
west barat 77
what apa 11
wheel roda 78
when kapan 11
where dimana 11
where from dari mana 93, 146
which yang mana 11
whisky wiski 17, 60
white putih 112
who siapa 11
why mengapa 11
wick sumbu 126
wide lebar 117
wide-angle lens lensa sudut-luas 125
wife isteri 93
wig rambut palsu 110
wild boar babi hutan 49
wind angin 94
window jendela 29, 36, 65, 69
window *(shop)* jendela 100, 111
windscreen/shield kaca mobil 75
windsurfer peselancar angin 91
wine minuman anggur 59
wine list daftar minuman anggur 59
wine merchant's pedagang minuman anggur 99
winter musim dingin 150
wiper *(car)* kipas kaca mobil 76
wish harapan 152
with dengan 15
withdraw, to *(from account)* penarikan 131
withdrawal penarikan 130
without tanpa 15
woman wanita, perempuan 114
wood kayu 85
wool wol 113
word kata 12, 15, 133
work, to bekerja 118
working day hari kerja 151
worse lebih jelek 14
wound luka 139
wrap up, to membungkus 103
wrinkle-free tahan kusut 113
wristwatch jam tangan 122
write, to menulis 12; tuliskan 101
writing pad buku catatan 105
writing paper kertas tulis 28
wrong salah 14, 77, 135

X
X-ray sinar X 140

Y

year tahun 149
yellow kuning 112
yes ya 10
yesterday kemaren 151
yet masih 15, 16, 25
yoghurt yogurt 41, 64
you anda 161
young muda 14
youth hostel graha wisata remaja 22

Z

zero nol 147
zip(per) kancing tarik 116
zoo kebun binatang 82
zoology zoologi 84

Indeks Bahasa Indonesia

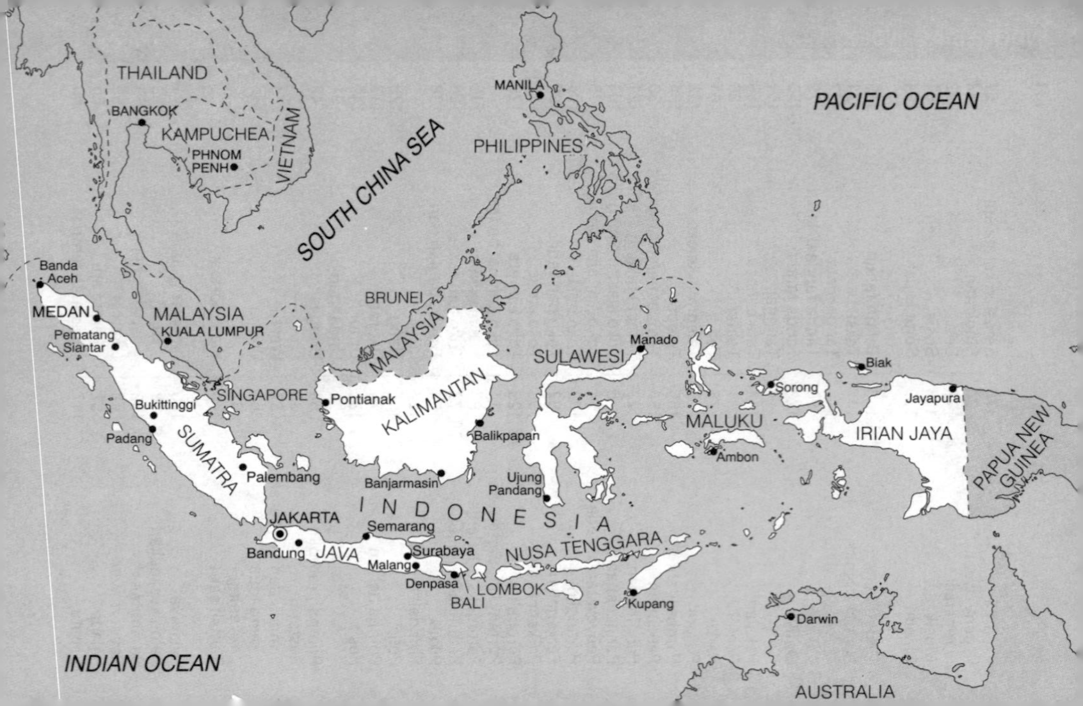
PACIFIC OCEAN
SOUTH CHINA SEA
INDIAN OCEAN
THAILAND
BANGKOK
KAMPUCHEA
PHNOM PENH
VIETNAM
MANILA
PHILIPPINES
Banda Aceh
MEDAN
Pematang Siantar
MALAYSIA
KUALA LUMPUR
SINGAPORE
BRUNEI
MALAYSIA
Bukittinggi
Padang
SUMATRA
Palembang
Pontianak
KALIMANTAN
Balikpapan
Banjarmasin
SULAWESI
Manado
Ujung Pandang
INDONESIA
JAKARTA
Bandung
JAVA
Semarang
Surabaya
Malang
Denpasa
BALI
LOMBOK
NUSA TENGGARA
Kupang
MALUKU
Ambon
Sorong
Biak
Jayapura
IRIAN JAYA
PAPUA NEW GUINEA
Darwin
AUSTRALIA